DISCARD

Bloom's Modern Critical Interpretations

The Adventures of Huckleberry Finn
The Age of Innocence
Alice's Adventures in Wonderland
All Quiet on the Western Front
Animal Farm
The Ballad of the Sad Café
Beloved
Beowulf
Black Boy
The Bluest Eye
The Canterbury Tales
Cat on a Hot Tin Roof
Catch-22
The Catcher in the Rye
The Chronicles of Narnia
The Color Purple
Crime and Punishment
The Crucible
Cry, the Beloved Country
Darkness at Noon
Death of a Salesman
The Death of Artemio Cruz
The Diary of Anne Frank
Don Quixote
Emerson's Essays
Emma
Fahrenheit 451
A Farewell to Arms
Frankenstein
The Glass Menagerie
The Grapes of Wrath
Great Expectations
The Great Gatsby
Gulliver's Travels
Hamlet
Heart of Darkness
The House on Mango Street
I Know Why the Caged Bird Sings
The Iliad
Invisible Man
Jane Eyre
The Joy Luck Club
Julius Caesar
The Jungle
King Lear
Long Day's Journey into Night
Lord of the Flies
The Lord of the Rings
Love in the Time of Cholera
Macbeth
The Man Without Qualities
The Merchant of Venice
The Metamorphosis
A Midsummer Night's Dream
Miss Lonelyhearts
Moby-Dick
My Ántonia
Native Son
Night
1984
The Odyssey
Oedipus Rex
The Old Man and the Sea
On the Road
One Flew over the Cuckoo's Nest
One Hundred Years of Solitude
Othello
Persuasion
Portnoy's Complaint
Pride and Prejudice
Ragtime
The Red Badge of Courage
Romeo and Juliet
The Rubáiyát of Omar Khayyám
The Scarlet Letter
A Separate Peace
Silas Marner
Slaughterhouse-Five
Song of Solomon
The Sound and the Fury
The Stranger
A Streetcar Named Desire
Sula
The Sun Also Rises
The Tale of Genji
A Tale of Two Cities
"The Tell-Tale Heart" and Other Stories
Their Eyes Were Watching God
Things Fall Apart
The Things They Carried
To Kill a Mockingbird
Ulysses
Waiting for Godot
The Waste Land
Wuthering Heights
Young Goodman Brown

Bloom's Modern Critical Interpretations

Charles Dickens's

Great Expectations

New Edition

Edited and with an introduction by
Harold Bloom
Sterling Professor of the Humanities
Yale University

Bloom's Modern Critical Interpretations: Great Expectations—New Edition
Copyright © 2010 by Infobase Publishing
Introduction © 2010 by Harold Bloom

All rights reserved. No part of this publication may be reproduced or utilized in any form or by any means, electronic or mechanical, including photocopying, recording, or by any information storage or retrieval systems, without permission in writing from the publisher. For more information contact:

Bloom's Literary Criticism
An imprint of Infobase Publishing
132 West 31st Street
New York NY 10001

Library of Congress Cataloging-in-Publication Data
Charles Dickens's Great expectations / edited and with an introduction by
Harold Bloom. — New ed.
p. cm. — (Bloom's modern critical interpretations)
Includes bibliographical references and index.
ISBN 978-1-60413-819-1 (hardcover : alk. paper)
1. Dickens, Charles, 1812–1870. Great expectations. I. Bloom, Harold.
PR4560.G688 2010
823'.8—dc22 2009049230

Bloom's Literary Criticism books are available at special discounts when purchased in bulk quantities for businesses, associations, institutions, or sales promotions. Please call our Special Sales Department in New York at (212) 967-8800 or (800) 322-8755.

You can find Bloom's Literary Criticism on the World Wide Web at http://www.chelseahouse.com

Contributing editor: Pamela Loos
Cover design by Alicia Post
Composition by IBT Global, Troy NY
Cover printed by IBT Global, Troy NY
Book printed and bound by IBT Global, Troy NY
Date printed: April 2010
Printed in the United States of America

10 9 8 7 6 5 4 3 2 1

This book is printed on acid-free paper.

All links and Web addresses were checked and verified to be correct at the time of publication. Because of the dynamic nature of the Web, some addresses and links may have changed since publication and may no longer be valid.

Contents

Editor's Note

My introduction explores some aspects of Pip's inwardness and speculates on Shakespeare's possible influence on Pip's capacity for change as he listens to his own narrative voice.

Stanley Friedman asserts that the novel's conclusion only deepens Pip's belief in providential design, after which Gail Turley Houston finds in the book an ambivalent account of Victorian consumer society.

The role of Christian allusion and, in particular, the rite of baptism are noted by John Cunningham, while Margaret Flanders Darby strives to rescue Estella from her one-dimensionality.

Robert R. Garnett also takes up the figure of Estella, placing her on the dividing line between the work's moderate and impassioned characters. The notion of baptism then returns, this time by fire, in Sara Thornton's appraisal of Miss Havisham.

The ethical implications of the suspense plot are explored by Caroline Levine, after which Wendy S. Jacobson considers the influences of *Hamlet* on Dickens's novel.

For Stewart Justman, the antiromantic nature of the narrative relegates the characters to a shared democracy of ignorance. The volume then concludes with Andrew Sanders's assessment of the novel's ambiguous comedy.

HAROLD BLOOM

Introduction

Pip is the most inward of all Dickens's major characters, and except for Esther Summerson in *Bleak House*, he also appears to be the Dickens protagonist most overtly affected by his own pathos. In particular, he has a tendency to feel excessively guilty, almost in the Kafkan mode. An anguish of contamination seems to have reached out from Magwitch and Miss Havisham and invaded Pip's sensibility; this is profoundly irrational and yet seems demonstrable. Himself not at all criminal, Pip carries an aura that we might associate with the hero-villain Hamlet. "Hero-villain" sounds odd for Hamlet, but pragmatically the prince of Denmark is quite deadly. At play's end, Horatio and Fortinbras are the only survivors of any importance whatsoever. Pip, a far gentler person than Hamlet, is bad luck for his sister and for Magwitch, for Miss Havisham and Estella, even for the wretched Pumblechook and the malevolent Orlick. After all the disasters, Pip suffers his brain fever and returns to an improved infancy with the Gargerys and their child, his godson, little Pip. Absorbing as all this is, it remains a puzzle why Pip should have tormented himself into a guilt-consciousness he simply did not deserve.

Dickens, unlike Jane Austen or Stendhal or Dostoevsky, is not a particularly Shakespearean novelist. He has more affinities with Ben Jonson than with Shakespeare, but if you go in search of inwardness, then you must go to school with Shakespeare. *David Copperfield*, despite its autobiographical elements, would not refute Henry James's judgment that Dickens "has added nothing to our understanding of human character." *Great Expectations*, because it enters the abyss of Pip's inner self, *does* refute James. Something in

Dickens, descending into Pip's psyche, called on Shakespeare for aid, perhaps not altogether knowingly.

Pip's social identity is fathered by the secret patronage of Magwitch, who is also Estella's actual father. For Dickens, that hardly counts as extraordinary coincidence; in the world of the novels, everyone is overconnected. But it does place a particular demand on Dickens's genius; there is a profound link between Magwitch's love for Pip and Pip's suffering passion for Estella, though the connection necessarily is an uncanny one. Pip's inwardness has to apprehend the symbolic incest of his desire for the mocking Estella without comprehending it. So subtle and persuasive is Dickens's art of representation in *Great Expectations* that the reader experiences no surprise when the identity of Estella's father is revealed.

Magwitch, confronting Pip and Herbert together, plays the ghost of Hamlet's father, but he is a ghost who has come too late. Pip, gentlest of Hamlets, is no avenger: "Pip, revenge!" would be the silliest of outcries. Neither a dramatist nor a dramatizer, Pip joins Hamlet only as a sufferer, guilty and grieving. Hamlet mysteriously returns from the sea transformed, beyond melancholia and mourning. Pip goes under, is reborn very differently, and becomes a companion of his godson, little Pip. Dickens, theatrical to the core, values Hamlet as a self-dramatizer but has little interest in Hamlet the intellectual. Pip does not feel disgust at unpacking his heart with words, and Estella is a counter-Ophelia. Perhaps Magwitch and Miss Havisham are counter-ghosts, truly bearing the authentic guilt of the story.

I hold with those who believe that Dickens ruined the original ending, which held out no hope for Pip and Estella. The revised ending is equivocal but perhaps not equivocal enough. You can end a *Hamlet* transcendentally but not happily.

STANLEY FRIEDMAN

Estella's Parentage and Pip's Persistence: The Outcome of Great Expectations

In *Great Expectations* Pip sinks into despair on learning that his true patron is the convict he once helped on the marshes: "it was not until I began to think, that I began fully to know how wrecked I was, and how the ship in which I had sailed was gone to pieces" (p. 307).[1] Even though he goes on to describe as his "sharpest and deepest pain" the awareness that "for the convict" he "had deserted Joe" (pp. 307–08), his greatest cause of distress actually seems to be the feeling that he has lost any chance of gaining Estella. During a later visit to Satis House, Pip tells her of his continuing affection, but adds, "I have no hope that I shall ever call you mine" (p. 343). He remains in extreme depression until his own observations and reports from others lead to a startling realization: "the man we have in hiding [Magwitch] . . . is Estella's Father" (p. 386). This extraordinary coincidence strangely induces Pip to find new hope and greatly affects his subsequent behavior. By focusing closely on the ways in which Pip's attitude and actions are influenced by his discovery, we can, I believe, gain a clearer understanding of the outcome of the entire narrative. For the hero's new awareness plays an especially significant part in forming his responses to the failure of his plan to marry Biddy and to the mysterious appearance of Estella on the site of Satis House in the ending that Dickens decided to publish.

From *Studies in the Novel* 19, no. 4 (Winter 1987): 410–21. © 1987 by *Studies in the Novel.*

1

As Neil Forsyth observes, the revelation of Estella's parentage has been slowly prepared for.[2] In Chapter 22, originally published as the fourteenth of the novel's thirty-six weekly installments, we are for the first time clearly told that Estella is only Miss Havisham's adopted child. In various succeeding installments, Pip gradually perceives the resemblance between Estella and Molly, Jaggers' housekeeper, and eventually asserts, "I felt absolutely certain that this woman was Estella's mother" (p. 370). Nevertheless, he afterwards seeks further information about Molly from Wemmick and then asks Miss Havisham about Estella's background. Later, when Magwitch's disclosures about his own past are reported by Herbert, the revelations conveniently dovetail with material previously gained from other sources and enable Pip to identify the convict as Estella's father. Surprising though this realization is, its credibility has been enhanced by the very deliberate manner in which diverse hints have been developed, for these are found in no fewer than eight of the seventeen installments published from March 2 through June 22, 1861.

Of course, Pip's discovery creates retrospective irony when we recall his earlier feelings about the "abyss" between Estella and Magwitch (p. 335), and the coincidence also makes the young woman still another link between her father and Miss Havisham, who have been previously connected not only through their interest in Pip, their alienation from society, and their employment of Jaggers, but also through their coincidental victimization by the same villain, Compeyson.[3] Even more interesting, however, is the way in which learning of Estella's true parents affects Pip.

Seeking to corroborate his guesses, he himself does not understand why he is intent on "tracing out and proving Estella's parentage" (p. 387). A clue, however, seems present in the timing of his perception about Molly. Just before this realization, we are told that Pip, eager to avoid proof that Estella has married Drummle, has refrained from reading newspapers. But a chance meeting with Jaggers leads to a dinner, during which the lawyer refers to Drummle's having "won the pool" and speaks of Estella as "Mrs. Bentley Drummle" (pp. 368–69). Just after hearing this distressing news, Pip looks at Molly and decides that she is Estella's mother.

Although the protagonist later speculates that his urge to confirm that Estella is the daughter of Magwitch may stem from a desire to "transfer" to the latter "some rays of the romantic interest" long associated with Estella (p. 387), Pip's excitement may be attributable to two other causes: first, a satisfaction in finding Estella to be the child of a convict, since the discovery would make her less lofty and possibly more within reach, even though her very recent marriage has seemingly made her truly inaccessible; and, second,

Pip's wish to find a coincidence so extraordinary as to justify a faith in the possibility of miracles. If Magwitch's daughter, lost, according to his words, for "a round score o'year" (p. 386), can be found, may not Pip's Estella, just lost to Drummle, still be recovered? Such may be Pip's implicit reasoning, perhaps similar to that of Sir Leicester in *Bleak House*: in Chapter 58 of that novel the stricken baronet finds in the marvelous reappearance of the long-lost George Rouncewell a cause for hope that the missing Lady Dedlock will also be safely returned. Pip, despite his earlier renunciation of all thought of winning Estella, and despite his later statement that he has "lost her and must live a bereaved life" (p. 390), seems after discovering her parentage to act as though his optimism had been rekindled, even though she has married Drummle.

In previous remarks Pip has repeatedly described his love for Estella as an obsession. Even after her marriage, Pip tells Jaggers that "whatever concerned her was still nearer and dearer ... than anything else in the world" (p. 390). Although he evidently accepts the lawyer's advice that Estella's background be kept secret, Pip's devotion to Magwitch, already strong by this time, appears intensified by the knowledge of the latter's relationship to Estella. We may wonder whether Pip seeks to prove his own worthiness to himself by aiding her father to escape. For there may be significance in the fact that Pip does not even mention the "vague something lingering in ... [his] thoughts" (p. 427), later disclosed to be the intention of proposing to Biddy (pp. 446–48), until after Magwitch has been mortally injured and captured. Indeed, before this, Pip's first fear when his life is threatened by Orlick is, "Estella's father would believe I had deserted him " (p. 403)—Pip here refers to his benefactor as "Estella's father," instead of using either the convict's name or the pseudonym "Provis."

Later, Pip feels compelled not only to tell the dying Magwitch that his daughter, thought dead for many years, is alive, but also to add, "She is a lady and very beautiful. And I love her!" (p. 436). But Pip seems misleading in not mentioning Estella's apparent failure to return his affection and in omitting any reference to her marriage, by what she calls her "own act" (p. 344), to Drummle, who is considered "a mean brute.... a stupid brute" by Pip (p. 345) and is seen as a potential wife-beater by Jaggers (pp. 368–69). Then, too, in his avowal to Magwitch of love for Estella, the protagonist intimates that she and he will eventually be married, an idea that he evidently believes will please her dying father.[4] At this point, Pip appears to forget that in the preceding chapter he told us of harboring a "vague something" in his thoughts. Only later do we learn that this refers to a plan to marry Biddy, but if we then remember the scene with the dying Magwitch, we must concede that Pip's loyalty, even while he is supposedly thinking of marriage to Biddy, is not to her but to Estella; and his avowal of love for a married woman certainly raises questions of propriety. Perhaps even after the failure of the attempt to help Magwitch escape, Pip still clings to the hope that his devotion to this man will, as in a fairy tale, miraculously win the hand of the latter's daughter. Pip, who once "resolved" never to "breathe" a "word of Estella to Provis" (p. 335), now seems to seek the old convict's blessing for a marriage that appears no longer possible.

Estella's parentage adds irony to her marriage to Drummle, "the next heir but one to a baronetcy" (p. 181), but she is, of course, unaware of her background, and her reasons for marrying Drummle remain undisclosed. Mrs. Oliphant, while attacking *Great Expectations*, asserts that Estella "breaks nobody's heart but Pip's," does not carry out Miss Havisham's vindictive plans, and "only fulfils a vulgar fate by marrying a man without any heart to be broken, and being miserable herself instead."[5] But this choice of Drummle can be regarded differently. William F. Axton sees Estella's marriage as "a masochistic union" intended to be a "perverse revenge on the woman who has warped her," while Lucille P. Shores argues that Estella selects Drummle because "she feels he is the only sort of husband to whom she can do no harm."[6]

One other possibility, however, is that Estella wishes to achieve her foster-mother's revenge on a victim who is like Compeyson in being a false gentleman. For Jaggers believes that the marriage may turn out to be difficult for Drummle (pp. 368–69); and we certainly would not grant the latter the status of "a true gentleman at heart" which Herbert's father denied to Compeyson (p. 171). Orlick, whose "slouching after" (p. 124) resembles the "lagging behind" of Drummle (p. 205), is evidently the man that Pip sees lighting Drummle's cigar (p. 339). Because Orlick later reveals that he has become Compeyson's employee (pp. 405–06), he serves to link the two false gentlemen.[7] Moreover, Jaggers' references to Drummle as "the Spider" (pp. 200, 205, 368–69) create an association between this character and the spiders on Miss Havisham's wedding-table (pp. 78, 289), emblems of ruin caused by the cruelty of Compeyson, whom we may also consider a spider if we recall the "nets" in which he entrapped Magwitch (p. 331). Drummle seems, therefore, a substitute for Compeyson and a suitable object on whom to obtain revenge for Miss Havisham. Although Estella does not escape unscathed from her marriage, she does survive her husband.

In addition, a few details raise the possibility that Dickens wishes us to link Estella with Drummle's death. After encountering Pip at the Blue Boar, Drummle is seen "seizing his horse's mane, and mounting in his blundering brutal manner" (p. 339). Later, we learn of his death, "from an accident consequent on his ill-treatment of a horse" (p. 458). Since Pip has just previously reported that Estella had been "separated from her husband, who had used her with great cruelty" (p. 458), we may tend to associate her with the horse, despite our not knowing the animal's gender, for both Estella and the horse are harshly treated by Drummle, and the prior image of "mounting" may carry sexual connotations. Just as Tolstoy, over a decade later, was to use Vronsky's mare, a creature ridden to death, to symbolize Anna Karenina (Part II, ch. xxv), so Dickens is perhaps suggesting that Estella, daughter of physically violent parents, may in some vague way be responsible for Drummle's destruction, thereby revenging Miss Havisham on a surrogate for her betrayer. Dickens does not wish to make Estella a killer like her mother, but he may want to hint that Drummle's death is an answer to Jaggers' toast concerning the marriage, "may the question of supremacy be settled to the lady's satisfaction!" (p. 369).[8]

Although speculations like these do not seem to rise to Pip's mind, he never escapes the effects of his startling discovery that Estella is Magwitch's child. His response to this coincidence evidently shapes his subsequent reactions to two crucial coincidences of timing: first, his arrival in the village for the purpose of proposing to Biddy occurs just after her marriage to Joe; and, second, in the revised ending his return, after eleven years, to the site of Satis House is on the same evening that Estella has chosen to visit this location.

2

The idea of Biddy as a possible mate for Pip is thought of and rejected by him early in the story (pp. 121, 123–25), before he learns of his "expectations." Apparently, he first begins to reconsider this option at about the time that Herbert, after the shock of Magwitch's capture and before the trial, mentions the possibility of obtaining a clerkship for him (pp. 426–27). But, as we have noticed, Pip's first reference to his intention of proposing to Biddy is so veiled—"a vague something"—that it is incomprehensible; and between this reference and the subsequent explanation we find him affirming his love for Estella to the dying Magwitch. Since at the time of this avowal the covert reference to marrying Biddy has not yet been clarified, we are prevented from initially regarding the comment about loving Estella as disloyalty to Biddy. Certainly, however, we may later view the hero's statement as indicating a lack of any deep attachment to the latter. Pip, despite his genuine remorse about his treatment of both Biddy and Joe (pp. 399, 403), has never had feelings for her other than those of respect and brotherly affection, her early residence in the same household having perhaps created an incest-prohibition similar to that which David Copperfield must overcome before recognizing his desire for Agnes.

Following Magwitch's death, Pip, having fallen ill and been nursed back to health by Joe, plans to tell the latter of the previously mentioned "vague something." Joe leaves unexpectedly, however, and only then are we told that the "something" involves proposing to Biddy. After three days, Pip travels to the village, but finds that Joe and Biddy have just been married.

Fainting at the surprise, the protagonist then reacts in an unusual way: his "first thought" is not one of disappointment but, instead, "one of great thankfulness" that he "had never breathed this last baffled hope to Joe" (p. 454). Pip may be truly grateful that he has caused his brother-in-law no discomfort, but he is perhaps also pleased that he has not given Joe a chance to relinquish Biddy in a display of noble-hearted generosity. The coincidence that Biddy's marriage comes just before Pip can propose saves him not only from potential rejection but also from the prospect of actually becoming Biddy's husband. He perhaps feels relieved to have escaped Biddy, for he may not really wish to face even the possibility that she would ask him to work at the forge.[9] Indeed, his previously declared intention of leaving all decisions to Biddy, should she accept him (p. 447), seems a plan to resign from adult responsibility. Most important, Pip has not overcome his obsession with Estella. At the time when she, after disclosing her plans to be married, told him that he would soon get over his disappointment, the response was really a promise, "Never, Estella!" (p. 345). His final words to Magwitch, while evidently meant to cheer the dying man, are perhaps also intended to comfort Pip himself. Many years before, after Pip once tactlessly exclaimed to Biddy, "If I could only get myself to fall in love with you," she perceptively replied, "But you never will, you see" (p. 123).

After learning that Biddy and Joe are married, Pip undertakes to cleanse himself by begging their forgiveness and then announces his intention to return almost immediately to London, where he will accept Herbert's offer of a clerkship and go, a voluntary exile, to Cairo. Although Pip's eagerness to depart hastily from Biddy and Joe may reflect either a wish to avoid obtruding on their early days of marriage or a desire to conceal his own disappointment, his behavior may also be prompted by an impulse to flee the scene of a close escape from a future that he did not really want, a future that would have been a final acknowledgment of the loss of the woman he still loves. With Biddy safely married, Pip is free to wait indefinitely for Estella.

Earlier, Pip has been dramatically saved from the murderous Orlick in a rescue made possible by two coincidences: Herbert's opportune finding of the letter summoning his friend to the marshes, and the availability of Trabb's boy to serve as a guide after Herbert and Startop reach the village. In Victorian fiction, such fortunate circumstances are often attributed to divine intervention.[10] Pip evidently sees his survival as a providential response to his remorse concerning his treatment of Biddy and Joe and to his sincere prayers for divine pardon (pp. 404, 407). Right after the rescue, he offers a "thanksgiving" (p. 408).

The subsequent coincidence that prevents Pip from even proposing to Biddy may also seem to him—and to us—a miraculous phenomenon that allows him to continue defying reason and hoping for further miracles. For, after "losing" Biddy, he considers no alternative other than bachelorhood. His eleven-year stay "in the East" (p. 457) seems a penance, a punishment like the one that society unfairly gave Magwitch, but Pip's removal from ordinary life is also like Miss Havisham's in being self-imposed. In fact, he may appear as emotionally arrested as the heiress,[11] and we may wonder whether he has welcomed exile in the exotic East because it has reduced his chances of meeting women whom British society would consider suitable marriage partners. Significantly, after the return of Pip to England, his assurance to Biddy that he does not long for Estella (p. 457) seems disingenuous—possibly a self-deception if read with the novel's original ending (never published by Dickens), for even that conclusion is marked, as John Kucich observes, by "the prominence Pip gives Estella at the end of his narrative."[12] When considered with the revised conclusion, the statement to Biddy is clearly a falsehood, for Pip concedes in the next sentence that, while speaking to her, he was "secretly" intending "to revisit the site" of Satis House, for "Estella's sake" (p. 458). In addition, both the original and revised endings contradict the last paragraph in Chapter 57, which affirms that the result of Pip's intention of going to the village to propose to Biddy is "all" that he has "left to tell" (p. 448).

3

Both conclusions describe a coincidental meeting with Estella when Pip returns to England. In the original version this encounter occurs on Piccadilly after two years have passed, while in the revised ending the meeting is much more remarkable, taking place on the very evening of Pip's homecoming visit to Biddy, Joe, and their children, and occurring at the deserted, desolate site where Satis House once stood. Not only is the location of the reunion in this revised ending far more significant than Piccadilly; in this version both Pip and Estella have coincidentally chosen to visit this particular place for nostalgic reasons. In the original conclusion the only point of the meeting is that Estella, who has remarried after Drummle's death, conveys "in her face and in her voice, and in her touch, . . . the assurance, that suffering had been stronger than Miss Havisham's teaching, and had given her a heart to understand what . . . [Pip's] heart used to be" (p. 461). Pip, in employing the words "used to be," suggests that by the time of this meeting his heart has changed, has perhaps become less romantic or less sensitive. But his insistence on bachelorhood in the preceding talk with Biddy may make us doubtful that any such change has occurred, and we may also wonder why in this final meeting, in the original version, Pip allows Estella to assume mistakenly that young Pip is his child.

In the revised ending Pip stresses the extraordinary nature of the encounter: he first perceives "a solitary figure," "the figure of a woman" that, on seeing him, falters "as if much surprised"; on hearing his name "uttered," he recognizes Estella and later remarks, "After so many years, it is strange that we should thus meet again, Estella, here where our first meeting was!" (pp. 458–59). Nevertheless, he seems less astonished than she, as though he possibly regards the meeting as a wonderful but not wholly unexpected event. Both he and Estella, in this revised ending, have lost their fortunes, but each has been improved by adversity.

In this conclusion, the one that Dickens decided to publish, the intention is, despite much speculation by scholars, to unite Pip and Estella in marriage. Indeed, any attempt to deny this must begin by countering the fact that Forster includes in his biography a reference to "an objection taken not unfairly [by some critics] to the too great speed with which the heroine, after being married, reclaimed, and widowed, is in a page or two again made love to, and remarried by the hero" (Bk. IX, ch. iii, p. 737). Forster adds that Dickens changed the conclusion because of Bulwer-Lytton's "objecting to a close that should leave Pip a solitary man" (Bk. IX, ch. iii, p. 737).

Various details in this second ending seem to confirm Forster's belief that it implies the protagonist's marriage. On sitting down with Estella, Pip thinks of his last words to Magwitch, a farewell expressing love for the convict's daughter. Moreover, Estella discloses that she has "often thought" of Pip and then makes an admission even more gratifying to him: "There was a long hard time when I kept far from me the remembrance of what I had thrown away when I was quite ignorant of its worth. But, since my duty has not been incompatible with the admission of that remembrance, I have given it a place in my heart" (p. 459). Pip has finally gained an answer to the question he had asked many years before: "When should I awaken the heart within her, that was mute and sleeping now?" (p. 230). For he has never believed her cold words, "I have no heart" (p. 224), and in this reunion she openly refers to her heart and the place in it devoted to the remembrance of Pip's love. Furthermore, her statement suggests that prior to Drummle's death—which released her from wifely "duty"—she had to exert an effort to keep the remembrance of Pip's love "far" from her. As for the hero, he immediately responds, "You have always held your place in my heart" (p. 459)—no ambiguous reference here by Pip to her understanding "what my heart used to be." Although Estella, in the revised conclusion, does comment that she now comprehends what Pip's "heart used to be" (p. 460), her remark seems not a recognition of change in the protagonist, but merely a defensive gesture, for she may fear—in her new vulnerability—that Pip, despite his reassuring words, no longer loves her.

There is significance, too, in the fact that Estella's proposal that she and Pip "will continue friends apart" (p. 460) elicits no response from the hero except for his taking of her hand. The final clause in the novel, "I saw no shadow of another parting from her," seems an improvement over the wording in the installment publication in *All the Year Round*, "*I saw the shadow of no parting from her*," a statement that may bring to mind the humorous possibility that the prospect of not being able to part from Estella ("no parting") might now be seen as a "shadow," a problem, facing Pip.[13]

But, if the book's revised conclusion includes an anticipation of marriage, we may question why Pip, as narrator, is not more lucid. Since he continues to use the past tense, we may surmise that he has had time to discover whether his expectation of "no shadow" was correct. As Milton Millhauser asks, "Why . . . does he not tell us what he knows?"[14] Nevertheless, the echo, noticed by Edgar Johnson among others, of the closing lines in *Paradise Lost*, in which a reconciled Adam and Eve go forth together, united, to face the world, suggests a basically positive outcome.[15] Moreover, the degree of improbability or surprise in the revised version's coincidental meeting is so much greater than that in the corresponding encounter in the original version that Pip and we are likely to see some supernatural cause at work once more—providence or destiny.

Pip is a decent, honorable, kind man, one whose sufferings seem disproportionate to his earlier moral errors. For him to be again disappointed would be a cruel conclusion, one that would condemn him to a life of only avuncular, limited involvement with others, the kind of role that even unselfish Tom Pinch, in Chapter 50 of *Martin Chuzzlewit*, accepts with resignation rather than joy. Marriage with Estella, who, like Pip, is in her mid-thirties, perhaps gives the protagonist a chance to have a child of his own, a desire that Biddy surmises he has when she replies, in response to his request that she "give" or "lend" her son to him, "No, no," and adds, "You must marry" (p. 457). Clearly, for Pip, only Estella can be his mate.

4

Pip's early romantic delusions serve in many ways to create his problems, but his views are in part imposed upon him by circumstances and by his understandable misinterpretation of these. Christopher Ricks, after referring to Jaggers' dual roles and to Magwitch's being Estella's father, asserts, "these improbabilities are gross enough," but maintains that they act to win sympathy for the protagonist: "The odds against him are shown to be pretty terrifying."[16] As a result of his own temperament, the expectations mysteriously announced to him, and his misunderstanding concerning Miss Havisham, Pip has become, in Herbert's words, "a good fellow, with impetuosity and hesitation, boldness and diffidence, action and dreaming, curiously mixed in him" (p. 234). Although Pip at the end of the novel appears to retain an unrealistic romantic outlook, it is largely purged of selfishness. As Robert A. Greenberg cogently argues, the revised conclusion is more appropriate than the original one to "the total coherence of the book."[17] And this ending is meant to be a happy one, even though Pip carefully avoids a totally clear account. Indeed, the remaining tinge of ambiguity may perhaps be Dickens' conscious or unconscious acknowledgment of a conflict. There is, on the one hand, the fear that Pip's moral education has come too late to save him from a saddened, diminished life, while, on the other hand, there is the intuition, first suggested by Bulwer-Lytton, but nevertheless endorsed by Dickens himself, that in the case of Pip one more last-minute rescue is not too much to hope for.

In addition, another element makes the revised ending particularly suitable. From the early chapters on, the novel seems to place great emphasis on the theme of revenge. Magwitch, Compeyson, Miss Havisham, her half-brother, Molly, Orlick, Pip himself (especially with regard to Trabb's boy)—all of these figures display vindictiveness.[18] Despite this extensive concern with revenge, however, the value that the narrator, Pip, eventually comes to embrace is clearly forgiveness. He learns that his sister, before her death, asked his pardon (p. 269), and his forgiveness is also sought by another erring mother-figure, Miss Havisham (pp. 377, 382). Overcoming his own pain, Pip readily forgives Estella, even without being asked (p. 345). In turn, he himself, when threatened by the murderous Orlick, requests divine pardon (p. 404) and, after his rescue, subsequently begs forgiveness of Biddy and Joe (p. 455). That Pip knows he will receive this is suggested by his earlier praise of Joe as "this gentle Christian man" (p. 439).

The forgiving of Miss Havisham—by Pip and by us—seems earned by her sincere repentance and by the expiation of her death from shock after she has been burned in a kind of purgatorial fire. But her regret and suffering may also make us wish her to be given a relatively full moral exoneration, and this seems to require a softening—a retroactive reduction—of the wrong she has done to both Estella and Pip. In effect, *only* the romantic reunion intimated in the revised ending can achieve this, since Estella has long been, in Pip's words, "part of my existence, part of myself" (p. 345), "impossible . . . to separate . . . from the innermost life of my life" (p. 223). We may here, too, be reminded of *Paradise Lost*, in which Eve reports Adam's words to her: "Part of my Soul I seek thee, and thee claim/ My other half" (Bk. IV, ll. 487–88).

The discovery of Estella's parentage lifts Pip from despair, reawakens his hope, and creates in him, and perhaps in us, the readers of his story, expectations that Dickens was later persuaded to satisfy. After recognizing Estella's relationship to Magwitch, Pip once again appears confident about the possibility of the miraculous in life. He therefore is free to persist in his desires and to interpret subsequent events such as his escape from Orlick, the removal of Biddy as a potential mate, and the meeting with Estella as confirmation of providential design. As his story concludes, his expectations, though modified, remain great.

Notes

1. In citing *Great Expectations* I use the volume in the Oxford Illustrated Dickens (London: Oxford Univ. Press, 1953) and provide page numbers in parentheses.

2. "Wonderful Chains: Dickens and Coincidence," *MP*, 83 (1985), 164.

3. Among the scholars who emphasize Dickens' linking of Miss Havisham and Magwitch are H. M. Daleski, *Dickens and the Art of Analogy* (New York: Schocken Books, 1970), p. 238; Ross H. Dabney, *Love and Property in the Novels of Charles Dickens* (London: Chatto & Windus, 1967), p. 126; and Forsyth, pp. 163–64.

4. Dabney, p. 147, maintains that Pip is giving Magwitch "a final illusion to die on," while Harry Stone, in *Dickens and the Invisible World: Fairy Tales, Fantasy, and Novel-Making* (Bloomington: Indiana Univ. Press, 1979), p. 311, asserts, "One part of Pip's rebirth consists in recognizing and accepting Estella's true identity and then confessing to her debased father—now under sentence of death—that he loves her."

5. *Dickens: The Critical Heritage*, ed. Philip Collins (New York: Barnes & Noble, 1971), p. 440.

6. Axton, "*Great Expectations* Yet Again," *DSA*, 2 (1972), 290; Shores, "The Character of Estella in *Great Expectations*," *MSE*, 3 (1972), 97.

7. For comments on the linking of Orlick and Drummle, see Karl P. Wentersdorf, "Mirror-Images in *Great Expectations*," *NCF*, 21 (1966), 212, 217–19.

8. In *The Life of Charles Dickens*, ed. J. W. T. Ley (London: Cecil Palmer, 1928), Bk. VIII, ch. ii, p. 636, n., John Forster observes of Dickens, "The question of hereditary transmission had a curious attraction for him, and considerations connected with it were frequently present to his mind." My later references to this volume appear parenthetically in the text of my essay.

9. Milton Millhauser, in "*Great Expectations*: The Three Endings," *DSA*, 2 (1972), 271, maintains that Pip "would probably have made a rather condescending husband for the Biddy he had determined on marrying, country school-teacher or no," while Melanie Young, in "Distorted Expectations: Pip and the Problems of Language," *DSA*, 7 (1978), 212, states that "experience and education have made him unsuited to a life at the forge (or anything similar with Biddy)." E. Pearlman, in "Inversion in *Great Expectations*," *DSA*, 7 (1978), 200, sees snobbery in "Dickens' unwillingness to allow his hero to sacrifice himself" by marrying Biddy. A very different view is offered by Jack P. Rawlins, who affirms, in "Great Expiations: Dickens and the Betrayal of the Child," *SEL*, 23 (1983), 679, that Dickens intends the loss of Biddy to be "a bitter pill" for Pip and does not realize that the reader will "gasp with relief."

10. Among those who see coincidence in Victorian literature as usually representing providential intervention are Harland S. Nelson, in "Dickens' Plots: 'The

Ways of Providence' or the Influence of Collins?," *VN*, No. 19 (1961), pp. 11–14, and David Goldknopf, in *The Life of the Novel* (Chicago: The Univ. of Chicago Press, 1972), pp. 164, 174. Harvey Peter Sucksmith, in *The Narrative Art of Charles Dickens: The Rhetoric of Sympathy and Irony in his Novels* (Oxford: Clarendon Press, 1970), p. 237, asserts that Dickens' "most important and extensive use of coincidence" is "to create an ironic effect" and to suggest "fate or design." See, too, the stimulating chapter on coincidence in John R. Reed's *Victorian Conventions* (Athens: Ohio Univ. Press, 1975), pp. 126–41.

11. Maire Jaanus Kurrik, in *Literature and Negation* (New York: Columbia Univ. Press, 1979), pp. 175–76, considers the resemblance between Pip and Miss Havisham.

12. "Action in the Dickens Ending: *Bleak House* and *Great Expectations*," *NCF* 33 (1978), 102.

13. Angus Calder, in his edition of the novel (Baltimore, MD: Penguin, 1965), p. 496, reproduces the original clause and maintains that with the emendation "Dickens deliberately made the last phrase less definite, and even ambiguous," since the shadow may have been there even though Pip did not see it.

14. P. 274.

15. *Charles Dickens: His Tragedy and Triumph*, 2 vols. (New York: Simon and Schuster, 1952), 2, 993–94.

16. "*Great Expectations*," in *Dickens and the Twentieth Century*, ed. John Gross and Gabriel Pearson (Toronto: Univ. of Toronto Press, 1962), p. 203.

17. "On Ending *Great Expectations*," *PLL*, 6 (1970), 154. J. Hillis Miller, in *Charles Dickens: The World of His Novels* (Cambridge: Harvard Univ. Press, 1958), p. 278, also finds the second ending "much truer to the real direction of the story," as does Marshall W. Gregory, in "Values and Meaning in *Great Expectations*: The Two Endings Revisited," *EIC*, 19 (1969), 407–08. Sucksmith, p. 112, in defending this revised version, maintains, "If we accept the account of Estella's regeneration in the rejected ending, then we should also accept the reconciliation between Pip and Estella in the new ending, since this is only a logical development of that regeneration." For a review of the scholarly debate over the two conclusions, and an argument in favor of the unpublished version, see Edgar Rosenberg, "Last Words on *Great Expectations*: A Textual Brief on the Six Endings," *DSA*, 9 (1981), 87–115. More recently, Rawlins, p. 680, n. 13, has also contended that the unpublished ending is more credible.

18. Julian Moynihan, in "The Hero's Guilt: The Case of *Great Expectations*," *EIC* 10 (1960), 71–77, and Wentersdorf, pp. 206–07, 214–16, 219–21, are among the commentators who consider Pip's covert desires for violent revenge, expressed through such surrogates as Orlick and Drummle.

GAIL TURLEY HOUSTON

"Pip" and "Property": The (Re)Production of the Self in Great Expectations

One of the important perceptions of Dickens' fiction is of Victorian society as one in which the weak support the strong, the starving underwrite the satiated, the poor prop up the rich, the children sustain the parents—and the female upholds the male. Indeed, the typical Dickensian heroine is a nourishing mother figure who herself is usually motherless. Central to most of Dickens' novels, this heroine in her self-denial creates for the hero a safe and sacred haven from the rapaciousness of the market. Nevertheless, these same heroines also underwrite the economic ambition they are intended to mediate. As Mary Poovey suggests, in Victorian England the alienation of male labor was made tolerable by representing female work within the domestic sphere as selfless and self-regulating, and therefore not alienated. Hence, it was assumed that the "non-competitive, non-aggressive, and self-sacrificing" private sphere of women domesticated without curbing the "competitive, aggressive, and acquisitive"[1] public sphere of the male dedicated to success and money.

This pattern is borne out in Dickens' fiction in a number of ways. For example, in *The Old Curiosity Shop*, Nell's ascetic control of her body and her maternal care for her grandfather mute but also magnify his grotesque obsession with gambling and wealth. Likewise, Mary Graham's "self-possession and control over her emotions" tame the senior Martin Chuzzlewit's selfish

From *Studies in the Novel* 24, no. 1 (Spring 1992): 13–25. © 1992 by *Studies in the Novel*.

materialism, and thus validate his wealth, as she makes him rich in feeling. Herself starved for affection, Florence Dombey becomes a nurturing angel to her financially and emotionally bankrupt father at the same time that she underwrites Walter Gay's "Dick Whittington" aspirations to marry the daughter and heir and become financially successful.

This pattern culminates in Dickens' autobiographical novel *David Copperfield*, in which David depends on Agnes to domesticate his "undisciplined heart." Thus, married to the self-denying Agnes, Copperfield's self-indulgent actions and thoughts are redeemed. Moreover, in depicting Agnes as a maternal, self-sacrificing heroine who is the inspiration for himself as aspiring author, David casts a positive aura on his own ambitions that might otherwise be construed as, in his words, "sordid things."[2] Hence, emphasizing Agnes' role as amanuensis, literary helpmeet, and Muse, David focuses on his motives as secular prophet and downplays his own profit motive.[3] Indeed, the underside of David's excessive humility about his own profession is Heep's aggressive profession of his "humble" aspirations.[4]

Great Expectations, Dickens' second attempt at a fictional autobiography, is an about-face, for the key women in the protagonist's life are anything but maternal. In fact, in this late novel, the long suppressed Dickensian female defies her maternal role. Clearly Pip seems doubly bereft of maternal nurture through the death of his mother and the accession to that role by Mrs. Joe. In fact, named after Pip's mother—and with everything that implies about the senior Georgiana Pirrip's nurturing abilities—Pip's sister regrets having to have been his second "mother."[5] Bitter that circumstances have forced her into being the self-denying mother figure, Mrs. Joe physically and emotionally starves her brother, become son. Likewise, she forces him to pay a high price—and that is to be taken literally—for her maternal service(s). With her arsenal of needles and pins sticking to the bodice of her apron, this "all-powerful sister" is literally the bad breast (p. 46). Miss Havisham, whom I will discuss in more detail later, is another surrogate mother to Pip. Not the "fairy godmother" Pip thinks she is, Miss Havisham manipulates Pip in order to enslave him emotionally in the same way that she forms her adopted daughter, Estella, in order to cannibalize her (p. 183).

Certainly Dickens sets Biddy up as a potential wife and mother figure for Pip, but here again a contrast with *David Copperfield* is enlightening. In *David Copperfield* Dickens describes David's romantic love for Agnes as the culmination of a ragged young boy finding his way home to his mother. Similarly, Pip romantically sees himself as "one who was toiling home barefoot from distant travel, and whose wanderings had lasted many years," and he hopes that Biddy can receive him "like a forgiven child (and indeed I am as sorry, Biddy, and have as much need of a hushing voice and a soothing hand)" (pp. 486, 481). But in a surprising scene, Dickens denies his hero the self-denying heroine. Indeed, Biddy will not be the mother figure—the good breast—for Pip, for she rather abruptly "baffles" Pip's plans by marrying Joe (p. 487). Nevertheless, she remains a touchstone for the hero's romantic intentions. For instance, pointedly questioning why he would love someone who calls him coarse and common, Biddy asks Pip if he wants to be a gentleman, "to spite her [Estella] or to gain her over?" Pip responds that he doesn't know, to which Biddy replies: "if it is to spite her . . . I should think . . . that might be better and more independently done by caring nothing for her words. And if it is to gain her over, I should think . . . she was not worth gaining over" (p. 156).

Thus, true to her name, Biddy is something of a hen pecker, but her catechisms of Pip are incisive and just. One wonders, then, why neither Pip nor Dickens is capable of taking her sensible advice. But, in fact, with Estella Dickens seems ready to delineate a very different kind of woman, for, considering her predecessors, the ingenue Estella is an astonishing Dickensian heroine. Like Nell, Mary Graham, Florence, Agnes, Esther, and Little Dorrit, she is without a nourishing mother figure, but in this novel the lack of a loving mother results in the creation of a "Tartar," Herbert Pocket's epithet for Estella (p. 200). Furthermore, as Estella tells Miss Havisham,

> Mother by adoption, I have said that I owe everything to you. All I possess is freely yours. All that you have given me, is at your command to have again. Beyond that, I have nothing. And if you ask me to give you what you never gave me, my gratitude and duty cannot do impossibilities (p. 323).

Obviously, Miss Havisham uses this child for her own warped purposes, but in producing Estella to take revenge on the men who took public and economic advantage of her private sexual desires, Miss Havisham only succeeds in duplicating the experience for her own adoptive daughter, making her a thing to be bartered in the marriage market.

Moreover, trained in the accomplishments of the ideal Victorian woman, Estella as Dickensian heroine has finally necessarily become what Victorian and Dickensian expectations must naturally—or, rather, unnaturally—result in: she is the nightmare version of the Victorian female bred to have no desires, no appetites, trained to be desired and to be the object of appetite. Clearly Estella views herself as Miss Havisham's ornamental object, to be dangled before men to tantalize them and break their hearts. Thus, groomed to be the absent center of the Victorian male's affections, Estella incites obsessive emotional responses in men while she herself is without feelings. Dickens, of course, reviles the kind of system that would create such a creature, yet it is undeniable that his own earlier powerful portrayals of ascetic heroines helped to create this distorted version of the ideal female. Pip's remark to Estella that "you speak of yourself as if you were some one else," reveals Dickens' implicit and incisive awareness of the results of Pip's—and for that matter, his own—sexual and economic obsessions (p. 286). Indeed, Estella's self-forgetfulness resonates on the self-forgetfulness of Dickens' previous heroines, for Estella's alienation from self is the underside of the earlier Dickensian heroine's self-denial.

Struggling with his own self-aggrandizing personality, Dickens' alter-ego, then, comes face to face with a ravishing, sensual, but heartless woman. Pip cannot help but empathize with her, but he also cannot rise above his own rationalization of his desire. If in Dickens' autobiographical *David Copperfield* Agnes' self-denying female economy underwrites David's self-indulgent, aggressive male economy, we must question what happens in Dickens' later semi-autobiographical novel when Estella's warped female economy underlies Pip's, for like David, Pip places the responsibility for his own character on the woman he loves:

> Truly it was impossible to dissociate her [Estella's] presence from all those wretched hankerings after money and gentility that had disturbed my boyhood—from all those ill-regulated aspirations that had first made me ashamed of home and Joe—
>
> . . . In a word, it was impossible for me to separate her, in the past or in the present, from the innermost life of my life (p. 257).

The ominous suggestion that Estella made Pip avaricious becomes almost a threat when Pip states to her, "Estella, to the last hour of my life, you cannot choose but remain part of my character, part of the little good in me, part of the evil" (p. 378). In contrast to *David Copperfield*, in which Dickens portrays male ambition as refined by an ascetic female, the reasoning of *Great Expectations* is that, not the devil, but Estella made me do it.

In his study of the Naturalist novel, Mark Seltzer tracks the ways that writers like Frank Norris counter two generative forces, production and reproduction, as signified in the masculine steam machine and the mother. Brilliantly arguing that Naturalist fiction assumes that genetically males live according to a principle of loss and females according to a principle of profit, Seltzer points out that such a discourse posits the contradictory spheres of the public and the private, work and home, the world and family, and the economic and the sexual.[6] Though Seltzer's focus is on American Naturalist fiction, his contrast of male production and female reproduction is useful in analyzing the meaning of *Great Expectations*, for in this later autobiographical novel Dickens is far more conscious of how economics infiltrate the construction of the self. Indeed, in *Great Expectations* the making of the self rests in the space between the meanings of reproduction and production, the maternal and the material, the home and the market. Thus, perhaps more so than in any other of his novels, in *Great Expectations* Dickens realistically examines the possibility of inhabiting the sphere of reproduction, which in his previous works was that place or person—usually female and maternal—through which the individual is validated as a human being with feelings. To put it more precisely, in Dickens the sphere of reproduction is in essence a kind of actual or metaphorical return to the bosom of the family.

The problem, as Seltzer is so aware in his analysis of the Naturalist novel, is that though the productive and reproductive spheres are separate, they also interpenetrate, for the one sphere produces the goods while the other produces the consumers of those goods.[7] Thus the sphere of production infiltrates that of reproduction, creating the self caught in the cycle of consumption, as the individual becomes a thing, reared to consume and to be consumed. Therefore, in contrast to Dickens' earlier works, in which he represents the heroine as a haven from aggressive economies, in *Great Expectations* both hero and heroine are constructed, that is, made economically. In fact, Dickens comes to realize that the possibility of escaping the market and effecting a return to the mother is practically nil. Indeed, Pip's—and, for that matter, Estella's—maternal guardians, who are supposed to be their nurturers, end up being their business managers.

That production infiltrates reproduction is apparent in the fact that the Victorians referred to private, sexual matters in rather public, economic terms. For example, the Victorian slang phrase for male organs was "to spend."[8] Therefore, when Victorian men were trained to "save" themselves for marriage it was in both economic and sexual terms: they were required to put off marriage until they had saved enough in the bank to be financially stable: but it was also necessary to put off "spending" in sexual terms. Hence, Samuel Smiles' blithe assertion that the capitalist is a man "who does not spend all that is earned by work," but rather is a man prepared to deny "present enjoyment for future good," results in the ludicrous situation that Fraser Harrison describes: "Celibate and capitalist alike resolutely fought off the desire to spend."[9] Herbert Pocket's emotional and economic reasoning regarding his engagement to Clara is a fictional example of this Victorian attitude: "the moment he [Herbert] began to realize Capital, it was his intention to marry this young lady. He added as a self-evident proposition, engendering low spirits, 'But you can't marry, you know, while you're looking about you'" (p. 273).[10]

In the opening chapter of *Great Expectations* Dickens immediately confronts the reader with this question of who "made" Pip. Indeed, in contrast to the young Copperfield's first sense of the "identity of things" as residing exclusively in the maternal reproductive sphere, Pip's budding sense of the "identity of things" is a combination of familial and economic bonds: in the graveyard scene Pip first registers his beginnings in the deceased father and mother and his kinship to five brothers, but then his "second father" Magwitch appears, who, of course, is the benefactor who will produce Pip and his great expectations (p. 337). What with the absent family unit, particularly the mother, very little in the way of maternal nurture protects Pip from falling from the sphere of reproduction into that of production, for in this state of affairs he is destined to become associated with property one way or another. As Biddy teaches Joe and Joe keeps repeating, when the hero first learns of his great expectations, there are really only two words to describe the change: "Pip" and "Property," and the sense is as much Pip becoming property as inheriting it (p. 170).

In fact, before he received his great expectations, Pip, who was "raised by hand," was in the same situation as Herbert Pocket, who is always "looking about me" for his opportunity to become a self-made "capitalist." Juxtaposed, the suggestion that Pip was "raised by hand," (pp. 39, 41, 78, 125, 180, 484) and Pocket's continual assertion that he is always "looking about" for something (pp. 207, 273, 293) seem to contrast the modes of reproduction and production: nevertheless, in actuality the two refrains tend to merge those meanings. For example, Herbert's "looking about" for a "capitalist" position refers to his economic need, but that stress is also partially the result of having to look out for himself as a child in a family that "tumbles" children up, clearly portrayed as more the fault of Pocket's mother than father (p. 209). As Herbert explains to Pip, the offspring of a family in which children are unfathomably produced rather than reproduced, are quick to look about them both for opportunities to marry and enter the market.

Of course "raised by hand," meaning literally the laborious and usually unsuccessful Victorian practice of feeding orphans or abandoned infants by hand rather than by bringing in a wetnurse,[11] signifies Pip's physical lack of the breast in the primal infantine stage, but it also implies his lack of maternal love. Thus, given her brother's fragile beginnings, it is ironic that the woman who raised him by hand, Mrs. Joe, believes that Pip should not be "Pompeyed," that is, pampered (p. 73). And, in fact, the phrase "raised by hand" comes to mean Mrs. Joe's physical abuse of her brother. Furthermore, Mrs. Joe also expects remuneration for having raised Pip by hand, for obviously she hopes to advance her own fortunes by placing him at Miss Havisham's. Her ally, Pumblechook, coopts the phrase, and, by acknowledging that his niece raised Pip by hand, gives added weight to his own claim that he is Pip's mentor in economic terms (and thus deserving of Pip's newly inherited "Capital") when he ludicrously suggests that he "made" Pip (pp. 431–32, 179). Pip thinks and hopes that "Miss Havisham was going to make my fortune on a grand scale," but he is repulsed that he is the gentleman Magwitch has "made" and "owns" (pp. 165, 337, 339, 346).

Fallen into the world of production and consumption, Pip is not born: he is made, and that makes him particularly vulnerable in the cannibalistic world of Victorian England. James E. Marlow suggests that for the reader of *Great Expectations* "the dread of being eaten structures the novel." Asserting that after 1859 "the themes of orality, predation, and the translation of human flesh into economic gain—all metaphoric cannibalism—dominate [Dickens'] fiction," Marlow argues that by this point Dickens believed that cannibalism was not just an "aberration" in ogres like Quilp, but rather "a custom sanctioned by the ideologues of capitalism" such as Merdle and Casby.[12] Indeed, in *Great Expectations* production displaces reproduction whenever the individual is abandoned or betrayed by family, more particularly, by the mother.

With no nourishing mother figure, Pip becomes the object of market relations, learning only to consume or be consumed. Certainly, the masterplot of Pip's rise to and fall from fortune indicates Pip's sense of self as devoured or devouring. Gluttony and starvation oscillate in Pip as his often violent assertion of hunger conflicts with his sense of being devoured. In his "first most vivid and broad impression of the identity of things," Pip is confronted by a convict who threatens to eat Pip if he does not bring him food and a file. As Magwitch later explains to Pip, he turned to crime because he was starving and no one ever "measured my stomach," for "I must put something into my stomach, mustn't I?" (p. 361). Furthermore, when asked what his occupation is, the convict replies, "Eat and drink . . . if you'll find the materials" (p. 362). However, eating and drinking in a society that tolerates starvation—physical or emotional—may be defined as robbery, and Dickens does seem to suggest that any kind of market relations between human beings is a kind of robbery, or, worse, cannibalism. Thus, Pip becomes like "my convict": the starving child of his sister's "bad breast," he broods "I was going to rob Mrs. Joe," and metaphorically assaults the surrogate mother's bad—unreproductive—breast by invading his sister's pantry (pp. 68, 46).

But, as Marlow suggests, the scene that follows indicates that "Pip's dread of being eaten was founded long before the arrival of Magwitch."[13] Young Pip seems in constant danger of being eaten by adult swine. In the Christmas Day feasting scene tales of the eating of children act as appetizers for the adults. Wopsle begins the linguistic cannibalism:

> "Swine," pursued Mr. Wopsle, in his deepest voice, and pointing his fork at my blushes, as if he were mentioning my christian name: "Swine were the companions of the prodigal. The gluttony of Swine is put before us, as an example to the young." (I thought this pretty well in him who had been praising up the pork for being so plump and juicy.) "What is detestable in a pig, is more detestable in a boy" (p. 58).

Pumblechook takes up the sermon, focussing on the "boy" Pip. He opines, "If you'd been born a Squeaker," which Mrs. Joe heartily affirms he was, "You would have been disposed of for so many shillings according to the market price of the article, and Dunstable the butcher . . . would have shed your blood and had your life" (p. 58). The suggestion, of course, is, and Marlow alludes to it as well, that Pip's relations with his sister and her uncle are "market" relations, their chief interest in him being both what fortune they can accrue through him, and making him repay them for how much effort and energy they have spent on raising him. To extend the metaphor, in a later scene, Joe clumsily remarks of Pip's London apartments, "I wouldn't keep a pig in it myself—not in the case that I wished him to fatten wholesome and to eat with a meller flavour on him" (p. 243). This remarkable statement by the "angel" of the novel suggests just how much Pip is consumable "property," subject to the market and its consuming practices (p. 168).

Nevertheless, the epithet "swine" indicts the hero as a devouring as well as devoured self, for, in addition to describing Pip as victim, it is also used, of course, to refer to a person with an inordinate appetite. Pumblechook notes that when Pip leaves for London to fulfill his expectations be is "plump as a Peach," whereas in his diminished state he returns as "little more than skin and bone" (p. 483). It might be taken literally, then, when Joe visits Pip in town and exudes that he has "growed" and "swelled" as he becomes "gentle-folked" (pp. 241–42). In fact, like most of Dickens' young heroes and heroines, Pip is "uncommonly small," yet like young Oliver and David, who are accused of wanting "more," and being a "boa constrictor," respectively, Pip is accused of "bolting." Like his predecessors, Pip is both innocent and guilty when it comes to being accused of gluttony. On the one hand, this ostensible ingestion is an empty consumption, for the hungry boy forgoes eating the bread in order to feed it to the escaped convict, yet his guardians accuse him of "bolting" (p. 43).

But, on the other hand, Dickens never leaves these accusations of his hero's inordinate appetite alone. Quite commonly he complicates the hero's motives, suggesting that there is a kind of oscillation between guilty desires and innocent victimization. Thus, when Pip feeds Magwitch with the hoarded slab of bread and butter, the convict actually does bolt the wadded up supper, as Pip watches with the fascination of revulsion: "He swallowed, or rather snapped up, every mouthful, too soon and too fast . . . In all of which particulars he was very like the dog" (pp. 50–51, see also p. 346). But, of course, Pip both directly and implicitly compares himself to "bolting" canines, an animal image like the swine imagery that implies both voracious gluttony and victimization and starvation. Estella otters Pip "bread and meat" as if he were "a dog in disgrace," and it is also telling that Pip's fanciful description of his first visit to Miss Havisham's includes four "immense" ravenous dogs that "fought for veal-cutlets out of a silver basket" (pp. 92, 97, 118). In the same interlude, after young Pip pummels Herbert Pocket, he regards himself "as a species of savage young wolf or other wild beast," an image reiterated at the end of the novel when a murderous Orlick refers to Pip as "wolf" (pp. 121, 439).

Pip's first impression of Miss Havisham, that she is "immensely rich" and lives in a "large and dismal house barricaded against robbers," also suggests his unconscious motives (p. 81). In other words, already having "robbed" his sister, Pip now desires to rob Miss Havisham of her material and maternal wealth. However, her domicile is a fallen and unfruitful paradise. Indeed, the home of Satis, which reproduced Miss Havisham, is infiltrated by the market because it is also the house of Satis, a brewery where her father produced the family's wealth. Likewise, market relations penetrate marital relations, for Satis House is where Miss Havisham has been the victim of her own brother's and lover's economic designs. Consequently, in the next generation, the cycle of production infiltrates reproduction again as the motherless Miss Havisham becomes the unnatural mother to Estella. Thus, though "Satis" is the root of satiation and satisfaction, Satis House is unsatisfying, unnourishing, and barren. Indeed, Satis House may represent a fundamental contradiction of the Victorian economy in the startling and simple revelation that abundant wealth is founded on deprivation. In other words, there must be poor Magwitchs for there to be wealthy Miss Havishams.

Nevertheless, in *Great Expectations* Dickens reveals that both rich and poor fill the roles of consumer and consumed, as consuming and being consumed almost become interchangeable states. Hence, caught in the cycle of production and consumption, Miss Havisham, like Pip, devours others and is herself devoured. Indeed, to a certain extent, Miss Havisham equates herself with her own digestive processes, about which she is morbidly self-conscious. In fact, the reader does not see Miss Havisham eat or drink: "She has never allowed herself to be seen doing either . . . She wanders about in the night, and then lays hands on such food as she takes" (pp. 262–63). Such self-imposed physical and emotional deprivation on the part of this wealthy woman reveals a number of things. Most important, I suggest, is the contrast of Miss Havisham's asceticism with Little Nell, Florence, Agnes, and Little Dorrit and their insistent indifference to eating. In fact, I believe that in *Great Expectations* Dickens faces the fact that in a consumer society the lack of appetite in a character like Miss Havisham is a grotesque display of the miraculous anorexia that the younger Dickens had expected to mediate aggressive market demands.

Indeed, as Miss Havisham ascetically nibbles in her decaying house, she watches the natural world—or rather, supernatural—mimic the intrusion of the economic and public into her very private sphere as spiders invade and devour her decomposing wedding cake. Dickens' representation of such public and private consumption is unforgettable, for Miss Havisham's bridal "feast" remains like "a black fungus" on the table where "speckled-legged spiders with blotchy bodies [run] home to it, and [run] out from it, as if some circumstance of the greatest public importance had just transpired in the spider community" (p. 113). At the same time, this "feast" also represents Miss Havisham's moral decay and her acquiescence to the demands of the market, revealed in the fact that she can only express her emotional responses in images of devouring. Indeed, in *Great Expectations* the cliche of being eaten up by revenge almost becomes actuality when Miss Havisham remarks, "The mice have gnawed at it [the wedding cake], and sharper teeth than teeth of mice have gnawed at me" (p. 117). A displaced representation of anthropophagy, the arachnid feast is not only a gothic image of the market dynamics that have also become Miss Havisham's bodily dynamics. This construct of consuming also displays the incursion of the financial into the familial, for Miss Havisham's cousins wait to "feast" on her at her death, on the same table where the spiders feed on her rotting bridal cake (p. 116).

Perhaps, then, it is not too far-fetched to suggest that the spider community may represent all England itself actively engaged in the perpetuation of its own consumption. In fact, *Great Expectations* suggests that consumer society is the ultimate gothic horror. Indeed, this novel almost endlessly produces gothic or comic oral images of ingestion for the reader's consumption, from Miss Havisham, who "feasts" on Estella, "as though she were devouring the beautiful creature she had reared"; to Wemmick "putting fish into" his "post-office" mouth, and bullying customers as a kind of "refreshment" or "lunch"; to the "heavy grubber" Magwitch who threatens Pip that "your heart and your liver shall be tore out, roasted and ate"; to the fish-mouthed Pumblechook who stuffs himself with food at Mrs. Joe's funeral (pp. 320, 402, 427, 346, 38, 299).

It is only natural, then, that Pip represents Orlick's attempt to kill him as an expression of violent appetite: Orlick "slowly unclenched his hand and drew it across his mouth as if his mouth watered for me" (p. 436). Obviously, such oral imagery may be Pip's projection of his own ravine, for as Pip explains, Orlick hates him because he fears Pip will "displace him," but in fact Pip displaces onto Orlick his own violent anger towards his sister and her bad breast (p. 140). As Orlick ominously reveals of the bludgeoning of Mrs. Joe: "I tell you it was your doing—I tell you it was done through you" (p. 437). I need not retrace Julian Moynihan's excellent essay on this projection;[14] suffice it to say, that like an Oedipus figure seeking the perpetrator of his sins, Pip "revengefully" vows to pursue Orlick, or "anyone else, to the last extremity," when it is his own tail he chases and swallows, and his own tale he must ingest (p. 297).

Once again, Pip is both innocent and guilty as Dickens dramatically underscores Pip's rationalized and displaced appetite for revenge at the same time asserting that Mrs. Joe, Miss Havisham, Estella, Pumblechook, and Magwitch are to blame for the hero's fall into the sphere of production. In any case, Dickens calls each to a violent accounting: Orlick brutally attacks Mrs. Joe and robs and beats Pumblechook, while Compeyson assaults Magwitch;[15] in two instances Pip fantasizes Miss Havisham as hanging, and he is there when she rather spontaneously combusts. And to punish the heartless heroine, heavy-built Drummle, nicknamed the "spider"—surely an evocation not only of the spider feast, but also of Miss Havisham feasting on her adopted daughter—beats Estella. His physical abuse, of course, leads to the abasement that purportedly makes the heroine worthy of Pip's love (p. 234).

The novel, then, persistently manufactures images of Pip's innocence and guilt. But it must stop somewhere, and Dickens must redeem his alter-ego from the cycle of production and consumption. Thus, in the end, after all those who claimed to have "made" Pip receive their just desserts, in Dickens' displaced system of tit for tat, Pip, as a kind of outcast in India, spends his energy for eleven years paying his financial and emotional debts. Obviously Dickens cannot fully disentangle his hero from market relations, because, in fact, Pip's calculated debt-paying really provides no redemption, nor does the protagonist's hinted marriage to Estella, for these only seem to perpetuate the dynamics of production. After all, in a capitalist society, the notion of paying for one's sins is hardly to the purpose.

Dickens allows Pip only a brief return to the ideal reproductive sphere through the characters who seem most immune to the desire for money: Joe and Biddy. Joe, for instance, shies away from a premium Miss Havisham offers him for putting Pip into his indentures. Likewise, he castigates the intimidating, money-conscious Jaggers for his "bull-baiting and badgering" insistence that "Money can make compensation to me for the loss of the little child—what come to the forge—and ever the best of friends!" (pp. 168–69). In fact, Pip's deepest regret is that he never acknowledges properly that it is

Joe who has made him, or rather, reproduced him. Joe, who has "the touch of a woman," spiritually and physically nurses Pip, acting in the end as his true mother; when Pip is ill, Joe wraps him up and carries him "as if I were still the small helpless creature to whom he had so abundantly given of the wealth of his great nature" (pp. 168, 476). This illness offers Pip his only chance in actual and figurative terms of having all his debts canceled. In fact, even the ideas of debt and the market dynamics of production and consumption are repealed when Joe freely pays Pip's creditors: Thus, for an Edenic while Pip is no longer equated with "property." That reproduction of Pip—"I again"—is wonderfully recreated in Joe and Biddy's young son, named after Pip, who under the "good matronly hand" of Biddy and the woman's touch of Joe, returns the protagonist, at least for awhile, to the condition of the child's bonding with the maternal (p. 490).

Nevertheless, the ending of *Great Expectations* is troubling, and we know, of course, that Dickens had difficulty concluding his story. The main problem with the ending(s) is not that Dickens cannot bring about his protagonist's permanent regeneration. I suggest, instead, that the conclusion is problematic because Dickens ends up affirming and advocating what he also reviles in a consumer society: the necessity for the powerless to underwrite the powerful. In Dickens' earlier fiction that quite typically means that the heroine, though herself motherless, must be a self-sustaining source of nurture and nourishment to the emotionally starved hero. In the later *Great Expectations*, though Dickens rigorously explores the effects of a market economy on his protagonist, Pip's momentary but transcendent rebirth is at the expense of the female, for Dickens fails to redeem Estella from the sphere of production. Indeed, he forces her back into the mold of his earlier ascetic heroines. Thus, this physically abused, motherless heroine is still an ornament, for neither Pip nor the reader has any conception of what Estella's desires or hungers might be, only that she has been "bent and broken" into "better shape" in order to fulfill Pip's desires (p. 493).

Notes

1. Mary Poovey, *Uneven Developments: The Ideological Work of Gender in Mid-Victorian England* (Chicago: Univ. of Chicago Press, 1988), pp. 77, 115.

2. Charles Dickens, *David Copperfield*, ed. Nina Burgis (Oxford: Clarendon, 1981), p. 145. Further citations will be noted parenthetically in the text.

3. See Alexander Welsh's discussion of Agnes as muse in *From Copyright to Copperfield: The Identity of Dickens* (Cambridge, MA: Harvard Univ. Press, 1987), p. 113.

4. As Poovey points out, Dickens defines the writer as self-effacing and idealistic in order to set himself apart from the alienation and acquisitiveness of the market. But obviously Dickens' profession depends on the crass reality of the product, the novel, being consumed, and Dickens' genius had much to do with the brilliant

marketing techniques (most importantly serialization) that he introduced into the profession of writing in the nineteenth century. Hence, in this novel, Dickens must avoid saying very much about the economic realities of David's and his own profession, and if he does speak of it, he always associates it with Agnes, for by locating in her the "source of every worthy aspiration," David redeems his rather more earthly economic and social aspirations (p. 740).

Thus Copperfield's longest discussion of his profession starts with the direct statement that "I have been very fortunate in worldly matters: many men have worked much harder, and not succeeded half so well," but then he quickly moves on to "humbly" numerate the "spiritual" qualities that have brought about his financial success, including "perseverance," "patient and continuous energy," "punctuality, order, and diligence," and "ardent and sincere earnestness." He ends, as he must, referring all his financial and personal success to Agnes: "How much of the practice I have just reduced to precept, I owe to Agnes, I will not repeat here. My narrative proceeds to Agnes, with a thankful love" (pp. 517–18). Thus Agnes is David's hidden—spiritualized—business partner. Indeed, Heep makes a grotesque conjunction between her business acumen and domesticity when he replies to Betsey Trotwood's assertion that "Agnes is worth the whole firm [Wickfield and Heep]." Uriah "fully agree[s] . . . and should be only too 'appy if Miss Agnes was a partner" (p. 441). But David sounds not much better in the final chapter when he permanently associates male and female economies, saying, in one breath, "I had advanced in fame and fortune, my domestic joy was perfect" (p. 741).

5. Charles Dickens, *Great Expectations*, ed. Angus Calder (1965: reprint New York: Penguin, 1985). p. 41: further citations will be noted parenthetically in the text.

6. Mark Seltzer, "The Naturalist Machine," in *Sex, Politics, and Science in the Nineteenth-Century Novel*, ed. Ruth Bernard Yeazell (Baltimore: Johns Hopkins Univ. Press, 1986), pp. 116–47.

7. Seltzer, p. 136.

8. Fraser Harrison, *The Dark Angel: Aspects of Victorian Sexuality* (London: Sheldon, 1977), pp. 21–22, 55.

9. Samuel Smiles, *Thrift* (New York: Harper & Brothers. 1876), p. 20: Harrison, pp. 20–21.

10. Victorian men were taught to be sexually economical even after marriage. Dr. William Acton believed that husbands should conserve energy, and thus he advocated indulgence in the sex act no more than once in seven to ten days. William Acton, *The Functions and Disorders of the Reproductive Organs* (n. p., 1857), as cited in Harrison, p. 22.

11. Valerie Fildes, *Wet Nursing: A History from Antiquity to the Present* (Oxford: Basil Blackwell, 1988), pp. 91–92, 191, 193; Virginia Phillips, "'Brought up by Hand': Dickens's Pip, Little Paul Dombey, and Oliver Twist," *Dickensian* 74 (1978): 144.

12. James E. Marlow, "English Cannibalism: Dickens after 1859," *Studies in English Literature* 23 (1983): 660, 655. Of all Dickens' novels, perhaps *Great Expectations* incorporates the most alimental images. The plot is structured round meals and hospitality; Barbara Hardy notes that in *Great Expectations* the meals offered to and by Pip vivify an important contrast between what she calls the "ceremony" of love and "failure in hospitality" in "Works in Progress IV: Food and Ceremony in *Great Expectations*," *Essays in Criticism* 13 (1963): 354, 361. Ian Watt has called

Great Expectations the best example in Dickens of "a comprehensive integration of eating and drinking into every aspect of the novel," for Dickens uses each character's attitude toward the subject of eating" as diagnostic of his moral essence and his social role ("Oral Dickens," *Dickens Studies Annual*, ed. Robert B. Partlow, Jr., vol. 3 [Carbondale, IL: Southern Illinois Univ. Press. 1974], p. 170).

13. Marlow, p. 660.

14. Julian Moynihan, "The Hero's Guilt: The Case of *Great Expectations*," *Essays in Criticism* 10 (1960): 60–79; regarding Orlick as Pip's doppelgänger, see also Alexander Welsh, *The City of Dickens* (1971; reprint Cambridge: Harvard Univ. Press, 1986), p. 131.

15. In the final scenes, Pip's seemingly merciful wish that Magwitch die before his execution, is replete with ulterior motives. Indeed, it is an opportune way to dispose of his "burden," a fact that becomes more ominous when Pip worries that the prison guards might suspect him of trying to poison Magwitch. Thus, he asks them to search him thoroughly at every visit (pp. 341, 468).

JOHN CUNNINGHAM

Christian Allusion, Comedic Structure, and the Metaphor of Baptism in Great Expectations

Critics have demonstrated the richly symbolic structure of *Great Expectations* by displaying such recurrent figurative motifs as those of, among others, fairy tale, parable, dream, and allegory; but one characteristic relevant to interpreting the novel that critics have no more than mentioned is a pattern of Christian allusion that Dickens so introduces into the novel that metaphors of baptism and of the redemption adumbrated by this sacrament take their place among the other controlling symbolic structures of the book. The novel opens, as I take it, with a parody of the Christian sacrament of baptism, by which (according to Prayer Book notions) people are born into a new life free of original sin; in Dickens's use of the figure, however, persons—namely Pip and Magwitch—are "born" instead into guilt and death. Janet L. Larson has written that the Bible in Dickens's mature novels is becoming "a locus of hermeneutical instability"; she speaks of the scriptures as a "broken" or "fractured code" (3). I take it that by perverting the stereotype of regeneration Dickens dislocates it from cliché; then as the novel comes toward its conclusion when Magwitch, Compeyson, and Pip plunge into the Thames (Byrd 262; Robison 436), he transforms the corrupted figures of baptism into genuine ones, and comic regenerations open onto new lives.[1] He restores the fractured or unstable meanings into Christian significance. Comic structure, as is often the case, regenerates its

From *South Atlantic Review* 59, no. 2 (May 1994): 35–51. © 1994 by *South Atlantic Review*.

images. Christian analogy and imagery suggest a providential order that works toward the comic conclusion that many critics have described in terms of regeneration and redemption. In this essay I offer a sustained account of Christian emblems and allusions in *Great Expectations* and indicate how they cohere to form a major pattern of meaning in the novel;[2] for Dickens uses analogies of Christian comic archetypes to effect the resolution of the moral problems posed as the book develops.

The matrix of baptismal imagery includes symbols drawn from Christian typology. This figurative way of reading the Bible sees imperfect types and shadows—anticipations—of Christ throughout the Old Testament. By the last decade of the eighteenth century, sermons, tracts, biblical commentaries, hymns, and stained-glass windows taught Christians of all stripes to read scripture in this figurative way (Landow, *Hunt* 12–13). Typological reading was so widespread in the nineteenth century that any person who could read, even an unbeliever, was likely to recognize allusions to Old Testament figures and to know that these worthies served as types of Christ; the antichrist was also prefigured in the Old Testament (Landow, *Victorian* ix, 22–34; *Hunt* 11–12). This figurative way of reading scripture will prove useful in discussing a novel that alludes to Abel and Noah (types of Christ) and to Cain (a type of the antichrist), for Dickens draws typological references into the metaphoric structure of his novel. Dickens's parody of Christian typology and of the baptismal rite manifests itself in figures of Noah and in several patterns of imagery: death-in-life, false resurrection, of the old man, of clothing, and of Christmas.

The type of Noah provides one example of Dickens's use of parody. From ancient times Christians have seen the ark—a means by which the righteous few were given a new beginning—as a type of baptism in which wickedness suffered death by water (see 1 Pet. 3.18–21). At the end of the first full day of the novel, Pip sees a "black Hulk," "cribbed and barred and moored by massive rusty chains," "like a wicked Noah's Ark" (71). Years later he recalls "the wicked Noah's ark lying out on the black water" (252). This typology of Noah and the ark appears in the Flood Prayer of the Prayer Book (1662) baptismal office that nineteenth-century Anglicans would have heard repeatedly in their parish churches.[3] In that rite the priest prays "that the old Adam in this child may be so buried that the new man [Christ, who is the second Adam]" may be "raised up in him."[4] But the ark Dickens described is "wicked," a prison ship lying on the "black waters," a parody of the new beginning, of the new life, and of the forgiveness suggested by the allusion to Noah.

The "birth" that Pip experiences at the opening of the book is not into new life but into metaphoric and moral death. In the churchyard on Christmas eve, Pip's "birth" comes with his "first most vivid ... impression of the identity of things" and of his own identity as "a small bundle of shivers," like a newborn babe (35–36); but Magwitch's actions associate Pip with death. The convict seats the boy directly on a tombstone, to which Pip clings. When he asks Pip where his mother is, the boy points to her grave as if death were his origin. Metaphors of death-in-life pervade the first two-thirds of the novel and carry forward the figurative birth-into-death introduced in the first pages; they parody both the new beginning suggested by the allusion to Noah and also the new life promised in baptism. Miss Havisham is "withered" and "shrunk," a skeleton, a "ghastly waxwork" like some "personage lying in state" (87). She is brokenhearted, emotionally, morally, and spiritually dead; and she has stolen the heart away from Estella and "put ice in its place" (88, 412). Estella's contempt is "infectious," and Pip catches it (90). In fact, Pip cannot separate Estella "from the innermost life of [his] life" (257); moral infection and death stand at the center of Pip. He visits Miss Havisham annually on his birthday, celebrating his introduction to Satis House, as it were, as a kind of anniversary of his birthday into moral death in the churchyard. Because of the convict, he chooses to steal; because of Miss Havisham and Estella, he chooses to lie. Metaphors of death follow Pip from the country to London. Jaggers's office with its domineering death masks is a "dismal" place, like the churchyard and like Satis House. Jaggers's chair with its deadly black and its rows of brass nails is like a "coffin" (188). Here the lawyer presides over Pip's twenty-first birthday in such a way as to remind the young man of "that old time when [he] had been put upon a tombstone" (305). Barnard's Inn, Pip's London residence, is in a "melancholy little square" that looks to Pip "like a flat burying ground" (196).

In the first scene of the novel, the presence of the burial ground beside a church should remind those alive, "the Church Militant on earth," of the unity of all "lively members of Christ's Church" with "the Church Triumphant" beyond the grave (Davies 20). This unity is achieved in baptism. But the churchyard at the beginning of *Great Expectations* is a parody of these themes; it is a place that speaks only of death, not of the expectant life mentioned in the baptismal office. The brambles there seem to the young Pip like "the hands of the dead people, stretching up cautiously out of their graves, to get a twist upon . . . [Magwitch's] ankle and pull him in" (38); and the graves of his five dead brothers suggest to Pip those who have given "up trying to get a living, exceedingly early in that universal struggle." Pip then repeats a phrase, twice saying that his parents and brothers are "dead and buried" (35); those as familiar as Dickens was with matins and evensong would easily recognize the phrase as coming from the Apostles' Creed,[5] the formula composed specifically for the rite of baptism (Shepherd 284). The creed goes on to add, but Pip does not, "and the third day he arose again from the dead."

Paul links baptism with resurrection (Rom. 6.4); but Magwitch's starting "up from among the graves" (36) represents an ironic parody of resurrection. He is like "the pirate come to life [but going back to the gibbet] . . . to hook himself up again" (39). Likewise, Miss Havisham's appearance suggests a false resurrection and makes Pip think of "a skeleton in the ashes of a rich dress, that had been dug out of a vault under the church pavement" (87). Seeming to Pip as if she "might rise in those grave-clothes of hers" (122), she is a parody of Lazarus rising in his "grave-clothes" (John 11.44).

Moreover, on Christmas Eve, Pip is also born into a guilt like the first Adam's, into something like the Fall and not into the new innocence and forgiveness of those just baptized. His growing guilt accounts for the moral death that comes more and more to possess him. Pip says, "I think my sister must have had some general idea that I was a young offender whom an Accoucheur Policeman had taken up (on my birthday) and delivered over to her, to be dealt with according to the outraged majesty of the law" (54). Later, by his own choice, he does consent to the guilt into which he is born; the guilt which he embraces from his first awareness is fixed and compounded by his association with Miss Havisham and Estella. He begins to love Estella "against reason, against promise, against peace, against hope, against happiness" (253–54). Pip "made [his] own snares" and became a "self-swindler" (374, 247). He returns home from Satis House oppressed by the "ungracious condition of [his] mind" and by his "ungracious breast" (134, 136).

For Pip, the guilt that he has acquired at Satis House is symbolized by the unwanted bloody fight with Herbert. When Pip admits that "the young gentleman's blood was on [his] head" (121), he introduces words that point to a series of scriptural allusions. These references associate him with both the shedding of Abel's blood and also the crucifixion of Christ.[6] Moreover, a "sponge dipped in vinegar"[7] forms part of the ritual of the fight (119). Pip covers the traces of Herbert's blood "with garden mould from the eye of man" and fears arrest and vengeance as a result of his assault. He then tries "to wash out that evidence of [his] guilt" (122), but his guilt cannot be thus washed out. The assault on Herbert that Pip does not initiate is like the assault on Mrs. Joe that Pip does not initiate either; yet he unexpectedly, even mysteriously, shares in the attack on his sister by helping Magwitch to free himself from the manacle that Orlick uses to attack her. Pip thinks that he must somehow share responsibility for the attack, as in fact Orlick says he does: "'It was you as did for your . . . sister'" (437). Pip may not literally kill his brother Abel when he bloodies Herbert nor even literally kill his sister; and yet in the metaphorical structure of the novel he takes his place beside Cain.

In so doing, he participates in the state of death-in-life that all the unredeemed share. Both Paul (Rom. 6.6; Eph. 4.22; Col. 3.9) and the baptismal office define this extreme state (see Col. 2.12–13) and the condition of guilt inherent in it by the term "old man." The purpose of baptism is to give the old man, the mortal and fallen Adam, the death blow. The dominant figure of the old man in *Great Expectations* is "old Orlick,"[8] who is driven by the bitterness, wrath, anger, clamor, evil speaking, and malice that Paul attributes to the old man in Ephesians 4.31. Twice Pip reports his belief that Orlick has assumed "Dolge" as his "pretended Christian name" to affront people (139, 158); metaphorically, then, Orlick has no baptismal name, no name of a new man. Adam was a creature of earth, and Orlick is one who seems to have "started up . . . from the ooze," one who is "very muddy" (158, 146). Moreover, Orlick is, in Pip's words, "like Cain" (140), a son of fallen Adam; and he is the agent of death for Mrs. Joe and the would-be agent of death for Pip. He is, also in Pip's words, "like . . . the Wandering Jew" (190), who, according to legend, taunted and rejected the new Adam.

In confronting Orlick, Pip also confronts the old man, the figure of death and guilt; as such, he is Pip's doppelgänger. Orlick is like Cain; but Pip is like Cain in relation to Herbert. Orlick is also a figure of the old man, the doppelgänger never on this side of the grave completely drowned even in the baptized; hence he is associated with many of the characters who are violent and often labeled as old. Orlick is linked with Mrs. Joe by her violent rage and blind fury; he is linked with Bentley, "an old-looking . . . man" (213), by malice and a sulky and unforgiving disposition. He comes into the employ of Miss Havisham, who has her own wrath and anger. Orlick also comes into the employ of Compeyson; and he utters a parody of the baptismal pattern of union when he says of Compeyson and Bentley, "'I've took up with new companions and new masters'" (438).[9] By the epithet "old"[10] he is linked to Barley who roars and growls, full of anger, wrath, malice.

That the old man has died in baptism is symbolized by new white clothes; they represent the new life and innocence conferred in the rite. Paul wrote to Christians in Ephesians 4.22–24 and Colossians 3.9–10 that those buried in the baptismal waters must "put off," like a suit of clothes, the old man and "put on the new." The church early introduced into the ceremonial of baptism the putting off of old clothes and the putting on of new white ones. Pip's new clothes, however, are not like these new clothes; rather they are like the clothes that God gave Adam and Eve in their guilt. In pride Pip goes to put on his new clothes at Pumblechook's, but they prove a disappointment as has "every new and eagerly expected garment ever put on since clothes came in" (183)—as they did, of course, with the Fall.

The baptismal imagery of clothing is inverted, then, in the first parts of *Great Expectations*, but so are other parts of Pip's world. No sooner does Pip come to his first impression of the identity of things than Magwitch places him upon a tombstone and literally turns him upside down. From almost the first, Pip's "interior landscape is inverted" (Van Ghent 135), as is the imagery of baptism, as is the presentation of Christmas in the opening chapters. The perversion of baptism enacted in the first pages of the novel takes place in the context of the perversion of Christmas, the birthday of the Last Adam. The book opens on a Christmas Eve as Pip experiences a kind of birth. Moreover, the names of his mother and his foster father are Georgiana Maria and Joseph. Christmas is important to baptismal themes because, according to the Prayer Book, the baptized is born into the second Adam (Christ). In fact, Christ's own baptism is observed in many calendars during the Christmas-Epiphany season.[11] Dickens carries the initial perversion of Christmas further by using imagery of darkness. The coming of light is part of the iconography of Christmas. The rite of a feast begins on its eve, and this novel begins on Christmas Eve; but darkness is the imagery of the opening pages as night comes on. And darkness closes Christmas day and the hunt for Magwitch; Pip says, "It had been almost dark before, but now it seemed quite dark, and soon afterwards very dark" (69). Light is put out as "the ends of the torches [are] flung hissing into the water . . . as if it were all over with [Magwitch]" (71). Dickens introduces the symbols of the gibbet and the beacon as Magwitch leaves Pip on Christmas Eve. Both are "ugly" and "black things" (39) because they are corruptions of Christian symbols—the gibbet suggesting the cross, and the beacon suggesting the "light [shining] in the darkness" of the gospel reading appointed in the Prayer Book for Christmas. The motif of light in darkness, in turn, suggests the story of the unbaptized Nicodemus, who came by night to Christ the light inquiring of salvation and learned that by water he must be born again; this lesson, from John 3, occurs in the Prayer Book rite of adult baptism and is the source of the ancient Christian iconography that associates light with baptism.

Pip in exile is like Nicodemus in the darkness; he is also like the fallen Adam in his clothes but, as will be seen, unlike Adam exiled from Eden. Pip alludes directly to the last lines of *Paradise Lost* as he sets out for London, saying, "The world lay spread before me" (186). After suffering and repenting and after having been given a vision of the new man, Adam in *Paradise Lost* is exiled but is given, like the baptized, a new beginning, and he journeys in hope of attaining the "paradise within," that is, the Kingdom of Heaven promised in the baptismal office. The night before he leaves for London, Pip suffers nightmares of failed journeys, of coaches going to wrong places. The allusion to *Paradise Lost* is followed by a description of London as "ugly, crooked, narrow, and dirty" (187)—hardly a paradise, more nearly exile.

Great Expectations attains a comic resolution as the perverted figures of baptism discussed hitherto are metamorphosed into true ones and as regenerations open onto new lives. Despite the almost pervasive presence of death in the novel, evidence of life nevertheless persists; but the life present in death must be freed, usually by the discipline of suffering that characterizes most comedy. Pip calls the night on which Magwitch comes to his London chambers "the turning point of my life" (318). That night is characterized both by figures of rain and flood (typologically associated with baptism) and by figures of destruction, of apocalypse (also typologically associated with baptism [Daniélou 75–85]). These images reach their symbolic completion in death-by-water when Magwitch, Compeyson, and Pip suffer shipwreck and descend into the Thames.[12] In the rhythm of the final chapters, the counter movements—one of death and one of life—come to their resolutions. Pip must come to see that his great expectations are not Estella and Miss Havisham's money but regeneration, which will offer him the paradise within that the allusion to Milton—"the world lay spread before me" (186)—finally invokes. Dickens renews the motifs of baptism that have had negative connotations throughout much of the novel and gives them positive meanings: the death of the old man makes possible the birth of the new man; unprofitable guilt gives way to fruitful contrition and humility; life comes out of living death through painful baptismal fire and through life-giving water, violence and malice metamorphose into forgiveness. Magwitch, Miss Havisham, and Mrs. Joe experience various aspects of regeneration that precede and anticipate Pip's rebirth. Light replaces darkness, and Dickens transforms the perverted Christmas of the opening chapters into genuine celebration at the end of the novel.

The drowning of Compeyson in the waters of the Thames is like the death of the old man in the baptismal office; he is everyone's secret companion, everyone's inner darkness. Like Magwitch he is a prisoner. Like Miss Havisham he is a failed marriage partner. Like Orlick he is a criminal. Like Pip he is a gentleman. He is ubiquitous; everyone may see his or her own likeness in him (Gilbert 98). Early in the novel we see Compeyson and Magwitch, linked like Cain and Abel, in a death-grip, splashing water and mud in the ditch; then we see them tied together to be taken to the hulks. They go overboard together; as in the scene in the ditch, they are fiercely locked in each other's arms. After "a struggle underwater," Magwitch disengages himself, finally, forever free of Compeyson, who goes to an "unshriven death" (Stone 687), "tumbling on the tides, dead" (Dickens 458). Like the newly baptized, Magwitch is given new clothes at the Ship. Simultaneously with the killing of Compeyson occurs the "death" of the old man in Magwitch, and Pip sees the new man "bearing towards [him] on the tide" (455), severely injured, the "old sound in his throat softened" (457).

The metaphors of resurrection associated with Magwitch at the beginning of the book are, as we have seen, perverted images; by the conclusion of the novel they have been metamorphosed into genuine figures of rebirth. Pip thinks that, as Provis, changes have already begun in Magwitch who has "softened—indefinably" (391); on the boat he sits, "smiling with that softened air upon him" (448). Magwitch knows full well that "'it's death'" to return to England (340). The cataclysmic shipwreck has sealed his transformation. He has begun his passage "beyond Gravesend," which Pip calls the "critical place" (429, 445, 449). Before his trial he shows "submission or resignation," knowing that he cannot "bend the past out of its *eternal* shape" (465; italics mine).

At his trial he can accept his "sentence of Death from the Almighty" and can bow to the sentence of death from the judge. Pip mentions at this juncture the "greater Judgment that knoweth all things and cannot err" (467); his words—"knoweth all things"—are quoted from the twentieth verse of 1 John 3, a chapter that speaks of the baptized as "sons of God" who will, when God appears, "be like him" (3.2) because in baptism they are "born of God" (3.9) and will pass "from death to life" (3.14). After the judgment Magwitch becomes more and more "placid" (468, 469) while Pip takes as "the first duty of life" to prepare Magwitch for death, "to say to him, and read to him, what I knew he ought to hear" (465). The collect for Ash Wednesday asks God to "create and make in us a new and contrite heart." Magwitch's heart, "humble and contrite" (466), has become the kind of sacrifice that, according to the psalm (51.17) appointed for Ash Wednesday, God will not despise. Abel can finally offer the acceptable sacrifice that makes him a type of Christ. "Mindful, then, of what [they] had read together," Pip can knowingly and deliberately apply to Magwitch specifically words applicable to all sinners generally and pray, "'O Lord, be merciful to him, a sinner!'" (470).

The rhythm of baptism by which the old dies and the new is born is also the pattern of comedy, in which life almost implausibly comes out of death and joy implausibly out of sorrow. In fact, in several cases in *Great Expectations*, literal death of the old is requisite for new life: old Barley must die in order that Clara may marry Herbert; Miss Havisham must die that Matthew and Herbert may be financially secure; Bentley must die that Estella may put her new heart into employ; Mrs. Joe and Mr. Wopsle's great-aunt must die that Biddy and Joe may wed; Compeyson must die for Magwitch to end well. As death has not in it the wherewithal of life nor sorrow the wherewithal of joy, Dickens's comedy implies the operation of a theistic providence that can use pain to effect joy.

John the Baptist announced that, while he baptized "with water unto repentance," one would succeed him who would painfully baptize "with fire" (Matt. 3.11). In the context of this passage, purification by water pertains to Magwitch, one of Pip's foster parents, and purification by fire concerns Miss Havisham, another of his foster parents. Pip holds the burning Miss

Havisham down "with all [his] strength, like a prisoner," "struggling [with her as if they were] . . . desperate enemies" (414); the struggle is desperate because the old man in her wants to flee his painful baptismal death. Miss Havisham becomes "insensible," as in death, later to revive and speak "collectedly." The fire destroys the old in her, the "faded bridal dress," "every vestige of [which] was burnt" and "all the ugly things that sheltered" in the decay on the table. The fire also makes way for the new, for the "phantom air [about her] of something that had been and was changed"; it is a kind of baptism (414–15). Likewise, the white cotton-wool and the white sheet that replace the old clothes suggest the baptismal change of apparel. Miss Havisham's hope that she might die on her birthday and that she might then be laid out on the feast table comes to pass when her bed is laid there upon this day in which she is "changed" and established in a new moral life.

The cleansing flame actually seals a work that has already commenced because Pip has led her to recognize the evil that she has perpetrated. In the "'looking-glass'" (411) of Pip's suffering she sees what she once felt and, we may suppose, can now see herself as like Arthur and Compeyson, who betrayed her; and she begs Pip's forgiveness. In granting it, Pip, who himself "'want[s] forgiveness'" (410), enters the rhythm of the Lord's Prayer; and in forgiving her he becomes an analogue of Christ.[13] In showing a "new affection" (411) toward Pip and in asking to serve him as well as Herbert, Miss Havisham is ready for her baptism by fire.

In fact, the theme of forgiveness, which is also a theme of baptism, becomes particularly of great import as the novel moves toward its conclusion. In Mrs. Joe, too, who is "left . . . for dead" (437) after Orlick's blow, the old dies.[14] It dies that the new may indeed come to life. Early in her infirmity, "her temper [is] greatly improved" (150); as she emerges from one of her bad states, she wants to put her arms around Joe's neck, and she asks pardon (302). The announcement of her death comes to Pip in the words "[She has] departed this life" (297); this locution comes from the prayer for the church in the Holy Communion. In this instance, too (see above 38), anyone as familiar with the liturgy as Dickens was would recognize this allusion immediately; that prayer speaks of those who have "departed this life in [God's] faith and fear." Penance, asking forgiveness, amendment of life, requisites for adult baptism, precede the entry of Mrs. Joe, as well as Miss Havisham, into death, which the church sees as a second baptism (Daniélou 24). In Estella likewise suffering brings life out of death. At an early stage of their acquaintance, she tells Pip, "'I have no heart'" (259); somewhat later she says to him, "'You address nothing in my breast, you touch nothing there'" (376). Then, in the first, more austere ending, Bentley's death releases her from the "suffering [that] had been stronger than Miss Havisham's teaching, and [that] had given her a heart to understand what [Pip's] heart used to be" (496). One may assume that the new heart and its ability to love are put into employ in her marriage with the Shropshire doctor. The second ending is even more hopeful for Estella.

Like Miss Havisham, Mrs. Joe, and Estella, Pip, too, experiences suffering, repentance, and regeneration. He is baptized by fire and then by water, and it is to his moral regeneration that Dickens gives the most attention. Even before his boat is wrecked and he is immersed in the Thames, Pip introduces imagery of a ship at sea. When Herbert announces his intention to go to the East, Pip says, "I felt as if my last anchor were loosening its hold, and I should soon be driving with the winds and waves" (427–28). Pip must cast away, or have cast away for him, all his anchors—his great expectations of being a gentleman and his hopes regarding Estella, his companionship with Herbert, his illusory "last baffled hope" (487) of marrying Biddy, even his life in England—and he must become fully a castaway before he can become a "twice-born" hero (Westburg 115). Drowned with Magwitch, burned with Miss Havisham and by his own fever, brought to the point of death by Orlick, reduced to debt and almost to imprisonment, bereft even of Biddy, sent for eleven years' exile into the East, Pip is drawn into the pattern of baptism and of comedy.

Pip experiences baptismal death-by-fire, first by participating in Miss Havisham's fiery baptism and then by confronting Orlick. As he struggles on the floor with Miss Havisham, he suffers a state like death until his awareness revives: "[T]hat [the events described] occurred I knew through the results, but not through anything I felt, or thought or knew I did," Pip says, "I knew nothing . . ." (414). Pip's encounter with Orlick, described repeatedly with imagery of fire, is, typologically speaking, a battle against the old man. Against his doppelgänger Orlick Pip "struggle[s] with all the [previously unknown] force . . . within [him]." When "after a blank . . . [he] recover[s] consciousness" (440), he thinks that he has been lying in the sluice house "two days and nights" (441). By the "noose" (434) that Orlick uses to capture Pip and by the "perpendicular ladder" (435) to which Orlick binds him, Dickens associates Pip, as he has associated Miss Havisham, with that figure of death and resurrection, the gibbet (see above 41).[15] Like a catechumen preparing for baptism, Pip admits his "miserable errors," "humbly beseech[es] pardon . . . of Heaven" (437), and intends amendment of life. In both fiery encounters Pip loses consciousness, as if he were dead, and regains it, as if he had come to life again; he participates in a kind of comedic baptismal death and rebirth.

The same rhythm that obtains in Pip's encounters with Magwitch, Miss Havisham, and Orlick also obtains in his descent into both debt and sickness and in his ascent out of them. Illness and the consequences of his debt come upon Pip simultaneously. In his sickness Pip descends into the isolation and the hell of his soul, confronts and rejects what he finds there, and rises to a new kind of life. In his fever he enters a "night . . . of great duration . . . which teem[s] with anxiety and horror"; he frequently loses his hold on reality (470–71). After a feverish delirium he "tries to settle" the details of his hallucination with himself and "to get [them] into some order" (471). As his encounters with Magwitch, Miss Havisham, and Orlick have the figurative shape of death followed by rebirth, so, too, does his encounter with the fever. In his sickness, Pip struggles with people whom he takes to be murderers and then understands that they intend to do him good and "sink[s] exhausted in their arms" (472). Apparently, however, all these "people" are Joe, to whom he is restored. As he gains strength he fancies himself "little Pip again," like a "child in [Joe's] hands" (476). Pip's metaphoric birth in the churchyard occurs in winter, a season metaphoric of death. Pip's recovery occurs during May and June; and his first outing is on Sunday, the day commemorating the resurrection that the "Sunday bells" celebrate (476). As a boy, Pip had looked at seeds and bulbs jailed in Pumblechook's drawers and wondered if they wanted "of a fine day to break out . . . and bloom" (83). But while Pip has now lain "burning . . . on [his] bed," the little wild flowers that he sees on his Sunday outing have been "forming" (476) and suggest the new life of springtime to which his own pip has come.[16] Baptized when he was given his "Christian name," Pip at seven falls into the world of guilt and sorrow; brought to repentance by several purgatorial ordeals of testing and trying, he asks forgiveness, recovers innocence, and regains a kind of paradise.

When the castings-off enforced upon Pip are complete—when he is fully a castaway with "no home anywhere" (461), a clerk from somewhere in the East—Pip can approach the paradise within only by working and repaying his debts. He leaves England, carrying out Christ's commandment to those who seek eternal life or the kingdom of heaven: "I sold all I had" (489). But Pip cannot redeem "his [own] soul" (Wentersdorff 224)—either in terms of baptism or in terms of the comic structure of the novel; for an act of substitution must occur in each. Baptism is validated only by Christ's actual death and resurrection; and in the comic rhythm of the novel Joe must redeem Pip's debt of "'hundred and twenty-three pound, fifteen, six'" (471). Likewise, Pip suffers and Miss Havisham is redeemed; Joe and Pip suffer and Mrs. Joe is redeemed. In order that Magwitch may know redemption Pip goes beyond Jaggers's prudential advice that he abandon the returned felon. These acts of substitution (of suffering and forgiving) essential to the economy of the novel partake in a pattern of Christian analogy. They are acts of charity, of disinterested love.

Dickens describes such love by imagery of light. One of the corrupted figures of baptism that the comic rhythm of the novel renews is that of light, which was perverted at the beginning of the novel into darkness. Before the novel ends, light becomes a genuine emblem of divinity. Dickens establishes this value of the metaphor when he allows Estella to describe her ignorance of love by using an analogy of the absence of sunlight. Having been taught from the first that daylight is her enemy and destroyer, that it would blight her, and having been brought up wholly in the "dark confinement" of Satis House, Estella cannot be expected "to understand the daylight" (324). Love is like the sunlight or the daylight. Moreover, Pip analyzes Miss Havisham's history in terms of the same analogy. "In shutting out the light of day," she has "shut out *infinitely* more" (italics mine), a "thousand natural and healing influences." Consequently, her mind has "grown diseased, as all minds do and must and will that reverse the appointed order of their Maker" (411). Light is like love: and both are like the healing influences that the "Maker" orders as remedies.

Imagery of fire in *Great Expectations* is figurative of the painful cleansing necessary to metaphoric death; imagery of light is figurative of the fertility of that new life. It describes the regeneration of Magwitch—and also of Pip. Two baptismal emblems govern Pip's interpretation of Magwitch's trial: "drops of April rain" and "rays of April sun" (466). The trial takes place during both the natural season of rebirth and fertility and also the liturgical season of resurrection. The sun striking the great court windows links the prisoners in a "broad shaft of light" suggesting to Pip a "greater Judgment," the justice of one whom Magwitch calls "the Almighty" (467).

Dickens metamorphoses his perverted figures of baptism, and he ends the novel by returning to Christmas; the imagery of this feast is also transformed. Roberta Schwartz points out that Pip's return "upon an evening in December" (489) from eleven years in Egypt completes the Nativity cycle (65).[17] The novel has come full circle; it ends where it began—but with a major difference. Pip finds that a proper father has married a proper mother to provide a proper family and a proper home; they have produced a new Pip, in whom the old can vicariously find his second chance (Meisel 329). Joe and Biddy have "'giv' him the name of Pip'" (490); that name they would have given him during the rite of his baptism. His name is not that of a dead father. He has not been baptized into the exile into which Pip was "born." The young Pip is about seven. Pip replaces Magwitch as a kind of adoptive father: on a visit to the churchyard, he repeats Magwitch's gesture by setting the young child upon a tombstone, but not in such a way as to invert his world.

* * *

Scholarship has informed us of the widespread understanding of biblical typology among the English public of the nineteenth century. At the same time, as Larson has argued in the passage I cited at the outset, the Bible was becoming for Dickens and his audience "a locus of hermeneutical instability," a "broken" and "fractured code." Larson recognizes Dickens's many allusions to the Bible and *The Book of Common Prayer* and displays ambiguities that Dickens introduces into the allusions; however, she does not suggest the strategies by which the novelist restores the meaning and significance inherent in them. Nor does she discuss *Great Expectations.* I believe my analysis of this novel helps us see just how Dickens breaks the code and how he then restores it. What is true of *Great Expectations*, I presume, is true of Dickens's other mature novels.

Dennis Walder records the equivocal remarks that Dickens made in places other than his novels about baptism and goes on to add that Dickens's beliefs are rarely made explicit; rather they are implicit in the texture of his novels. One must study them as they are embodied in "significant moments," in images, themes, and structures. The novels are the only expression of the inner life of Dickens. In *Great Expectations*, Dickens relies "on the familiar underlying pattern of sin, repentance and regeneration" (Walder 200, 3, 14, 15, 209); this pattern is the rhythm of baptism and implies a providential order.[18] Dickens mentioned this order in a letter to Wilkie Collins. He said that the "business of art is to lay all [the] ground carefully..., to show ... what everything has been working to.... These are the ways of Providence, of which ways all art is but a little imitation" (125). We may say that Dickens's allusions define this shaping order as Christian.

Notes

I am grateful to Professors George Walton Williams, Clyde Ryals, Eric Trethewey, Brian Gillespie, Iain Crawford, and Nickolas Pappas, to the late Doctor John Kassman, and to Mr. Robert Whitaker for suggestions toward the improvement of this essay.

1. The Christian figure of the wedding feast and the sacrament of the eucharist of which it is an emblem also occur in *Great Expectations.* Like the metaphor of baptism, they appear first in a perverted form and then in a genuine one. I discuss the pattern of this other transformation in "The Figure of the Wedding Feast in *Great Expectations.*"

2. I do not, however, find the pervasive "allegory" in *Great Expectations* that Jane Vogel does, nor do I find the profusion of Christian allusions that she sees (45–80).

3. That prayer addresses God, the one who did "save Noah and his family in the ark from perishing by water ... figuring thereby [his] holy baptism" and asks that the baptismal candidate may be "received into the ark of Christ's church," may "safely pass the waters of this troublesome world," and may be led to the "land of everlasting life." The office speaks of the baptized as "regenerate and born again," as "lively members of Christ's church," who by "mystical" and "heavenly washing" have experienced "remission of sin"; therefore, they may be "partakers of Christ's resurrection."

4. Behind the Prayer Book formularies stands Paul's discussion in Romans 6. There the apostle says that the faithful have been "baptized into Christ's death" and have been "buried with him by baptism into death" so that they may be "raised into likeness of his resurrection, . . . knowing that the old man is crucified in him."

5. Dennis Walder writes that Dickens demonstrates his intimate knowledge of the Bible and of *The Book of Common Prayer* (1662) "by frequent, accurate, and often surprisingly relevant allusion throughout his works" (290).

6. See Matt. 27.25; Luke 11.51; Acts 18.6.

7. See Matt. 27.48.

8. At the climax of his attempt to destroy Pip, Orlick calls himself "old" twelve times (437–39); five other times in the novel he uses this adjective to describe himself. Dickens's insistence on the old raises it to a metaphoric significance.

9. See the passage from the baptismal office in the Prayer Book where the priest gives thanks for receiving the "Child by adoption" and for incorporating him into God's "holy Church" and when he announces that the child has been "receive[d] into the congregation of Christ's flock." By the adoption, the child receives a new master and enters a new society.

10. Used eight times to describe Orlick in two pages (389–90).

11. As in the office lectionary of *The Book of Common Prayer.*

12. Landow shows that Christian writers since Augustine have used the voyage as an image of movement toward the second Eden; the traditional use of the figure of the voyage allows for such a cataclysmic event as shipwreck that may result either in a failure to reach the second Eden (as with Compeyson) or in testing and trying (as with Pip and Magwitch). See *Images* 16, 7, 20, 17, 91.

13. In so doing, Pip fulfills a role foreshadowed in his baptism, for in the metaphor of baptism he had already become an analogue of Christ when he received his "Christian name." Allusions to one's "Christian name," given at baptism, occur throughout the novel: 58, 105, 139, 202, 215, 362.

14. If a lime kiln had been nearby, Orlick says, "She shouldn't have come to life again" (437).

15. "I fancied that I saw Miss Havisham hanging to the beam" (413).

16. In this connection, Dorothy Van Ghent cites John 12.24: "Except a corn of wheat fall into the ground and die, it abideth alone: but if it die, it bringeth forth much fruit" (379).

17. See Matt. 2.19–21. See also Matt. 2.15: " . . . that it might be fulfilled which was spoken of the Lord by the prophet, saying, Out of Egypt have I called my son."

18. Walder concludes that Dickens "did not ever break entirely his connections with broadly Anglican faith and practice."

Works Cited

The Book of Common Prayer (1662). Crown copyright, various editions.

Byrd, Max. "Reading in *Great Expectations.*" *PMLA* 91 (1976): 259–65.

Cunningham, John. "The Figure of the Wedding Feast in *Great Expectations.*" *Dickens Quarterly* 10.2 (1993): 87–91.

Daniélou, Jean. *The Bible and the Liturgy.* South Bend, IN: U of Notre Dame P, 1956.

Davies, Horton. *From Watts and Wesley to Maurice, 1690–1850.* Vol. 3 of *Worship and Theology in England.* Princeton, NJ: Princeton UP, 1961. 5 vols. 1961–75.

Dickens, Charles. *Great Expectations.* Ed. Angus Calder. Harmondsworth, Middlesex: Penguin, 1965.

———. *The Letters of Charles Dickens.* Vol 3. Ed. Walter Dexter. Bloomsbury: Nonesuch, 1938. 3 vols.

Gilbert, Elliott L. "'In Primal Sympathy': *Great Expectations* and the Secret Life." *Dickens Studies Annual* 11 (1983): 89–113.

Landow, George. *Images of Crisis: Literary Iconology, 1750 to the Present.* Boston: Routledge, 1982.

———. *Victorian Types, Victorian Shadows: Biblical Typology in Victorian Literature, Art, and Thought.* Boston: Routledge, 1980.

———. *William Holman Hunt and Typological Symbolism.* New Haven, CT. Yale UP, 1979.

Larson, Janet L. *Dickens and the Broken Scripture.* Athens: U of Georgia P, 1985.

Meisel, Martin. "The Ending of *Great Expectations.*" *Essays in Criticism* 15 (1965): 326–31.

Robison, Roselee. "Time, Death and the River in Dickens' Novels." *English Studies* 53 (1972): 436–54.

Schwartz, Roberta. "The Moral Fable of *Great Expectations.*" *North Dakota Quarterly* 47 (1979): 55–66.

Shepherd, Massey Hamilton, Jr. *The Oxford American Prayer Book Commentary.* New York: Oxford, 1950.

Stone, Harry. "Fire, Hand, and Gate: Dickens' *Great Expectations.*" *Kenyon Review* 24 (1962): 662–91.

Van Ghent, Dorothy. *The English Novel: Form and Function.* New York: Holt, 1953.

Vogel, Jane. *Allegory in Dickens.* Studies in the Humanities 17. University: U of Alabama P, 1977.

Walder, Dennis. *Dickens and Religion.* London: Allen, 1981.

Wentersdorff, Karl P. "Mirror-Images in *Great Expectations.*" *Nineteenth-Century Fiction* 21 (1966): 203–24.

Westburg, Barry. *The Confessional Fiction of Charles Dickens.* DeKalb: Northern Illinois UP, 1977.

MARGARET FLANDERS DARBY

Listening to Estella

In 1860 Charles Dickens had this to say about the difficulties of weekly serial publication: " . . . one of its most remarkable and aggravating features is, that if you do not fix the people in the beginning, it is almost impossible to fix them afterwards" (*Letters* 9:327–8). Just beginning to write *Great Expectations*, Dickens would have intended "fix" in the sense of establishing character, but the word resonates in interesting ways when we consider Pip's fixations, especially his obsession with Estella.

In remembering her, Pip, or rather Mr. Pirrip the narrator, follows Dickens's advice so thoroughly that he never reconsiders his initial impressions of her, and straight through to their last encounter, acts as though he has never listened to the woman he claims to love. Having fixed her in the beginning, Pip stops paying attention to *her*, and thereby enacts one of the deepest ironies of his obsession. So permanently are their first encounters incorporated into "the innermost life of my life," (236; ch. 29) so painful are her childish insults, so traumatic is her part in his introduction to the cruelties of class distinction, that in his self-absorption Pip locks this star into a whole constellation of rigid emotional patterns.

Mr. Pirrip's success with Dickens's principle is in this way simultaneously his failure, but it is a failure Dickens himself avoided, for the text gives us an Estella beyond her narrator's understanding. If we attend to what she

From *Dickens Quarterly* 16, no. 4 (1999): 215–29. © 1999 by the Dickens Society.

has to say for herself, we discover not only an Estella Pip does not know, but a Pip Mr. Pirrip never knows. Although Mr. Pirrip does not seem to transcribe all of what she said to Pip, he does reproduce some of it, and those conversations between Pip and Estella, as well as those with Miss Havisham, give Dickens his chance: to identify with, yet undermine his protagonist, and to sympathize with, yet question the integrity of unrequited love. But especially they give Dickens his chance to decide what it means to learn how to learn by looking back. Estella learns more by retrospective reflection than Pip does, and Pip's persistent blindness throughout the story of his romance enables Dickens to complicate conventional paradigms of moral growth as much in the second of his first-person "autobiographies" as in the first. Just as Dora's point of view undermines David's, Estella's shows us what Pip could learn from her if he would.[1]

It is time to abandon the one-dimensional Estella, the capricious-heart-breaker. She is "much maligned yet much neglected," as Juliet John says of other Dickens women (68). Herbert Pocket expresses the received opinion of Estella: "hard and haughty and capricious to the last degree," (177; ch. 22) and in company with all the novel's characters, Herbert will not notice that Estella grows into someone else. It is against multiple fixations—for Miss Havisham has fixed her most rigidly of all—that she must try to find her way.

Readers, too, often fix Estella into the Pirrip pattern: they find their sense of her entirely in the first encounters, and after her return from Paris at the beginning of what Dickens calls the "Second Stage of Pip's Expectations," they stop listening. Then they reduce her to one or two adjectives as Herbert does, but without Herbert's excuse; when he sums up her character he has not seen Estella since childhood. Critics, in contrast, have read the whole novel, have examined its brilliantly recursive structure, always doubling back on itself to reconsider its preoccupations,[2] yet such labels as "cruel, capricious, money—and status—grasping" (Alexander 127), "egotist" (Morgan 121), without "a self" only a "role" (Waters 159), and, of course, "heartless," recur again and again. They write as if to *say* one has no heart is the same thing as not having one. Harry Stone, after quoting her at length from Pip's initial encounter with her at Satis House sees no need to quote her again, but limits her to Pip's associations with her name: "cold and remote yet ever luring him on" (364–66). For some, she simply is a star (Brooks-Davies 56; Marlow 101). In focusing on his created Estella, insightful discussions of Pip's obsession often say little about Estella herself (Polhemus, Kusnetz), and Anny Sadrin has claimed that she is the heroine of a novel Dickens did *not* write (177). Only Hilary Schor listens to Estella as she deserves, but without considering fully how she changes.[3] This brief survey of critical response goes back no further than 1985, and ranges widely over theoretical orientations, see, for example, Connor, Stone and Flint, yet as far as Estella is concerned, little has changed since 1947, when George Bernard Shaw's wit fixed her into her place in the Dickensian critical tradition: "Estella is a born tormentor. She deliberately torments Pip all through for the fun of it."[4] The critical tradition has been mistaken about Estella; if we listen to what she says and pay attention to what she does, we understand how much even Shaw could be wrong. Estella is not "born" to a unified, consistent stance "all through" the novel; she is not having fun in *Great Expectations*; and the torment is all the other way.

It will be the purpose of this essay to trace the evolution of her growth from the Second Stage through the Third Stage to the end, and especially to consider her challenge both to Pip and to Mr. Pirrip. In that evolution, we hear an Estella very different from her reputation as a heartbreaker indifferent to Pip's suffering. More important, we see the extent of Pip's failure to learn—exactly the ostensible task of his story—his clinging in spite of those extraordinary reversals to his first immature judgments. An Estella-centered reading of their relationship reveals her greater capacity for change, illuminates his obsession, and documents the deafness of her world. In giving her the heroine's place, Dickens emphasizes how uncomfortably she occupies it, even how emphatically she tries to reject it; she resists both Pip's and Miss Havisham's obsessive love. No character, least of all Pip, cares to ameliorate her victimization, yet she speaks eloquently the lesson that Pip above all needs to learn and might be expected to sympathize with: how it feels to be used by others to the point of an alienation so complete that self-regard finds its ultimate expression only in self-abandonment.

The tri-partite structure of *Great Expectations*, with each stage doubling back on the past in the light of transforming revelation, enables Dickens to play the static Pip against the changing one, and both against Estella's greater development. In the Kent childhood of the First Stage, Pip freezes her disdain into a shame that quickly escapes any connection with Estella herself. In the rising expectations of the Second Stage, while passively expecting marriage to accompany money, he creates a fantasy romance which enables him to ignore Estella's refusal of it, while paradoxically excusing his failure to declare his love. In the Third Stage, under the pressure of multiplying revelations, he turns his back on their significance, refusing to ham the hardest lesson of all: that he has used Estella exactly as they both have been used, forced to embody their benefactors' obsessions. To face the implications of Estella's Third Stage choices would be to see that Herbert's characterization of Magwitch as "an ignorant determined man, who has long had one fixed idea" (343; ch. 41) applies equally to Pip himself, but with less excuse. Not only does Pip never fully acknowledge the parallels Dickens so carefully establishes between his experience and hers, but he misses her offer of solace in fellowship. She wants a comrade and tells him so, but he wants only to adore his star.

First Stage

"Why, he is a common labouring-boy!" (ch. 8)

and looking back:

> "Estella . . . said she had no doubt of my having been quite right, and of her having been very disagreeable." (ch. 29)

Dickens establishes parallels within the triangle of children at Satis House that will remain unnoticed even by Mr. Pirrip. Estella and Herbert treat Pip with the same initial disdain; Herbert's first reaction is to ask, "Who let *you* in?" (90; ch. 11). Mr. Pirrip also fails to notice that Pip and Estella have the same role to play there, the differences in social class notwithstanding. Both of them at the beck and call of Miss Havisham's authority, answering the bell, running errands, walking the wheeled chair, they seem "born only to be the victim of others' needs," as Douglas Brooks-Davies has written (45). Clearly both are victim to Miss Havisham's "sick fancy" of watching a man-child's humiliation at the hands of her woman-child, as she feeds voraciously on Estella's scorn and Pip's debasement.

Estella disappears from the First Stage only halfway through; her last directly quoted words as a child follow the fight between the "prowling boy" and the "pale young gentleman:" "Come here! You may kiss me if you like" (93; ch. 11). Emblematic of its juvenile class and gender triangle, the fight establishes the tangle of Pip's desire, the humiliation and guilt of his working-class physical strength, Herbert's importance as social guide, and Estella's mysterious link with violence. Both Herbert and Estella trade on Pip's bewilderment as the social interloper, but Estella is easier to blame than Herbert because two boys are equipped to bridge the social gap with contest. Herbert knows the rules, but Pip has the nascent blacksmith's arm. So it is Estella's disdain, "so strong, that it became infectious, and I caught it" (60; ch. 8) that will be blamed for controlling Pip's mind, in spite of the fact that Pip is infected with class contempt much earlier, at Mrs. Joe's prickly breast. Herbert's class superiority can be challenged in a fight, but gender and class together, attraction frustrated by inferiority, hurt far more.

In the second half of the First Stage, Pip fixes Estella in his mind and fixes his self-contempt in fixing her, organizing all his aspirations, shames and fears around her words "coarse" and "common." Working at the forge, he worries about the event that never occurs, that "at my grimiest and commonest" he will look up and see her looking in at him "doing the coarsest part of my work" and that she will "exult over me and despise me" (108; ch. 14). Although sensing that his struggle is primarily an internal one, Pip does not realize that his labeling that struggle "Estella" divorces it from her. He cannot imagine taking action himself to become a gentleman; in his mind such a transformation must come from the outside. In his heart he suspects it can never come at all. He can only dream about Miss Havisham's intentions, speculations that will reinforce his failure to court Estella throughout the second stage of his narrative.

Second Stage

> "We have no choice, you and I, but to obey our instructions. We are not free to follow our own devices. . . ." (ch. 33)

and looking back:

> "It is my own act." (ch. 44)

In beginning the Second Stage by reiterating the experiences that formed Pip's obsessive fixation of Estella—the class/gender triangle of Satis House's children, the association with criminality—Dickens reminds us of Pip's self-absorption as he meets the new Estella, as well as the older Herbert's independence of mind from Satis House, so much in contrast with Pip's continued dependence. Herbert serenely dismisses his earlier experiences and all they stand for as he looks back on how he was tried and found wanting: "if I had come out of it successfully, I suppose I should have been provided for; perhaps I should have been what-you-may-called it to Estella" (176; ch. 22). This is how one feels if secure in a bourgeois identity and not possessed by a sense of inferiority, of being an impostor, of being a toady.

In contrast, as he listens to the convicts discuss his most important secret on the coach to Rochester, Pip relives his most degraded associations. He cringes under his fellow travelers' revulsion as they repudiate the convicts, and he is overwhelmingly relieved, thanks to the alternate identity of his nickname Handel, that no one can tell who he "really" is. Pip can no more ignore his empathy than his fear and disgust:

> Then, they both laughed, and began cracking nuts, and spitting the shells about. As I really think I should have liked to do myself, if I had been in their place and so despised. . . . It is impossible to express with what acuteness I felt the convict's breathing, not only on the back of my head, but all along my spine. The sensation was

> like being touched in the marrow with some pungent and searching acid, and it set my very teeth on edge. (228; ch. 28)

In the social microcosm of the coach, journeying back to the scenes and voices of his defining humiliations, Pip is trapped in this confined space by his sense of being what he most loathes. By means of this newly reiterated duality, Dickens makes it clear that Estella's adult beauty will only intensify Pip's sense of immaturity. The coach incident shows that his new identity as a gentleman is so unstable that only romantic dreams of his "patroness and . . . brilliant pictures of her plans" can bridge his self-divisions:

> She had adopted Estella, she had as good as adopted me, and it could not fail to be her intention to bring us together. She reserved it for me to restore the desolate house, admit the sunshine into the dark rooms, set the clocks a going and the cold hearths a blazing, tear down the cobwebs, destroy the vermin—in short, do all the shining deeds of the young knight of romance, and marry the princess. . . . a rich attractive mystery, of which I was the hero. (231–2; ch. 29)

In Pip's romance Estella may be the "inspiration [and the] heart," but she is not a partner; she is not in on the plan. Sleeping beauties never have any say; if the hero has a partner, it is the fairy godmother, not the princess. It is the fantasy, not Estella, that has taken possession of Pip, and Mr. Pirrip is still in its thrall:

> But, though she had taken such strong possession of me, though my fancy and my hope were so set upon her, though her influence on my boyish life and character had been all-powerful, I did not, even that romantic morning, invest her with any attributes save those she possessed. I mention this in this place, of a fixed purpose, because it is the clue by which I am to be followed into my poor labyrinth. (232; ch. 29)

Looking back, Mr. Pirrip still confuses the fantasy with the person, and it is the former that he takes credit for viewing objectively. The crucial attribute Estella herself indeed will prove not to possess is a readiness to play the role Pip assigns her in his chivalrous romance. The masculine autobiographer's fixed purpose has been to place the feminine object into his narrative at the beginning, never thereafter altering it, making this unacknowledged purpose the most ironic of clues into his labyrinth:

> The unqualified truth is, that when I loved Estella with the love of a man, I loved her simply because I found her irresistible. Once for all; I knew to my sorrow, often and often, if not always, that I loved her against reason, against promise, against peace, against hope, against happiness, against all discouragement that could be. Once for all; I loved her none the less because I knew it, and it had no more influence in restraining me, than if I had devoutly believed her to be human perfection. (232; ch. 29)

Mr. Pirrip chooses to be aware only of the hopelessness of Pip's love, taking credit for abjuring an even more impossible yardstick of perfection than convention allows the eager young lover on a romantic morning. The younger Pip is indistinguishable from Mr. Pirrip here; their joint fiction will remain proof against all realities—reason, hope, happiness, discouragement—because those realities would necessarily involve interaction with a person, as opposed to internal struggles with an obsession. The repetition of "once for all" drives home the central fact: that as a child grievously hurt, he developed a sore he could keep forever raw, and he named it "Estella."

Yet the Estella who returns from Paris has clearly changed. No longer the child who taunted the small labouring boy, she is prepared to offer Pip a unique companionship based in her very different memories, as well as to ignore her foster mother's need to add him to the list of suitors whose hearts must be broken. Miss Havisham is the one who meets Pip's stereotypes with her own; both try to reimpose their narratives on Estella, who refuses both definitions of love and speaks with piercing honesty of her difficulties throughout the Second Stage, shaped as she has been. Her words are never indifferent; what Pip finds heartless is her insistence on her own point of view, a perspective that is chilled, sardonic, unable to love, but ready to be friends. She offers Pip a clear alternative to his self-casting as hero of romantic chivalry, a position that would be, if he would accept it, quite different from that of her other admirers. But she will wait in vain for him to acknowledge her individuality; the reasonable expectation that he would reciprocate her honesty, that he would perceive her as the unique person he claims she is, proves as false and cruel as any in the novel. He does not even tell her he loves her until his secret complicity with Miss Havisham is broken.

Pip's first impression is of "an elegant lady whom I had never seen" (234; ch. 29), but although he will claim to recognize her eyes, he will refuse to see the person behind her beauty who wants to escape the expectations it creates, and so he cannot hear her when she tries to tell him so. He will never be able to reconcile her beauty with her sexual indifference to him. On being together again, Pip and Miss Havisham fall immediately back into the old struggle of insult and shame, but the new Estella chooses the alternative of an apology, that she was "no doubt . . . very disagreeable" (235; ch. 29). When they revisit the scene of the fight, Estella shows that, unlike Pip, she is capable of a more detached self-judgment in looking back on an earlier self—"I must have been a singular little creature"—and she explains that she wanted Pip to win because she "took it ill that [Herbert] should be brought here to pester me with his company" (236; ch. 29).

Especially she abjures the stereotypes surrounding the word "heart" as she tries to explain why she does not remember making him cry as a child: "You must know . . . that I have no heart—if that has anything to do with my memory." Pip gets "through some jargon to the effect that . . . there could be no such beauty without it." Mr. Pirrip's choice of "jargon" suggests some awareness that not only is Pip's language at cross purposes with Estella's, but that his is the rhetoric to be found wanting. Estella tries again: "But you know what I mean. I have no softness there, no—sympathy—sentiment—nonsense." Pip is not listening, in spite of her "attentive" look, so she tries again to get his attention: "I am serious. . . . I have not bestowed my tenderness anywhere. I have never had any such thing." Pip still is not listening and says he does not believe her; he cannot believe anything so far from his romance.

Her reply acknowledges the conventional expectations of sentiment that burden the beautiful woman, while insisting, first, on her right to express herself, and second, on the possibility of something better than conventional flirtation. This seriousness is not the way Miss Havisham has brought her up to talk to men:

> "Then you don't [believe me]? Very well. It is said, at any rate. Miss Havisham will soon be expecting you at your old post, though I think that might be laid aside now, with other old belongings. . . . Come! You shall not shed tears for my cruelty to-day; you shall be my Page, and give me your shoulder." (237–8; ch. 29)

She will be the knight and he will be the page, but she is not going to avoid chivalry altogether; she just wants to reverse the roles. This encounter is typical of the adult Estella's refusal to follow Miss Havisham's script with Pip, of her lightly mocking tone as she articulates her own point of view, typical as well of her appreciation of a mutuality that could enable a more congenial relationship, and of her instinct to ignore the past that Pip and Miss Havisham remain enmeshed in. But above all, it is typical of Pip's refusal to believe that she does not want to be a belle, does not want to marry, does not want to marry *him*.

Just as Pip first travels to see Estella with the felons on the coach, so is Newgate round the corner as he waits for her to arrive in London; his imaginary criminality again stops his ears. He is baffled by her careful sarcasm: "I hoped there was an inner meaning in her words." She takes up her new life ironically, emphasizing her sardonic awareness that she and Pip share their victimization, and clearly inviting Pip to join her in sabotaging Miss Havisham's agenda:

> "I am going to Richmond. Our lesson is, that there are two Richmonds . . . and that mine is the Surrey Richmond . . . I am to have a carriage, and you are to take me. . . . We have no choice, you and I, but to obey our instructions. We are not free to follow our own devices, you and I. . . . I am to rest here a little, and I am to drink some tea, and you are to take care of me the while." She drew her arm through mine, as if it must be done. (265; ch. 33)

But literal-minded Pip cannot keep up; he hears only the offhand composure:

> "You speak of yourself as if you were some one else."
>
> "Where did you learn how I speak of others? Come, come," said Estella, smiling delightfully, "you must not expect me to go to school to *you*; I must talk in my own way."

We will learn later that she does want to be someone else; she is not happy with her life, and Pip is the only person in it who might understand. But he speaks only the conventional rhetoric of his romance: "[I live] as pleasantly as I could anywhere, away from you." She will have none of that: "You silly boy . . . how can you talk such nonsense?" (266; ch. 33).

She would rather talk of what they really have in common: despising the Pockets. She invites Pip to share her accurate analysis of the toadyism at Satis House: "It is not easy for even you to know what satisfaction it gives me to see those people thwarted. . . . You had not your little wits sharpened by their intriguing against you, suppressed and defenceless, under the mask of sympathy and pity and what not that is soft and soothing." Pip can see that "It was no laughing matter with Estella now, nor was she summoning these remembrances from any shallow place," but he fails to perceive her superior understanding of adult manipulation of children, and he continues to treat her as if she had no more depth than the princess of romance. She offers the handshake of fellowship, but he insists instead on bestowing a chivalrous kiss upon that hand:

> "I am beholden to you as the cause of their [the Pockets] being so busy and so mean in vain, and there is my hand upon it."
>
> As she gave it me playfully—for her darker mood had been but momentary—I held it and put it to my lips. "You ridiculous boy," said Estella, "will you never take warning? Or do you kiss my hand in the spirit in which I once let you kiss my cheek?"
>
> "What was it?" said I.
>
> "I must think a moment. A spirit of contempt for the fawners and plotters."
>
> "If I say yes, may I kiss the cheek again?" (267–8; ch. 33)

Pip uses a flirtatious courtesy to evade the implications of her friendly handshake, because to join her in her contempt for fawners would be to come too close to the discomforts of his own relations with Miss Havisham. He is not willing to go to school to her.

> "It is part of Miss Havisham's plans for me, Pip . . . I am to write to her constantly and see her regularly, and report how I go on—I and the jewels—for they are nearly all mine now."
>
> It was the first time she had ever called me by my name. Of course she did so, purposely, and knew that I should treasure it up. (270; ch. 33)

She asks him to understand her reluctance to do what Miss Havisham wants her to do, but he is counting on her doing exactly what he thinks Miss Havisham wants. In her "I am to do this and you are to do that . . ." is captured their shared humiliation; this insight is muffled by his romantic clichés. Dickens conveys the immediacy, even tragedy, of her perspective, "I and the jewels" said with a tired sigh, but Pip hears only his own name. Even Mr. Pirrip, writing with hindsight, falls back on comedy at this point over the waiter and the tea, evading, as Pip does, the central fact that he appears to be the kind of man prepared to marry a woman he knows does not love him. Even what most obliges the knight, to rescue the damsel in distress, Pip refuses to attempt in their final Second Stage encounter, when Estella is most articulate and clearsighted about the damage that has been done to her. So much for Pip's chivalry.

In that final encounter, the last dramatized trip to Satis House, Estella reveals the dark side of Pip's fantasy; she has been waiting for him to "take warning" (her words) and abandon his role in her Havisham-appointed task of "teasing" (his word) her admirers. She then analyzes Miss Havisham's parenting, finally reproaching her adoptive mother: "I am what you have made me. . . . I was no party to the compact, for if I could walk and speak, when it was made, it was as much as I could do." She acknowledges the "set purpose" and the "steady memory"—the fixation—that have formed her from "when your face was strange and frightened me!" She asks: "When have you found me false to your teaching?" And so, "I must be taken as I have been made" (304–6; ch. 38). But the very fact that she can articulate what Miss Havisham has done gives her a perspective more acute that Pip's, just as her frequent warnings that she has no heart suggest the reverse, that she has a heart for kindness, if not for love. In her ability to analyze what has been done to her is made clear her power to act alone and leave it behind. It is her tragedy that she chooses Drummle as means of escape, but he cannot command her kindness or her respect as Pip does.

When Pip reproachfully asks her to look across the room at Drummle, she replies, "Why should I look at him? . . . with her eyes on me instead" (310; ch. 38). When he emphasizes how much Drummle is generally despised, she asks "Well?" and then again "Well?" and then again "Well? . . . and each time she said it, she opened her lovely eyes the wider." But Pip disregards her challenge to understand the privileged place she has given him in her life.

She declares that it is for her to "bear it" not Pip, unless he wants her to "deceive and entrap" him. Her readiness to wreak Miss Havisham's revenge is at most half-hearted, and in Pip's case, clearly reluctant. She would rather make Pip the exception to Miss Havisham's agenda: "all of them but you" (311–12; ch. 38). Even marriage to Drummle is better than her entrapment in the destructive manipulations of those who love her.

Third Stage

> "It is in *my* nature. It is in the nature formed within me. I make a great difference between you and all other people when I say so much." (ch. 44)

and looking back from the revised ending:

> "suffering has been stronger than all other teaching, and has taught me to understand what your heart used to be." (ch. 59)

When Pip discovers the mistake that has excused his failure to court Estella, he is forced to discover that Estella has acted independently, that he can "touch nothing" in her, that his idea of a beautiful woman does not correspond to her inner nature, that she warned him many times, "but you would not be warned, for you thought I did not mean it" (362; ch. 44). She had invited him to look at the Havisham game from her side rather than from his; now she offers him the compliment of honesty—"I make a great difference between you and all other people when I say so much"—(362–3; ch. 44). When he finally pours out his fantasy—"The rhapsody welled up within me, like blood from an inward wound, and gushed out" (365; ch. 44)—her response to his eloquence is "incredulous wonder." With most readers, Pip attributes this surprise to emotional incapacity, but it could with equal justice be attributed to amazement that Pip, notwithstanding his rhetoric of adoration, has not listened to her since she allowed a childish kiss.

When Pip discovers Estella's biological parentage, the secret knowledge brings him no closer to her own perspective, but it does bring him power over Jaggers, because for once he knows more than Jaggers and is capable of surprising him; still better, power over Estella herself, because he knows more than she does about her own identity. The conference of men in which it is decided that no one else will know the truth does not include her or her mother. Pip has lost Estella to Drummle, but he has gained the knowledge that reduces her to his own level. Yet he never acknowledges that they are siblings in a terrifying ambiguity: low born, tainted by criminality, raised to a false gentility. The truth does not cause the revolution it should, the revolution of his relations with Magwitch and Joe and Miss Havisham, because what he has loved all along is her inaccessibility; in his fantasy she is a beautiful luxury, an object, that social climbers like himself can buy only with cash. It is then the perfect irony that of her own will she chooses the undoubted aristocrat—Drummle is in line for a baronetcy—who does not know of her false pretensions, but who will abuse her just as if he did. Her hidden identity reduces her in Pip's eyes to a person with whom he has too much in common. In the Second Stage he rejected her personhood because his romance called for her love if only she would accept his adoration, or if she could not love in exchange for worship, then it called for marriage because she had no choice. Knowledge of their equal class backgrounds ought to bring the power of liberation, ought to release him into action, ought to enable acceptance of the comradeship she has offered him. But that would involve him in too close an examination of what it means to be a gentleman. He cannot modify, let alone refuse, a status he feels at the deepest level he has no right to. He cannot meet her on either high ground or low, nor can he emancipate himself from the distinction.

Estella's choice of Drummle dramatizes her alienation and challenges both Pip and the reader to accept her rejection of romance. It enables Dickens to insure that she disappoint everyone, while keeping sexual passion safely beneath the surface of the text, displaced onto Orlick, onto Molly, onto Drummle. Having been used and manipulated all her life by others, Estella puts such a low value on herself that she does not seem to care much whom she marries, so long as "It is my own act," and so long as it breaks the pattern of her life, always suspended in the moment of teasing coyness that feeds Miss Havisham's insatiable desire: "Miss Havisham would have had me wait, and not marry yet; but I am tired of the life I have led, which has very few charms for me, and I am willing enough to change it" (364; ch. 44). In this decision she joins all the characters in *Great Expectations* who in making perverse, self-punishing choices forge their own chains: Miss Havisham, Mrs. Joe, Magwitch, Pip.

Rather than her choice of Drummle, it is Magwitch's death that elicits the final summary and farewell to Pip's romance of Estella. Pip's last words to Magwitch can comfort the dying, but sum up a romance that could not be sustained in life:

> "You had a child once, whom you loved and lost. . . . She lived and found powerful friends. She is living now. She is a lady and very beautiful. And I love her!" (460; ch. 56)

This account neatly, if ironically, sums up what matters to Pip, leaving out all that he still refuses to try to understand. In his mind, the child grew up to become, not a person, but a coveted abstraction of social and sexual assets: "She is a lady and very beautiful." This is what he loves. Since he has refused to know her as an individual, the fact that she never loved him can be denied again for the few moments that remain of her father's life.

This reading of Estella is consistent with the ending to the novel that Dickens published after being influenced by Lytton, the so-called happy ending.[5] Only this ending is sufficiently equivocal, and only this one does justice to the incompatibility of desire that Pip and Estella have faced throughout: his inability to perceive the Estella who has wasted her wisdom on him. To the final sentence he does not notice that she speaks from an intransigently independent point of view.[6] Estella says they will "continue friends apart" but Mr. Pirrip sees "no shadow of another parting" between them. The romance convention assumes on the part of the heroine a modest, silent acceptance, the speaking eyes that convey the heart, so Pip feels justified, as does Mr. Pirrip and the Bulwer-Lyttons to this day among the novel's readers, in expecting that Estella's silence gives consent as he takes her hand in his.[7] This is what he means by seeing no shadow of another parting. But throughout this novel the conventional courtship roles have broken down: Pip has not been the eloquent lover, and Estella has not been silently, modestly acquiescent. Dickens gives Pirrip the "last word" in a nonverbal gesture, following her last words, enabling both points of view to stand unreconciled at the end.

She never lured him, rather warned him repeatedly to no avail. Hard and haughty she was as a child, but capricious, never. Quite the reverse, with almost no room to manoeuvre through Miss Havisham's careful training, she found the strength, without Pip's help, to end Miss Havisham's abuse. That she ends it by choosing another kind of abuse, by punishing herself, is to fulfill the destiny shared by most of the characters in the novel. Mr. Pirrip claims new vision of the men he has misread—Joe, Herbert, Magwitch—but although he is burned with her, he does not share Miss Havisham's realization of what they have done to Estella. Instead, with us, Mr. Pirrip is allowed only the consolations of romance. We are one with Bulwer-Lytton in longing for the happy ending that Dickens did not write.

For Dickens resists genre, the story of the moral growth of the self-made gentleman as well as the story of love. In creating an Estella who refuses the romance script, he brings us up short in undermining his hero's claims. The hard truth is that Mr. Pirrip has wounded everyone he claims to love, beginning with the wound in himself, and those wounds remain. Mr. Pirrip is indeed sadder, but he is not wiser. He does not acknowledge the plain sense of her last words to him. The romance genre allows him to hear only coyness, the no that is really yes, because the claim of possession is the man's prerogative. As Mr. Pirrip writes his autobiography, he sees Pip's inner conflicts, he even can mock Pip's humiliations in the romance game through the comedy surrounding the scenes with Estella, but he can only report her words, and not many of those, said from a point of view that remains inexplicable to him. It is for Dickens to imagine the person who would say them, the person who refuses to stay fixed.

Notes

1. See Darby, "Dora and Doady," where I develop an argument about Dora that parallels the one here about Estella. For their patient critiques, I would also like to take this opportunity to thank particularly Vincent DiGirolamo, Bruce Pegg and Philip Rogers.

2. See in particular, Brooks-Davies and Meckier, 1998.

3. See Schor's reading of Estella, which is closer to my own than anything else I have read, and which stimulated me both to agree and, in disagreeing, to extend my own account.

4. Quoted in Cotsell, 42. The original reference is to the Foreword to *Great Expectations*, 1947 Hamish Hamilton/Novel Library Edition.

5. See also Jordan 1996 and Meckier, 1993.

6. See Schor, who credits this observation to D.A. Miller in *Narrative and its Discontents: Problems of Closure in the Traditional Novel* (Princeton: Princeton UP, 1981).

7. See Rosalind Coward's discussion of romance novel conventions.

Works Cited

Alexander, Doris. *Creating Characters with Charles Dickens*. University Park [PA]: Pennsylvania State UP, 1991.

Brooks-Davies, Douglas. *Great Expectations*. London: Penguin, 1989.

Connor, Steven. *Charles Dickens*. Oxford: Basil Blackwell, 1985.

Cotsell, Michael. *Critical Essays on Charles Dickens's 'Great Expectations'*. Boston: G.K. Hall, 1990.

Coward, Rosalind. "The True Story of How I Became My Own Person." *The Feminist Reader*. Eds. Catherine Belsey and Jane Moore. 2nd Ed. Maldon [MA]: Blackwell, 1997.

Darby, Margaret Flanders. "Dora and Doady." *Dickens Studies Annual* 22 (1993): 155–69.

Dickens, Charles. *Great Expectations*. Ed. Charlotte Mitchell. London: Penguin, 1996.

———. *The Letters of Charles Dickens*. Pilgrim Ed. Ed. Graham Storey. Vol. 9. Oxford: Oxford Clarendon, 1997.

Flint, Kate. *Dickens*. Brighton [Sussex]: Harvester, 1986.

John, Juliet. "Dickens' Deviant Women: A Reassessment." *The Critical Review* 34 (1994): 68–84.

Jordan, John O. "Partings Welded Together: Self-fashioning in *Great Expectations* and *Jane Eyre*." *Dickens Quarterly* 13 (1996): 19–33.

Kusnetz, Ella. "This Leaf of My Life: Writing and Play in *Great Expectations* (Parts One and Two)." *Dickens Quarterly* 10 (1993): 91–103 and 146–160.

Marlow, James E. *Charles Dickens: The Uses of Time*. Selinsgrove: Susquehanna UP, 1994.

Meckier, Jerome. "Charles Dickens's *Great Expectations*: A Defense of the Second Ending," *Studies in the Novel* 25 (Spring 1993): 28–58.

———. "*Great Expectations*: Symmetry in (Com)motion." *Dickens Quarterly* 15 (1998): 28–49.

Morgan, Nicholas H. *Secret Journeys: Theory and Practice in Reading Dickens*. Rutherford [NJ]: Fairleigh Dickinson UP, 1992.

Polhemus, Robert M. "The Fixation of Love: Charles Dickens's *Great Expectations* (1860–61)." *Erotic Faith: Being in Love from Jane Austen to D.H. Lawrence*. Chicago: U of Chicago P, 1990.

Sadrin, Anny. *Great Expectations*. London: Unwin Hyman, 1988.

Schor, Hilary. "'If He Should Turn to and Beat Her': Violence, Desire, and the Woman's Story in *Great Expectations*." *Great Expectations*. Ed. Janice Carlisle. Boston: Bedford, 1996.

Stone, Harry. *The Night Side of Dickens: Cannibalism, Passion, Necessity*. Columbus [OH]: Ohio State UP, 1994.

Waters, Catherine. *Dickens and the Politics of the Family*. Cambridge: Cambridge UP, 1997.

ROBERT R. GARNETT

The Good and the Unruly in Great Expectations*—and Estella*

Dickens's adoration of womanly tenderness and daughterly devotion is routinely evident in his fiction; but *Great Expectations* is distinctive for drafting its leading male characters into the traditionally feminine role of nurse. After Pip is burned at Miss Havisham's, Herbert Pocket "was the kindest of nurses, and at stated times took off the bandages, and steeped them in the cooling liquid that was kept ready, and put them on again, with a patient tenderness that I was deeply grateful for" (301; ch. 50). Later, Joe nurses Pip: "For, the tenderness of Joe was so beautifully proportioned to my need, that I was like a child in his hands" (346; ch. 57). Wemmick is a devoted nurse for his father. During a visit to Walworth, for example, Pip admires his solicitude for the Aged P: "As he wanted the candles close to him, and as he was always on the verge of putting either his head or the newspaper into them, he required as much watching as a powder-mill. But Wemmick was equally untiring and gentle in his vigilance, and the Aged read on, quite unconscious of his many rescues" (225; ch. 37). Biddy and Clara perform nursing duties as well—Biddy for Mrs. Joe after she is bludgeoned, and Clara for her roaring, rum-soaked father; but as nurses, these two admirable females are upstaged by the males in *Great Expectations.*

Pip's faithful attendance on Magwitch, sliding toward death in the prison infirmary, confirms his own softening and moral reformation. He praises the

From *Dickens Quarterly* 16, no. 1 (March 1999): 24–41. © 1999 by the Dickens Society.

prisoners who work as sick nurses, "malefactors, but not incapable of kindness, GOD be thanked!" and spends every possible hour at Magwitch's bedside, giving religious instruction: " . . . it became the first duty of my life to say to him, and read to him, what I knew he ought to hear"—just as Woodcourt had catechized the dying Jo in *Bleak House* (341, 338; ch. 56). Stationing Pip at Magwitch's prison deathbed, Dickens drags his erring hero into the company of the righteous—characters like Joe, Herbert, Wemmick and Woodcourt:

> Then shall the righteous answer him, saying . . . when saw we thee sick, or in prison, and came unto thee? And the King shall answer and say unto them, Verily I say unto you, Inasmuch as ye have done it unto one of the least of these my brethren, ye have done it unto me. (Matthew 25.37, 39–40)

Pip's Christian solicitude for Magwitch, for whom he earlier felt the greatest repugnance, atones for his addictive, decidedly unchristian passion for Estella—or so we are meant to believe.

How convincing is this renunciation of desire, and conversion to tenderness and virtue? When Magwitch's end arrives, he and Pip are holding hands: "He smiled, and I understood his touch to mean that he wished to lift my hand, and lay it on his breast. I laid it there, and he smiled again, and put both his hands upon it" (341; ch. 56). A pretty gesture, but who can doubt that Pip would prefer that it were Estella drawing his hand to *her* breast? For all Dickens's efforts to reform him, Pip is incorrigible, and resists his author. Even at the very end, after eleven years of respectable diligence as a merchant and "already quite an old bachelor," he remains haunted by his old passion, secretly revisiting Satis House "for her sake. Yes, even so. For Estella's sake" (356; ch. 59). He mentions no plans to revisit the marshes or prison for Magwitch's sake.

Pip flaunts his latter-day code of diligence, moderation, and humility: "But that poor dream, as I once used to call it, has all gone by, Biddy, all gone by!" he claims, immediately before sneaking off to Satis House, and "I work pretty hard for a sufficient living, and therefore—Yes, I do well," he informs Estella, piously, when he meets her amidst the ruins (356, 357; ch. 59). But his relapse into his old desire for her reveals the continuing conflict between passion and virtue in Pip's character, a conflict echoed in the sharp division of the novel's characters into two mutually exclusive parties—the moderate, and those governed by unruly passions. The moderate characters display to perfection the genial domestic and social virtues Dickens had been applauding for a quarter century. The passionate, on the other hand, with all their intense, self-absorbed desires, he disapproved of—but understood.

I

Joe, Wemmick and Herbert are the novel's leading moderates, along with the women who become their wives, Biddy, Miss Skiffins and Clara Barley, respectively. Despite their differences in personality, circumstances and class, all have fundamentally similar temperaments. The males are mild-mannered, cheerful and patient, their merits emphasized by the difficult figures they endure—Joe's vixen wife Mrs. Joe, for example. They are temperate, stable, and steady. "He is very regular in his walks, is my son," the Aged P says of Wemmick. "Very regular in everything, is my son"—in this steadiness, of course, a world apart from the restless Pip, with his "inability to settle to anything," "surely the most unsettled person in all the busy concourse" (222; ch. 37, 236; ch. 39, 289; ch. 48). This basic disparity in temperament between moderate and passionate characters is evident, for example, in Pip's comically elaborated invasion and derangement of Herbert's quiet, orderly life at Barnard's Inn. Moderate characters are unambitious; Joe is contented with forge and hearth, Wemmick shuttling between Little Britain and the Castle, Herbert "looking about" in the counting-house. Were it not for Pip's subvention, Herbert might still be looking: " . . . I do not remember that I ever saw him do anything else but look about him," Pip remarks. "If we all did what we undertake to do, as faithfully as Herbert did, we might live in a Republic of the Virtues" (209; ch. 34).

In effect, Herbert and his fellow moderates of *Great Expectations* constitute a circumscribed but admirable Republic, or even Church, of the Virtues—the usual Dickens Virtues, that is: domestic and childlike rather than heroic. The males are boyish—Wemmick with his toy castle, Joe with his unlettered simplicity, Herbert with youthful cheer, optimism and candor: "generous, upright, open, and incapable of anything designing or mean" (269; ch. 44). The moderate women enjoy less girlish license and fancy. Biddy, Clara and Miss Skiffins are nest-builders, highly valued for their contributions to domestic comfort and harmony. As a girl still, Biddy arrives to keep house for Joe and Pip "and became a blessing to the household," Pip says admiringly. "She managed our whole domestic life, and wonderfully too" (98; ch. 16, 100; ch. 17). Clara is a patient housekeeper to her drunken, ranting father, and even Miss Skiffins, though lacking the modesty and sweetness of Biddy and Clara, presides over a cozy tea-table and washes up the tea-things "in a trifling lady-like amateur manner"; contrasting sharply with the brusque, prickly "slapping dexterity" of Mrs. Joe's tea-making ritual and her manic housekeeping, the "exquisite art of making her cleanliness more uncomfortable and unacceptable than dirt itself" (225; ch. 37, 23; ch. 4).

Almost as a matter of course, the moderate women of *Great Expectations* are gentle and nurturing. Biddy is "pleasant and wholesome and sweet-tempered." Mrs. Joe may be violent and combustible, and Estella's touch a provocative slap, but Biddy is a peaceful, calming presence, and her touch is anodyne: "She put her hand, which was a comfortable hand though roughened by work, upon my hands, one after another, and gently took them out of my hair. Then she softly patted my shoulder in a soothing way . . ." Clara is "confiding, loving, and innocent" and "gentle." Even the "wooden," garish Miss Skiffins is "a good sort of fellow" (100, 103; ch. 17, 281; ch. 46, 223; ch. 37).

More striking, however, is the gentleness of the males. "Wemmick, I know you to be a man with a gentle heart," Pip remarks, urging him to intercede with Jaggers. Even the amelioration of the rough and violent Magwitch is repeatedly described as a "softening" process: " . . . it struck me that he was softened"; " . . . smiling with that softened air upon him which was not new to me"; " . . . I heard that old sound in his throat—softened now, like all the rest of him." This celebration of softness illuminates the complexity of the novel's impulses; for whatever shining virtues Dickens himself might have boasted, no one ever called him "gentle," "soft" and "tender" (306; ch. 51, 282; ch. 46, 325, 333; ch. 54).

The temperate characters naturally and inevitably pair off with one another. Just as Joe believes in social parity in marriage—"Whether common ones as to callings and earnings . . . mightn't be the better of continuing fur to keep company with common ones, instead of going out to play with oncommon ones"—so Dickens subscribes to an analogous system of matching moderates with one another; characters with modest desires and aspirations are best off marrying their like (60; ch. 9). Happy marriage is the pre-ordained future of moderate characters. Warming to the admirable domesticity of the bachelor Wemmick, Dickens belatedly introduced Miss Skiffins solely to furnish him with the requisite wife. The marriages of the moderates in *Great Expectations* are rewards for, and emblems of, their high moral value, as well as a guarantee that, inoculated against the fever of strong desire, they will enjoy the same rational happiness as David Copperfield, whose "domestic joy" with the sedate Agnes "was perfect" (*David Copperfield* 727; ch. 63).

If the temperate characters are the elect of Dickens's church, Joe is the elect of the elect. Dickens first conceived of him as "a good-natured foolish man" (*Letters* 9:325). He is initially described as a simpleton with weak coloring, weak character, and weak intelligence:

> Joe was a fair man, with curls of flaxen hair on each side of his smooth face, and with eyes of such a very undecided blue that they seemed to have somehow got mixed with their own whites. He was a mild, good-natured, sweet-tempered, easy-going,

> foolish, dear fellow—a sort of Hercules in strength, and also in weakness. (12–13; ch. 2)

There is nothing particularly child-like about Joe in this description, but his companionship with Pip naturally led to the idea of Joe as a fellow child—the young Pip regards himself and Joe as "equals"—and soon Dickens began to imagine Joe not as a weak adult but as a burly Oliver Twist at the forge, trailing clouds of glory well into a merely nominal adulthood. Joe waxes more saintly through the novel. In a world of strong-willed, manipulative adults—Magwitch, Miss Havisham, Herbert's mother, Clara's father, Pumblechook, Mrs. Joe—Joe's meekness becomes his virtue, his folly his wisdom. To exculpate him from his inability to protect either himself or Pip from his virago wife, Dickens concocts for Joe the lame explanation that he suffers her abuse because his father had beat his mother—cold consolation, one would think, for the sting of "Tickler"; yet Pip "dated a new admiration of Joe" from the night of this disclosure (43; ch. 7). "Long-suffering and loving Joe" actually fills the role of Pip's mother, comforting him under the lash of their common tyrant (312; ch. 52). Yet whether Joe is surrogate father or mother, one wonders if Dickens himself would have been so forgiving of such a patently inadequate parent.

Joe's truckling to Mrs. Joe ends when Orlick deals with her more forcibly, allowing Joe's virtues to flourish. As a blacksmith, he practices one of the manly professions—like soldier, sailor, fisherman—that Dickens greatly admired, but Joe's particular merit derives from his fusion of two of Dickens's favorite moral patterns, childlike innocence and simplicity joined to womanly tenderness and compassion. "Joe laid his hand upon my shoulder with the touch of a woman"; Joe "ever did his duty in his way of life, with a strong hand, a quiet tongue, and a gentle heart"; "Exactly what he had been in my eyes then [in Pip's childhood], he was in my eyes still; just as simply faithful, and as simply right" (111; ch. 18, 216; ch. 35, 347; ch. 57). Nursing Pip (as well as paying his debts) during his long fever, Joe exhibits both the charity of the Good Samaritan and the forgiveness of the Prodigal Son's father. Religious fervor is rare in Dickens's fiction, so that Pip's invocation "O God bless him! O God bless this gentle Christian man!" ratifies in the most high pontifical manner Joe's sainthood (344; ch. 57).

The novel's sanctification of the moderate characters, led by Joe, is particularly evident when Pip is *in extremis* in the old sluice-house. While Orlick rants and threatens, Pip's "dread of being misremembered after death" culminates in a vision of Estella's descendants: "My mind, with inconceivable rapidity, followed out all the consequences of such a death . . . I saw myself despised by unborn generations—Estella's children, and their children—while the wretch's words were yet on his lips."[1] But as death approaches and Pip's thoughts turn eternal, he prays: Orlick "flared the candle at me again, smoking my face and hair, and for an instant blinding me, and turned his powerful back as he replaced the light on the table. I had thought a prayer, and had been with Joe and Biddy and Herbert, before he turned towards me again" (316–7, 319; ch. 53). Noticeably absent from this prayer is Estella. Though his lifelong passion, she has no place among the saints who might intercede for him now—as Herbert presently does.

II

One might reasonably object, however, that it is easy enough for the moderate characters to be good and do good, because they feel little temptation to be or do otherwise. Their virtue lies not so much in resisting evil, as in lacking any strong inclination to it; they have no compelling desires to lure them into danger or error. While Herbert lackadaisically "looks about him," Pip is driven by desire for what is out of reach. Gazing out across the river, he is stirred by inexpressible longings: "Whenever I watched the vessels standing out to sea with their white sails spread, I somehow thought of Miss Havisham and Estella; and whenever the light struck aslant afar off, upon a cloud or sail or green hill-side or water-line, it was just the same" (88–9; ch. 15). The moderates are not strongly moved by those clouds or green hillsides beyond the marshes, and never voyage out onto risky emotional seas. Like Wemmick, they remain moated in safety; their imaginations bounded by the Castle, the forge, the counting house, the kitchen hearth. "What I wanted, who can say?" Pip wonders, and when he unfavorably contrasts "restlessly aspiring discontented me" with "plain contented Joe," we realize that the contented characters enjoying Dickens's approbation are those least like Dickens himself—suggesting the ambiguity of his feelings during the Ellen Ternan years (87; ch. 14).

Pip and Miss Havisham are the most prominent of the novel's passionately discontented characters, both desiring with ruinous intensity. Narrating Compeyson's pursuit of Miss Havisham, Herbert explains: "I believe she had not shown much susceptibility up to that time; but all the susceptibility she possessed, certainly came out then, and she passionately loved him. There is no doubt that she perfectly idolised him" (143; ch. 22). Miss Havisham herself exclaims:

> "I'll tell you," said she, in the same hurried passionate whisper, "what real love is. It is blind devotion, unquestioning self-humiliation, utter submission, trust and belief against yourself and against the whole world, giving up your whole heart and soul to the smiter—as I did!" (184; ch. 29)

So, too, Pip, who loves "against reason, against promise, against peace, against hope, against happiness, against all discouragement that could be" (179; ch. 29). Miss Havisham burns with passionate love, passionate resentment, passionate despair; when she catches fire, it is only an outward and visible sign of her inner fires: "I saw her running at me, shrieking, with a whirl of fire blazing all about her, and soaring at least as many feet above her head as she was high" (299; ch. 49). The same flames burn Pip, just as, years earlier, Miss Havisham had kindled his desire for Estella. The fierce self-consuming appetite of fire fascinated Dickens; just before beginning *Great Expectations* he enjoyed a symbolic bonfire of his own past, burning "the accumulated letters and papers of twenty years" in the field behind Gad's Hill (*Letters* 9:304).

Pip and Miss Havisham are the novel's most spectacular, but not the only, cases of self-consuming passion. Also fiery, in the termagant way at least, is Mrs. Joe, whose irascibility and "Rampages" suggest strong amatory desire diverted from satisfying channels: a sort of Wife-of-Bath figure in a misalliance with the "mild, good-natured, sweet–tempered, easy-going, foolish, dear fellow" Joe (12–13; ch. 2). Whereas Miss Havisham's love is warped into an excess of grief, Mrs. Joe's erotic energies erupt in pyrotechnic violence. The only (reported) conjugal embrace between Joe and Mrs. Joe, just after she has witnessed him drubbing Orlick in the forge, shows her unmistakably aroused. Swooning, she "was carried into the house and laid down . . . and would do nothing but struggle and clench her hands in Joe's hair" (93; ch. 15). Joe's response is doubtful; soon we find him sweeping up the blacksmith shop, an activity not particularly suggestive of post-coital lassitude. Their unhappy coupling illustrates the Dickens principle of emotional parity in marriage: moderate characters should seek out their own kind.

Even more violent than Mrs. Joe is Estella's mother Molly, "a wild beast tamed," "a perfect fury in point of jealousy," according to Wemmick, while Jaggers explains that "passion and the terror of death had a little shaken the woman's intellects," so that after her murder trial he employed her as his housekeeper and "kept down the old wild violent nature" (157; ch. 24, 293; ch. 48, 307; ch. 51). Like Miss Havisham, Molly is associated with flame: " . . . her face looked to me as if it were all disturbed by fiery air, like the faces I had seen rise out of the Witches' caldron [in *Macbeth*]. . . . She set on every dish; and I always saw in her face, a face rising out of the caldron" (165; ch. 26).

Even Jaggers himself, Molly's cool, domineering lord, seems a crypto-passionate figure. Referring to Pip's "poor dreams" of Estella: "'Pip,' said he, 'we won't talk about "poor dreams;" you know more about such things than I, having much fresher experience of that kind,'" and a little later he remarks, with plain self-reference, that "those 'poor dreams' . . . have, at one time or another, been in the heads of more men than you think likely" (307–8; ch. 51). Despite his present clam-like self-sufficiency, Jaggers too has evidently loved and suffered. His finger chewing habit suggests self-gnawing discontent; his "distrustful manner" suggests disappointment; his legal bullying suggests aggressive compensation for the loss of his "poor dreams." Returning each evening from his busy, crowded legal practice to his barren house in Gerrard-street, Jaggers is a lonely figure. But not entirely lonely; Pip's laconic comment to Estella that Jaggers's house "is a curious place" may hint that there is more to his private life than Pip (or Dickens) is willing to state openly (205; ch. 33). "How did Mr. Jaggers tame her, Wemmick?" Pip inquires with reference to Molly. Wemmick replies: "That's his secret. She has been with him many a long year" (293; ch. 48). Perhaps Gerrard-street harbors other secrets, too. Is the fiery Molly Jaggers's concubine as well as housekeeper, and in their loveless embraces does he spend the base coin of his lust, because the better tender of his love was once spurned ("I have been faithful to thee, Cynara! in my fashion")?

III

Desire springs from the sensual imagination, and the passionate are the novel's imaginative characters—dreamers and artists. Dickens may frown on their aspirations and their art, but the passionate are, figuratively, the novel's novelists. Miss Havisham is a flamboyant actress, her dramatic genius prompted by grief. Tormented by Estella's ingratitude, she is Lear; wracked by guilt and regret, she is Lady Macbeth (229–32; ch. 38). These are only occasional roles, however; in her principal role Miss Havisham creates herself, taking justifiable satisfaction in the staging of her own gothic melodrama. Wopsle's Hamlet is ludicrous, but Miss Havisham playing Miss Havisham is inspired. Like Dido, she has constructed a funeral pyre on which to sacrifice herself to thwarted passion, but she stretches out her theatrical holocaust into years of smouldering decay—grief among the ruins. Pip may (priggishly) rebuke her "vanity of sorrow," but Dickens could create an actress of Miss Havisham's flair only because of his own like genius; he may censure her, but his imaginative sympathies are very much with her.

Pip the blacksmith's apprentice is a dreamer seduced by his restless fancy. His first visit to Satis House awakens his imagination, inspiring extravagant fantasies; he confesses to Joe "that there had been a beautiful young lady at Miss Havisham's who was dreadfully proud, and that she had said I was common, and that I knew I was common, and that I wished I was not common, and that the lies had come of it somehow, though I didn't know how." Pip comments:

> This was a case of metaphysics, at least as difficult for Joe to deal with, as for me. But Joe took the case altogether out of the region of metaphysics, and by that means vanquished it.
>
> "There's one thing you may be sure of, Pip," said Joe, after some rumination, "namely, that lies is lies." (59; ch. 9)

The "metaphysics" of Pip's lies is more complex than Joe appreciates, however. Joe's simple, pious explanation, that "they come from the father of lies, and work round to the same," savors of puritan rhetoric that Dickens would despise in the mouth of someone like *Bleak House*'s Chadband. Pip is perplexed by his own particular demons, but his Satis House fictions come not from the devil but from a susceptible imagination quickened by Estella, "the embodiment of every graceful fancy that my mind has ever become acquainted with" (272; ch. 44). She is an intimation of more intense experience; she rouses more intense feelings; she is a liberation from the mundane, the plausible and the practical.

Unlike David Copperfield, Pip does not become a writer, yet he appears a more likely novelist than David, who of all the characters in *David Copperfield* seems the most conventional and least imaginative. Dreamy and restless, Pip lacks David's application, but he belongs among the lunatics, lovers and poets—along with *David Copperfield*'s Mr. Dick, with his kite and his mad memorial; or little Emily, with her colorful fancies about her fisherman uncle Mr. Peggotty transformed into a dandy: "If I was ever to be a lady, I'd give him a sky-blue coat with diamond buttons, nankeen trousers, a red velvet waistcoat, a cocked hat, a large gold watch, a silver pipe, and a box of money." And so saying, Emily "looked up at the sky in her enumeration of these articles, as if they were a glorious vision."(38; ch. 3). Pip too is a visionary—a "visionary boy—or man" as Estella says (272; ch. 44). Both as boy and man he "sees" Miss Havisham hanging from the rafters in the ruined brewery: "A figure all in yellow white, with but one shoe to the feet; and it hung so, that I could see that the faded trimmings of the dress were like earthy paper, and that the face was Miss Havisham's, with a movement going over the whole countenance as if she were trying to call to me" (55; ch. 8). At the forge, he sees "Estella's face in the fire with her pretty hair fluttering in the wind and her eyes scorning me," and at the window: "... often at such a time I would look towards those panels of black night in the wall which the wooden windows then were, and would fancy that I saw her just drawing her face away, and would believe that she had come at last" (87; ch. 14). Pip sees her everywhere, in fact: "You have been in every prospect I have ever seen since—on the river, on the sails of the ships, on the marshes, in the clouds, in the light, in the darkness, in the wind, in the woods, in the sea, in the streets" (272; ch. 44). Perceiving Estella as omnipresent and immanent, Pip reveals an essentially sacramental imagination.

IV

Against the intensity of such strong, restless feelings, the usual platitudes—including Dickens's own—are inadequate. Desire leads into a wilderness of moral complexity and ambiguity. Co-existing with the comic universe of the novel's more fortunate moderates, destined for connubial felicity, glooms a tragic universe of unattainable desires, fatal choices, and dead hopes. Happiness for the passionate is as "far out of reach" as Estella in Paris (and for that matter, always). "O the sense of distance and disparity that came upon me, and the inaccessibility that came about her!" Pip complains when she returns from Paris, and "Oh! She is thousands of miles away, from me," he tells Herbert (181; ch. 29, 190; ch. 30). The nature of desire is to imagine what is beyond reach; the *OED* and Skeat speculate that *desire* derives ultimately from the Latin *sidus*, a constellation or star. And desire for the unreachable star introduces Pip to passion in its root sense, suffering. Estella is "the theme that so filled my heart," Pip relates, "and so often made it ache and ache again" (235; ch. 38). Burning and wounding are frequent images for the passionate. During an attack of "the horrors," Miss Havisham's brother Arthur tells Compeyson: "And over where her heart's broke—*you* broke it!—there's drops of blood" (261; ch. 42). Pip's "rhapsody" on Estella "welled up within me, like blood from an inward wound, and gushed out" (272; ch. 44).

But apart from such acute agonies, the passionate endure chronic loneliness and homelessness. *Great Expectations* opens in bleak outdoor isolation, at the graves of Pip's family. In the churchyard beside the marshes, he first becomes aware of himself, and the self he becomes aware of is lonely, cold and frightened. Later, when his great expectations are revealed, he feels it "very sorrowful and strange that this first night of my bright fortunes should be the loneliest I had ever known" (114; ch. 18). Desire for Estella alienates him from home—"Now, it was all coarse and common, and I would not have had Miss Havisham and Estella see it on any account"—and after his great expectations dissolve, "I had no home anywhere" (86; ch. 14, 335; ch. 55). Jaggers returns every evening to his lonely house in Gerrard-street, relieved only by the doubtful companionability of Molly. Miss Havisham too is a forlorn figure, with "an air of utter loneliness upon her"; Satis House is not a home but a ruin and a wilderness, as desolate as Pip's marshes (295; ch. 49). Even when ostensibly mixing in the life around them—Pip among the Finches of the Grove, for example—the passionate are preoccupied by private desires and griefs, neither seeking, nor fit for, a wider community. Pip's desideratum is virtually his identity. "In a word, it was impossible for me to separate her, in the past or in the present, from the innermost life of my life," he reflects; and "You are part of my existence, part of myself," he tells Estella, " . . . to the last hour of my life, you cannot choose but remain part of my character, part of the little good in me, part of the evil" (182; ch. 29, 272; ch. 44).

V

What of Estella herself? At first glance she seems a *tertium quid*, neither passionate nor moderate. Everyone in the novel, including Estella herself, regards her as unfeeling and emotionless. Her icy detachment is explicitly contrasted both to Pip's yearning and to Miss Havisham's "fierce" and "flashing" passions:

> . . . Miss Havisham still had Estella's arm drawn through her own, and still clutched Estella's hand in hers, when Estella gradually began to detach herself. She had shown a proud impatience more than once before, and had rather endured that fierce affection than accepted or returned it.
>
> "What!" said Miss Havisham, flashing her eyes upon her, "are you tired of me?"
>
> "Only a little tired of myself," replied Estella, disengaging her arm . . . (229; ch. 38)

On the other hand, Estella plainly does not belong among the novel's temperate homebodies, either; she is the very antithesis, for example, of Biddy's contented domesticity.

Despite her anomalous position, few critics find Estella as intriguing as Pip does. In the 144 pages of Patricia Ingham's *Dickens, Women and Language*, for example, Estella is dispatched in a single, not overlong, paragraph. In *Dickens and Women*, Michael Slater concedes her several unenthusiastic pages, regretting that she is not "a character with whom the author lovingly makes the reader intimate as he does with Dora" in *David Copperfield*:

> She is there in the book as a necessary, and necessarily disastrous, object for Pip's passion, not there for her own sake. Dickens's imagination is concerned with the effect she has on Pip rather than with how Estella herself lives and moves and has her being.

Slater doubts that she really belongs in a novel "in the realist tradition" at all: " . . . the adult Estella must, it seems to me, be considered more as a fictive device than as a character in the mode of psychological realism"; and "what

Miss Havisham is supposed to have done to Estella surely belongs more to the realm of moral fable or fantasy than to that of psychological realism." She is basically "a fairy-tale ice maiden" (275–81).

Unlike Pip, Estella does not explain herself; we know her only from his account, and his knowledge of her is limited and unhappy. As an element in his life, she has a specific and well-defined role, and from his point of view her meaning is plain enough—she is what he desires but can never possess. Pip's narration concerns itself with his problems, not Estella's. But even his simplified version reveals complexities in her character that interested Dickens, if not Pip himself. Noting that Estella is not invariably a straightforward ice maiden but on several occasions surprises us with "natural emotions," Slater complains that "Dickens confuses us by not consistently presenting Estella as . . . preternaturally passionless" (281). But rather than a defect in her characterization, emotional ambiguity *is* Estella's character as Dickens understands it. She is a fairy-tale ice maiden; but at the same time she is intensely passionate.

Estella's passion scarcely resembles Pip's burning desire, or Miss Havisham's smouldering wrath. Like Yeats's Connemara fisherman, Estella is "cold and passionate as the dawn." Herbert describes her as "hard and haughty and capricious to the last degree" (139; ch. 22). She seems as glittering and unfeeling as her jewels, as cold and remote as the stars. "I have no heart," she claims, and she doesn't miss it: "I have no softness there, no—sympathy—sentiment—nonsense" (183; ch. 29). This self-admission, or boast, is usually taken as an accurate description of Estella's emotional frigidity. "But as she grew, and promised to be very beautiful," Miss Havisham asserts, " . . . I stole her heart away and put ice in its place." Estella concurs: "I am what you have made me," she taunts Miss Havisham. And Herbert, as the voice of popular opinion, offers the same version: Estella "has been brought up by Miss Havisham to wreak revenge on all the male sex," he tells Pip (298; ch. 49, 230; ch. 38, 139; ch. 22).

This straightforward, rational explanation of Estella's character conveniently serves both Pip's autobiographical and Dickens's homiletic purposes: Pip needs to console himself for his inability to win Estella, while Dickens never loses a chance to condemn selfish parents and emotional repression. But he provides contrary evidence to subvert his own argument. When Estella asserts that her capacity for love has been crushed by Miss Havisham (in an educational program never really explained), Pip exclaims that such emotional insensibility surely "is not in Nature":

> "It is in *my* nature," she returned. And then she added, with a stress upon the words, "It is in the nature formed within me." (271; ch. 44)

But her "nature," of course, pre-dates the influence of Miss Havisham. Estella is the daughter of the violent convict Magwitch and the even more violent Molly—both fierce characters; both, in fact, murderers. As the daughter of Molly, Estella has "some gypsy blood in her," denoting for Dickens a dark, hot-blooded, sexually passionate nature (293; ch. 48). Miss Havisham has not eradicated—could not eradicate—this inheritance; she has merely taught Estella to conceal her strong natural feelings behind a mask of cool indifference and glittering inaccessibility. But Pip detects the passionate blood in Estella. "What *was* it that was borne in upon my mind when she stood still and looked attentively at me?" he wonders, as Estella's resemblance to Molly dawns on him (183; ch. 29). Estella has even inherited Molly's mysterious, flame-like aura. When Pip passes through "a sudden glare of gas" with Estella beside him, "It seemed, while it lasted, to be all alight and alive with that inexplicable feeling I had had before; and when we were out of it, I was as much dazed for a few moments as if I had been in Lightning" (206; ch. 33). Estella's essence is fire, not ice.

Her intense scorn is like a photographic negative of intense desire; hers is not a dull, impassive frigidity, but a "burning" chill. She descends from a well-established line of Dickensian women of "cold" passion—Edith Dombey, Lady Dedlock, Louisa Gradgrind—silent, self-contained, self-possessed figures who suggest his fascination with the mysteries of eros. Estella adopts a passionless, scornful manner as a defense against both her desirability and her own susceptibility to desire. Miss Havisham is not Estella's teacher, but her textbook; Estella has profited from the fearful spectacle of Miss Havisham's diseased indulgence in her passions. "I, who have sat on this same hearth on the little stool that is even now beside you there," Estella exclaims, "learning your lessons and looking up into your face, when your face was strange and frightened me" (230; ch. 38). The lesson Estella has learned, however, is not frigidity—Miss Havisham cannot educate away Estella's "gypsy" blood, her aura of flame; what she has learned, rather, is self-command. While Miss Havisham rages like Lear, "Estella looked at her with perfect composure, and again looked down at the fire. Her graceful figure and her beautiful face expressed a self-possessed indifference to the wild heat of the other, that was almost cruel" (229; ch. 38). A proud, aloof manner, Estella has learned, subdues the unruly passion which has "blighted" her mentor and threatens herself. Gazing at the fire—frequently a sign in Dickens's fiction of intense, suppressed feeling—Estella reveals another trait inherited from earlier passionate characters, brooding fire-gazers like *Hard Times*'s Louisa Gradgrind and *Our Mutual Friend*'s Lizzie Hexam, for example, who find in the glowing coals an image of their own emotions.

Estella's kinship with the other passionate characters is suggested by the virtuoso quality of her beauty. While Miss Havisham is a flamboyant actress, and Pip a visionary, Estella's genius creates a perfect, aloof loveliness. "To be born woman is to know / . . . That we must labor to be beautiful," Yeats's "beautiful mild woman" says; far from "mild," however, Estella wields her beauty like a weapon, a jeweled sword that dazzles and destroys. Pip recognizes the artifice in it: "Proud and wilful as of old, she had brought those qualities into such subjection to her beauty that it was impossible and out of nature—or I thought so—to separate them from her beauty" (181–2; ch. 29). Her hauteur is provocative, heightening her fascination: "'Moths, and all sorts of ugly creatures,' replied Estella, . . . 'hover about a lighted candle. Can the candle help it?'" (234; ch. 38). But here she is being disingenuous; her indifference deliberately allures. "She treated me as a boy still, but she lured me on," Pip observes, and "It was impossible for me to avoid seeing that she cared to attract me; that she made herself winning; and would have won me even if the task had needed pains" (181; ch. 29, 206; ch. 33). It is easy enough for her to dazzle a young puppy like Pip or an oaf like Drummle, of course; a better challenge to her mastery is the imperturbable Jaggers. Dining with him at Miss Havisham's, Estella is at first discomposed by his "determined reticence"; then with Miss Havisham as her squire, she arms herself for combat:

> In the interval, Miss Havisham, in a fantastic way, had put some of the most beautiful jewels from her dressing-table into Estella's hair, and about her bosom and arms; and I saw even my guardian look at her from under his thick eyebrows, and raise them a little, when her loveliness was before him, with those rich flushes of glitter and colour in it. (186; ch. 29)

Estella matches, even defeats, Jaggers's masterful personality with the power of her beauty.

Her marmoreal loveliness convinces Pip that she is sexually frigid. "I leaned down [to kiss her], and her calm face was like a statue's," he complains on one occasion (204; ch. 33). But there are signs that she is, to the contrary, readily aroused, and ready to be aroused. On his second visit to Miss Havisham's, she "slapped my face with such force as she had," a precocious provocation which baffles the less precocious Pip—"She seemed much older than I, of course, being a girl, and beautiful and self-possessed" (68; ch. 11, 49; ch. 8). After his triumph over the pale young gentleman, she greets him (just as Mrs. Joe responds to Joe's thrashing of Orlick) with signs of arousal:

> . . . there was a bright flush upon her face, as though something had happened to delight her. Instead of going straight to the gate, too, she stepped back into the passage, and beckoned me.
>
> "Come here! You may kiss me, if you like." (75; ch. 11)

It is, alas for Pip, the last time that she displays any amatory interest in him.

Estella's indifference is nothing personal, he likes to imagine; she does not love him because she cannot love anyone. In fact, however, it seems to be the case that she feels no desire for Pip simply because she feels no desire for Pip—not because of any general incapacity for love, or lack of desire. As with her sister characters in earlier novels, Estella's contemptuous aloofness hints at unsatisfied longings. Perhaps her imagination carries her to reach for some visionary love as inaccessible to her as she herself is to Pip. Her decision to settle for a loveless match with the brutish Drummle, "a mere boor, the lowest in the crowd," recklessly flaunts her consequent despair (235; ch. 38).

To Pip's thinking, certainly, she acts perversely in choosing the worst of the moths who flutter about her—not a moth at all, in fact, but a spider, "a deficient, ill-tempered, lowering, stupid fellow" (234; ch. 38). Estella cites boredom: " . . . I am tired of the life I have led, which has very few charms for me, and I am willing enough to change it" (272; ch. 44). Such caprice seems lunatic: "It's certain that fine women eat / A crazy salad with their meat," Yeats grouses about Maud Gonne, and Pip feels the same about Estella. But these, of course, are the predictable complaints of disappointed suitors. In fact, despite Estella's contempt for Drummle, there may well be more to her decision to marry him than just "money, and a ridiculous roll of addle-headed predecessors" (234; ch. 38). And there is certainly more to her rejection of Pip than his vulnerable feelings: "Should I fling myself away upon the man who would the soonest feel (if people do feel such things) that I took nothing to him?"[2] Dickens and Estella are both too genteel to suggest that, though she despises Drummle, he is nonetheless sexually more interesting to her than Pip. "Come! Here is my hand," she bids Pip farewell. "Do we part on this, you visionary boy—or man?" (272; ch. 44). Given the choice between "visionary boy" and "a mean brute, such a stupid brute!"—a choice between soul and earth, between adoration and carnality—Estella chooses (without much hesitation, it seems) the earthy brute—not despite his brutishness, perhaps, but because of it.

We are given few privileged glimpses into Estella's feelings. Pip's divergent impulses are embodied in the two women he loves in different ways, Estella representing the lure of emotional and sexual intensity, Biddy the appeal of domestic moderation and stability. "And now," Pip explains the conflict, "because my mind was not confused enough before, I complicated its confusion fifty thousand-fold, by having states and seasons when I was clear that Biddy was immeasurably better than Estella, and that the plain honest working life to which I was born, had nothing in it to be ashamed of, but offered me sufficient means of self-respect and happiness" (105; ch. 17). Such allegorical oppositions and explicit self-analysis give us insight into Pip's feelings; but Dickens is content to leave Estella's character mysterious, her motives perplexing. There are adequate narrative reasons for this reticence, but perhaps the additional reason that Dickens too was uncertain about her.

Nonetheless, what we do learn about Estella suggests that, far from being a simple case of emotional sterility—an ice-maiden—she struggles with a dilemma as difficult as Pip's. It too is adumbrated by a choice between potential mates. She may fling herself away on Drummle, or she might marry the worshipful Pip himself. Pip can later console himself that Drummle turns out as nasty a husband ("quite renowned as a compound of pride, avarice, brutality, and meanness") as anyone could have wished, but it hardly follows that Pip would have been the better choice (356; ch. 59). The pattern for the hypothetical union of Estella and Pip is the marriage of Lady Dedlock and Sir Leicester in *Bleak House*. Pip and Sir Leicester are both snobs, one parvenu, the other to the manner born; despite which, both are essentially decent characters, each devoted to a lovely, cool, unresponsive woman. And like Lady Dedlock with Sir Leicester, Estella—married to Pip—would in all likelihood be comfortable, doted on, bored and unhappy, her gypsy passions frustrated. Unlike Lady Dedlock, however, Estella has no memories of a Captain Hawdon to flee to; her heart has never found the key to unlock it.

As with Edith Dombey and Louisa Gradgrind, as well as Lady Dedlock, wasting loneliness and despair drive Estella to willful self-destruction. As Louisa remarks of the chimneys of Coketown: "There seems to be nothing there, but languid and monotonous smoke. Yet when the night comes, Fire bursts out, father!" (*Hard Times* 135; ch. 15). Estella too is a victim of the strong feelings she has tried to suppress. Her stillborn marriage to Drummle, for whom she feels "the indifference of utter contempt," repeats Edith Dombey's aborted elopement with Carker and Louisa Gradgrind's aborted elopement with Harthouse (271; ch. 44). For Dickens, Desire is a tragic goddess, embodied in lovely, lonely, passionate women like Estella, who fling themselves away on what they despise. "Wretches!" she exclaims upon seeing Newgate, but whether contemptuous or pitying, her comment is unintentionally ironic; the wretched in *Great Expectations* are not the prisoners in Newgate, but characters of strong desire like Estella herself.

VI

As often happened with Dickens, his sympathy with his erring female grew as the novel progressed; conceived as an accessory to Pip's delusive great expectations, Estella gradually assumes her own autonomous identity. Her argument with Miss Havisham, for example, contributes little to Pip's progress, but evokes our admiration for Estella's cool intelligence, strong will, and defiant spirit. And just as Pip can't get her out of his mind, the narrative itself irresistibly returns to Estella at the end, after she has dropped out of sight for eleven years; Dickens must have realized that she had attained such independent interest that she demanded not only a curtain call, but some kind of resolution. His first (and probably better) notion, in fact, was to conclude the novel with a short coda on the redemptive quality of Estella's suffering:

> . . . for, in her face and in her voice, and in her touch, she gave me the assurance, that suffering had been stronger than Miss Havisham's teaching, and had given her a heart to understand what my heart used to be. (359; "Original Ending")

In its poignant cadences and terse finality, this brief reunion on a London street "marries" Pip and Estella with an artistic economy lost in the hand-in-hand fade-out of the revised ending. But both endings are Dickensian enough in insisting on Estella's moral regeneration; she, too, is finally humbled and softened. In this, she and Ebenezer Scrooge become unlikely cousins, but *Great Expectations* infuses into Dickens's much-loved conversion theme a somber moral realism: Estella has been chastened not simply by a night of troubled dreams, but by years of unhappiness, and the experience has scarcely left her feeling light as a feather, happy as an angel and merry as a school-boy. In the original ending, she and Pip look "sadly enough on one another"; in the final version, "what I had never seen before, was the saddened softened light of the once proud eyes" (359; "Original Ending"; 357; ch. 59).

Estella the penitent resolves the problematic character of Estella the cool, passionate enigma; moral reformation simplifies and clarifies her as a fictional character, sweeping away her puzzling ambiguities. But even if the new, improved Estella now has a heart to understand what Pip's heart used to be, does he—or do we—understand what *her* heart used to be? Stars are not only unreachable, but unknowable, and much of Estella's character—the early Estella—remains cloaked in Dickens's reticence or uncertainty. Though seldom lacking confidence in his penetration, he hesitated to intrude on her shadowy inner life. That we never quite understand Estella's character, however, paradoxically deepens our understanding of her. Musing on Estella, Dickens found himself straying into a labyrinth of sexual fascination and desire, far from his usual moral certitudes, and far from the sunlit, genial world of *Great Expectations*' moderate characters.

Notes

1. In fact, Pip need not have worried about Estella's descendants—like Pip himself, she appears to be childless at the end of the novel. Although sexually charged, Dickens's passionate characters are seldom fruitful. Of the passionate characters in *Great Expectations*, only Molly has a child—Estella herself. It must be admitted, however, that the novel's domestic characters seem equally short of offspring. After eleven years of marriage, Joe and Biddy have but one child, and there is no mention of Herbert and Clara having any children at all. In his somber, self-absorbed mood at novel's end, Pip neglects to bring us up to date on the other characters, so that this omission may mean nothing—but it nevertheless seems curious. Happy is the man with a quiver full of sons, the Psalmist says, but by 1861 Dickens—with seven sons—may have had some reservations.

2. Estella's rhetorical question—"Should I fling myself away upon the man who would the soonest feel (if people do feel such things) that I took nothing to him?" (271; ch. 44)—is a good example of her "deconstructing" her own ice-maiden character, for even as she tosses off an obligatory scoff at "such things" as the pain of unreturned love, she is sensitive to Pip's wounded feelings, tactfully attributing her rejection of him to her own emotional incapacity, and to his keen sensibility.

Works Cited

Dickens, Charles. *Bleak House*. Norton Critical Edition. Ed. George Ford and Sylvère Monod. New York: Norton. 1977.

———. *David Copperfield*. Norton Critical Edition. Ed. Jerome H. Buckley. New York: Norton. 1990.

———. *Great Expectations*. Norton Critical Edition. Ed. Edgar Rosenberg. New York: Norton. 1999.

———. *Hard Times*. Penguin Classics edition. Ed. David Craig. Harmondsworth: Penguin. 1985.

———. *The Letters of Charles Dickens*. Pilgrim Edition. Ed. Nina Burgis, et al. Oxford: Clarendon Press. 1965.

Ingham, Patricia. *Dickens, Women and Language*. Toronto: U of Toronto Press. 1992.

Slater, Michael. *Dickens and Women*. Stanford: Stanford UP. 1983.

SARA THORNTON

The Burning of Miss Havisham: Dickens, Fire and the "Fire-Baptism"

Like Frankenstein's monster, Miss Havisham has entered that ever-evolving textual space which is our cultural heritage: filed away under "weird spinsters: various" we retrieve her periodically in her yellowed bridal dress, the light of day shut out from the decaying feast chamber in which she sits. If she is not sitting when we conjure her up, she is burning; a flaming figure forever either running towards us or writhing in Pip's arms—an ambiguous accident or immolation rich in connotations and spreading its tentacles through the novel and beyond it. It is hinted at many times as the novel progresses in a series of eerie premonitions which gain in force as the scene approaches and continue to multiply when the flames are out. If the lady is for burning, so too are other marginal or dangerous witch-women in and outside of *Great Expectations*, Miss Havisham owing some of her power to women such as Hortense in *Bleak House* (1853) and Madame Defarge in *A Tale of Two Cities* (1859). But to fully understand the value of the burning scene within *Great Expectations* we need to examine the other examples of burning within the novel and in other Dickensian novels such as that of Krook in *Bleak House*, and the conflagrations in *The Tale of Two Cities* and *Barnaby Rudge* (1841). We also need to consider Miss Havisham not as burning solely for her aberrant female status but also for her textual entrenchment in the economics and industry of her time: a figure of that failure cleansed by a liberating fire. The

---

From *Q/W/E/R/T/Y* 9 (October 1999): 105–14. © 1999 by Publications de L'Université de Pau.

fire is also an aesthetic one which shares certain traits with an anatomy of fire established on the basis of Victorian prose such as Carlyle's *Sartor Resartus* (whose writings greatly influenced Dickens) and certain Turner paintings.[1] Thus Miss Havisham's fire is also Pip-the-narrator/creator's fire; it both figures and disfigures the Dickensian text, speaks of both acts of creation and destruction. Most of all, as a piece of writing it invites the reader to sift the ashes for signs of the phoenix.

A Witch-Burning

Unlike the witch in Grimm's "Hansel and Gretel" Miss Havisham has no gingerbread house to tempt Pip with. She has every intention of devouring him as she "devours" (228) Estella "greedily," with "relish" (77) and "ravenous intensity" but makes no attempt to entrap her victim by sprucing up her environment. She sees herself as sweetmeat enough, a delicious bait on any terms, and tells her relatives where they will sit at table when they come to "feast upon" (72) her. She has status as a supernatural bad spirit being called a witch many times in the narrative and is also a "fairy godmother"—a weird one wielding a "crutch" (122). She appears to her brother Arthur as a bleeding bride—a grotesque virgin with a bleeding sacred heart carrying a shroud. Miss Havisham has all the accoutrements of the witch figure—the evil crone who will be burnt as a scapegoat, the bewitching succubus who lays her head on a pillow next to Pip's in his dream and is a "shrieking" medusa figure mesmerising him in the burning scene.

She needs firstly to be placed in the context of other occult female figures already present in Dickens's novels and sharing certain traits with them. Her reclusive qualities link her to Mrs. Clennam in *Little Dorrit* (1857) shut up in her dark, crumbling house in a wheelchair with her family secrets until her death and the literal collapse of the miserable home which is finally reduced to dust and rubble. She too favours a young girl as a companion—this time a poor serving girl linked to her own history whom she has deprived of her inheritance. But it is Miss Havisham's devouring and cruel qualities which link her to other fiery and dangerous women destined for destruction in Dickens. Their "fire" comes not from their deaths but from the same self-consuming fire of revenge which slowly burns Miss Havisham and fuels her "burning love" for Estella. Moreover, Hortense of *Bleak House* and Madame Defarge of *A Tale of Two Cities* are French and associated with the images of conflagration in Carlyle's writing of the French Revolution.

It is Hortense's name which links her to this group of marginal women: she is tense, hot and if the name is mispronounced *à l'anglaise* she is a whore. She is described as "mortal high and passionate—powerful high and passionate" (312). When Jarndyce asks why she walks "shoeless" through the water, the gamekeeper's wife suggests that "she fancies its blood" (312). Being "shoeless" is a sign of revolt or a sign of some aberrant passion and we see Miss Havisham with her one shoe as a signal of her fall from grace and her rejection of patriarchal norms. The shoeless peasantry become the *sans-culottes* of revolt in *A Tale of Two Cities* while in other novels those who are "*sans chaussures*" also prepare revolutionary conflagrations.[2] Like Miss Havisham, Hortense spends all her forces in taking revenge for a rejection—this time from her mistress Lady Dedlock—and is ready to do murder to this end. Tulkinghorn as a figure of male power becomes her target while Miss Havisham turns her anger upon herself and upon others through Estella. Both have a pent up anger which is "devouring" in Miss Havisham and tiger-like in Hortense.

Both women wait patiently for the right moment to wreak havoc. This deadly staying-power is shared with Mme Defarge whose quality of steely determination is suggested in the metaphor of knitting—an uncanny mixture of gentle domesticity and the meticulous drawing up in the knitting's pattern itself of a death list of those who will die during the revolution. This knitted list evoked in the chapters "Knitting," "Still Knitting" and "The Knitting Done" gains in length as the narrative progresses and culminates when Mme Defarge realises her dream by hewing off the head of the governor of the Bastille. Thus we see that quiet domesticity leads to dangerous outbursts: the contemplative domestic scene can become a gothic drama. We see such a configuration when Pip turns to leave Miss Havisham as she sits quietly by her hearth:

> In the same moment I saw her running at me, shrieking, with a whirl of fire blazing all about her, and soaring at least as many feet above her as she was high. (299)

Miss Havisham's hair like that of the often predominantly female revolutionary crowd in *A Tale of Two Cities* is wild and streaming as she advances towards Pip, a frightful medusa paralysing her foe as Miss Havisham paralyses Pip by making him love Estella. This fear of the castrating woman is also relevant to Defarge and her guillotine and her actual decapitation of a man (*A Tale* 302). Hortense and Mme Defarge are both presented to the reader as witches and moulded like Miss Havisham in the "furnaces of suffering" (*A Tale* 249) and pitiless in their revenge. Thus as Mme Defarge sits and knits as the heads fall—associated as she is with the guillotine, the "figure of the sharp female called La Guillotine" (283), so Miss Havisham sits with Estella in Pip's sight knitting as the latter bares his soul to them. Like Madame Defarge, Estella has icy control which is suggested in her inexorable knitting: "All this time, Estella knitted on" (270). Even during

Pip's painful revelation of his feelings and accusation of cruelty directed at Miss Havisham "her fingers plied their work, and she looked at me with an unmoved countenance" (270) or "looking at me perfectly unmoved and with her fingers busy" (270). This might be contrasted with the pleading and kneeling woman at the feet of a male figure, her loss of control quite unlike the knitting and unmoved female whose hands are economically at work. Pip can only use his hands to bury his face (271) and hide his feelings. Both Estella and Madame Defarge face out their interlocutors and their manual dexterity is intensely threatening: hands that can manipulate needles can also manipulate Hortense's gun and Defarge's knife.[3] It is also the indecipherability of repetitive manual work which terrifies those associated with these women and although Pip fancies he "reads" "in the action of her fingers" (268) what Estella's thoughts might be, he remains unable to predict her moods and actions.

These qualities are what determine the fate of such figures in the text—cleansed from the pages of these urban novels of manners which practice a quite extraordinary violence towards women. The death toll is impressive: Defarge shot, Hortense hung, while in *Great Expectations* Molly is narrowly saved from hanging for a life of slavery to Jaggers, Mrs. Joe bludgeoned to death, Estella bludgeoned into submission by Drummle and thus replaced by a new submissive Estella. Miss Havisham's own burning is inscribed everywhere in the text of *Great Expectations* and she is seen hanging, bleeding and burning in fantasies of her destruction which are linked to the two other figures of the novel—the three Macbeth witches imagined by Pip when looking at Molly. These are the fiery faces of Miss Havisham, Molly and Estella, all medusa figures.[4] All are put into the fire as part of the presentiments of her death imagined by Pip.[5] He sees her hanging from a beam in the brewery and imagines her execution three times in terms of hanging—firstly during his first visit to Satis House (55), then in a memory of that moment, and just before the burning scene itself. She burns once in actuality then again in Pip's dreams (301)—the density of these executions stretching to a hanging and two burnings in three pages.

But before ever Miss Havisham burns both Estella (as bewitcher of men) and Molly (murderess like Hortense and Madame Defarge) burn as forerunners. Estella burns firstly when Pip watches her during his first visit to the ruined brewery when he sees her with her "pretty brown hair spread out in her two hands . . . pass among the extinguished fires, and ascend some light iron stairs, and go out by a gallery high overhead, as if she were going out into the sky" (54). This walk among ghostly extinguished fires and rise to the heavens implies a death and resurrection. Fire also engulfs her in the forge when Pip thinks back to his work as a blacksmith when "all those visions that had raised her face in the glowing fire, struck it out of the iron on the anvil, extracted it from the darkness of night" (182). The face in the fire is a foretaste, a pyromantic vision of the face of Miss Havisham who is seen by Pip "running at me, shrieking, with a whirl of fire blazing all about her, and soaring at least as many feet above her head as she was high" (299). Miss Havisham's face is framed in flame like a medusa head where snakes become fire, and Estella's face in Pip's vision is also framed in "glowing fire." There is also another witch-woman or medusa head who anticipates the burning of Miss Havisham, this time in the person of Molly who like the former has "a quantity of streaming hair." The description of Molly serving at Jaggers' dinner party is uncannily like the description of the burning of Miss Havisham since all the same motifs are present—agitation and a face surrounded by flames:

> I cannot say whether any diseased affection of the heart caused her lips to be parted as if she were panting, and her face to bear a curious expression of suddenness and flutter; but I know that I had been to see *Macbeth* at the theatre, a night or two before, and that her face looked to me as if it were all disturbed by fiery air, like the faces I had seen rise out of the Witches' caldron. (165)

In the next paragraph the narrator insists again on the caldron and then gives another image of a face in flames:

> She set on every dish; and I always saw in her face, a face rising out of the caldron. Years afterwards, I made a dreadful likeness of that woman, by causing a face that had no other natural resemblance to it than it derived from flowing hair, to pass behind a bowl of flaming spirits in a dark room.

"Years" later means that Pip remembers Molly's face *after* seeing Miss Havisham's burning and there seems to be a fusion or confusion of the two older women since the face is caught in the same fiery air. On a more sinister level this voluntary recreation of the burning face "by causing" it to pass behind flaming spirits implies a desire to see the burning of Miss Havisham again—this time Pip burns her voluntarily, and punishes her once again for her betrayal of him. Pip and his feeling of great guilt (65, 76, 85, 177) which has often been the focus of critical research might suggest a secret gratification at the deaths of the witch-women of his existence—Mrs. Joe and Miss Havisham—who pay for their misdemeanours in gruesome fashion.

A Bonfire of the Vanities

Yet Miss Havisham's burning cannot be seen solely in terms of a personal punishment and it is at this point that we need to examine her status as wealthy woman. We might see her demise as part of a renouncement of the beautiful items which become purchasable when one has, like her father, made a fortune. Is this Savonarola's fire into which he heaped all the jewels, paintings and vanities of a decadent Florentine people? We certainly find descriptions akin to the much later seventeenth-century Dutch vanity paintings[6] in which worldly goods are heaped up to emphasise their precarity and their imminent destruction at the hands of time. In the darkened chambers of Satis House the reader finds jewels, trinkets, flowers "all confusedly heaped about the looking-glass" (50):

> Some bright jewels sparkled on her neck and on her hands, and some other jewels lay sparkling on the table. Dresses, less splendid than the dress she wore, and half-packed trunks, were scattered about. She had not quite finished dressing for she had but one shoe on—the other was on the table near her hand—her veil was but half arranged, her watch and chain were not put on, and some lace for her bosom lay with those trinkets, and with her handkerchief, and gloves, and some flowers, and a prayer-book, all confusedly heaped about the looking-glass. (50)

The element of confusion and haphazardness is important here since the effect is of someone being caught in the act, frozen in a moment of time with the superfluous appendages of existence lying uselessly about as if to emphasize their transience and worthlessness. The death-head or *memento mori* which often lurks in such paintings as a contrast to youth and beauty is present in the form of Miss Havisham's body itself—a fleshly oxymoron—which like the wedding feast has decayed within the virgin bridal dress—a *nature morte* in which perfect ripeness has tipped over into corruption.

The seventeenth-century vanity paintings also favoured depictions of Mary Magdalene at a moment of her renunciation of earthly wealth; she is often shown on her knees, her hair and clothes in disarray, her jewels strewn about her. Miss Havisham appears in the role of Mary Magdalene asking for Pip's forgiveness: "dropped on her knees at my feet; with her folded hands raised to me." Pip goes on to remark: "To see her with her white hair and her worn face, kneeling at my feet gave me a shock through all my frame" (297). He seems to dwell on her humiliation with a certain pleasure: "She wrung her hands and crushed her white hair" (297). Pip judges her coolly and without haste—his forgiveness of her attenuated by the enumeration of her sins concerning Estella and the addition of a supplementary sin of vanity:

> And could I look upon her without compassion, seeing her punishment in the ruin she was, in her profound unfitness for this earth on which she was placed, in the vanity of sorrow which had become a master mania, like the vanity of penitence, the vanity of remorse, the vanity of unworthiness, and other monstrous vanities that have been curses in this world? (297–8)

This mention of vanity points to the discourse on vanity in Ecclesiastes (chapter 1, verse 8) "the eye is not satisfied with seeing, nor the ear with hearing" which is the fate of all who enter Satis House. There are also echoes of chapter 2, verse 11. "Then I looked on all the works that my hands had wrought, and on the labour that I had laboured to do: and behold, all was vanity and vexation of spirit, and there was no profit under the sun." So all Pip's acquisitions are seen by himself as coming to naught, and it is Miss Havisham who had tempted him with worldly goods and the beauty of Estella whom he blames for his own emptiness; the bonfire, then, is the bonfire of his vain and vexatious expectations. Just before the burning Pip recognises the fact that Satis House is a wasteland and that he too as time had gone by "had come to be part of the wrecked fortunes of that house" (295).

If Miss Havisham is cast, if only briefly, in the role of the Magdalene—an irony in itself since she is an unmarried virgin—she also appears in a more terrifying role as the "great whore" of the apocalypse. Raphael makes the point that Miss Havisham embodies "the mythic horrors of countless cruel mothers, stepmothers, and witch-like figures" (218) and notes the "unsatiated female passion and desire that smoulder in Miss Havisham" (220). Pip sits in judgement over her and her sins and in the last burning scene he struggles with her in a sexual embrace which suggests a fusion of murder and fornication rather than a saving of life. It is a moment when Miss Havisham's sexuality seems to ignite and has, as Walsh says "overtones of assault and rape" (718): "Pip works hard to extinguish not so much the return of the repressed but the last, furious eruption of the all-too-expressed" (718). She later appears succubus-like in a vision with her head on his pillow and indeed seems to embody the fornicating whore. In the Revelation (chapters 17–18) St. John the Divine is shown "the judgment of the great whore that sitteth upon many waters" who is a metaphor for the city of Babylon itself: "And the woman which thou sawest is that great city, which reigneth over the kings of the earth." Miss Havisham too is a symbol of the "city" of Victorian commerce. It is interesting to note that the fall of Babylon is precipitated as much by commercial success as sexual proclivities: "For all nations have drunk of the wine of the wrath of her fornication . . . and the merchants of the earth are waxed rich through the abundance of her delicacies."[7] Hubris is also one of her crimes: "How much she hath glorified herself." The wailings of the merchants can be heard as they see "the smoke of her burning" which whisks away great lists of goods: "The merchandise of gold, and silver . . . and all manner of vessels of most precious wood, and of brass, and iron, and marble." They make great lament as the flames consume the city: "What city is like unto this great city!" Surely at the time of the Great Exhibition and the achievements in iron and steel, this section of the Revelation would have spoken to readers and church-going listeners. Is not Miss Havisham's burning with its suggestion of sexual embrace and the destruction of the "heap" of objects on her feast table an echo however distant of this fundamental linking of the female body with the commercial life of a city found in Revelations. Walsh makes this link between Miss Havisham and the sick economy around her and here we see a final conflagration to cleanse the world of the taint of that acquisitiveness.

The burning of Miss Havisham marks the demise of Satis House yet the silence and the lonely desolation of the aftermath of the fire in Revelations ("And the voice of harpers, and musicians, and of pipers, and trumpeters, shall be heard no more at all in thee; and no craftsmen, of whatever craft he be, shall be found any more in thee; and the sound of a millstone shall be heard no more at all in thee.") is already part of the house and brewery when Pip first visits them. This image of the sad remains of destruction found in *Barnaby Rudge* and other Dickens novels "a blackening heap . . . a dreary blank . . . the silence and solitude of utter desolation"[8] is found in Satis House which is a blank, empty "desolate" (356) space long after and long before the fire which signals its final demise: it is a "cleared space" and, as in the Revelation, a series of negatives define it: "no house now, no brewery, no building whatever" (356). But what is strange is that the brewery is already destroyed and empty with "no craftsman" or merchants well before the fire begins. Babylon has fallen, the Garden has already cast out Adam and Eve before the final burning of the "mother of harlots" which Miss Havisham is seen to be as the mother of Estella.

The reader discovers Satis House and the brewery which provided the money to build it when the destruction has already occurred—after the fire of the vanities—in a world where the cobwebs cover the feast table as if they were ashes. If the bonfire of the vanities destroys not beautiful objects but fallen ones then the fire is also a means of liberation rather than a mere punishment.

Fire as a Liberating Energy

We have seen that the fire gets rid of dangerous and fallen women, as well as of the vanities or detritus of a Victorian Babylon. It seems then to be a purifying fire, one which clears ground and creates new space. In this connection we might begin by considering another death by fire—this time an inner fire which destroys Mr. Krook in *Bleak House.* A spinster burns, an old bachelor explodes: Miss Havisham catches fire, Krook spontaneously combusts. Both are examples of death by fire even though Krook's fire is one which bursts out from within him; there are also some interesting contextual similarities: the victims live isolated from others mentally, Krook being turned in upon himself through his obsession with a document he cannot find. He runs a rag and bottle shop and accumulates and hoards papers which he cannot read because he is illiterate. Living in the dark confines of his cluttered shop he slowly poisons himself with gin just as Miss Havisham poisons herself with hatred and like Krook prepares her doom by drying her body up by denying it food. Both bodies become flammable material just waiting to ignite and it has been suggested that Miss Havisham's death is a combustion. She has been consuming herself slowly as Krook does and finally both ignite in an instant. Both their bodies are associated gruesomely with food, the implication being that their bodies will be consumed in twisted acts of transubstantiation: in Cook's court the inhabitants smell Krook's burnt body, ingest it and taste it in the air, while Miss Havisham is laid out on the wedding banquet table like a burnt offering. These deaths are, it is implied, precipitated by the victims who bring their ends upon themselves and punish themselves for their crimes. But what exactly is the effect of their removal from the scene? When Krook dies there is a clearing of ground in that his shop is opened up and searched, his papers sifted through and secrets gradually brought to light. This is akin to a bonfire of the vanities since it is a purification of superfluous objects including the owners themselves; yet it is a "heap of ugly things" which is destroyed not the staple goods of bourgeois contentment. There is a respect for property[9] in the Dickens novel which is counterbalanced by a delight in the energy of change and particularly in fire as a vehicle for change—in particular the clearing of blockage in circulation, the thwarting of hoarding, stagnation, constipation.

The life of the fire itself in Dickens is worth considering here since the other examples of burning often bring out a dynamic force of change, a baroque awe of the power of the element of fire. Here the perverse Marquis murdered in his bed burns with his château:

> The château was left to itself to flame and burn. In the roaring and raging of the conflagration, a red-hot wind, driving straight

> from the infernal regions, seemed to be blowing the edifice away. With the rising and falling of the blaze, the stone faces showed as if they were in torment. When great masses of stone and timber fell, the face with the two dints in the nose became obscured: anon struggled out of the smoke again, as if it were the face of the cruel Marquis, burning at the stake and contending with the fire.
>
> The château burned; the nearest trees, laid hold of by the fire, scorched and shrivelled; trees at a distance, fired by the four fierce figures, begirt the blazing edifice with a new forest of smoke. Molten lead and iron boiled in the marble basin of the fountain; the water ran dry; the extinguisher tops of the towers vanished like ice before the heat, and trickled into four rugged wells of flame. Great rents and splits branched out in the solid walls, like crystallisation; stupefied birds wheeled about and dropped into the furnace. (261–2)

Just after this paragraph, fire becomes a metaphor for the crowds themselves and for the energy which fuelled the revolution:

> In such risings of fire and risings of sea—the firm earth shaken by the rushes of an angry ocean which now had no ebb, but was always on the flow, higher and higher, to the terror and wonder of the beholders on the shore—three years of tempest were consumed. (263)

Notice that after the restraint imposed on the populace by the *ancien régime* in *A Tale of Two Cities*—when the death of a child at the hands of the Marquis is not mourned—we have an explosion of excess, the excess of pent-up emotion which has all the joy of relief and the excitement of flow after much congestion. The sea is the crowd and the fire is the energy flowing from them and adding to the force and verve in the description of the burning château (the boiling lead, structures vanishing like ice, rents and splits). Even though there is horror at the *foule* and its destruction there is also delight. The Marquis like Miss Havisham is seen as a face engulfed in flames—like her punished for his self-indulgence and selfishness. The liveliness of the description implies the same sense of release and relief. That the fire should consume and destroy Miss Havisham is cause for celebration since like the decadent Marquis she embodies the congested sick body of society; both indulge in repetitive and ritualistic behavior (her endless rounds in her wheelchair, his endless social calls). Just as Krook's explosion releases tension and lets in light and air so the two must burn to allow new circulation. Strangely, Miss Havisham's movements—so restricted and deformed by her sick mind—take on new life in the flames when she performs a dance of death. For the first time we see her animated and running, running indeed into the wild embrace of a young man for the first (and the last) time. These actions are signs of youth grotesquely manufactured by the fire. The constrictions of the old world are thrown out and the narrator, like the scientist Frankenstein, animates the tired mummy with fire—forces her into life and then to extinction. The fire brings light to Satis House only to eradicate it like the Marquis's château, the Bastille, and Newgate prison all gloomy hulks brought to life at the moment of their destruction.[10]

Industrial Gothic or an Industrial "Vanity"

Miss Havisham is a complex nexus of meanings which associate her with a society and a historical conjuncture. She both represents and is part of a heap, not of beautiful objects which the spectator must renounce, but the heap of rubbish of disused machines and discarded goods. Keeping in mind the energy of fire which can move a stagnant situation forward we might dwell on the figure of Miss Havisham as a representation of the now derelict factory which was the source of her fortune. The brewery is first described thus:

> there were no pigeons in the dovecot, no horses in the stable, no pigs in the sty, no malt in the storehouse, no smells of grain and beer in the copper or vat. All the uses and scents of the brewery might have evaporated with its last reek of smoke. In a by-yard, there was a wilderness of empty casks, which had a certain sour rememberance of better days lingering about them; but it was too sour to be accepted as a sample of beer that was gone—and in this respect I remember those recluses as being like most others. (54)

There is a link here with Miss Havisham herself who was once a young active body in the bridal dress which is now inhabited by a ghost of herself, a dried husk. Nothing has been produced in her womb—a true sign of bankruptcy for the Victorian woman; like the brewery she is reduced to an empty vat. In "the large paved lofty place in which they used to make the beer, and where the brewing utensils still were" (54) he sees a vision of Miss Havisham hanging which suggests that her death and the death of the brewery are part of the same decadence. The ruined garden echoes this. This is part of a vein in Dickens's novels which I would describe as industrial gothic: the emblems of decay are not used to criticise the aristocracy or the Catholic church as in the late eighteenth century gothic tale and its later neo-gothic progeny such as *Dracula* but used to create a critique of industrial capitalism. This "industrial gothic" involves an uncanny vision of a post-industrial world, a millennialist fantasy of a post-cataclysmic wasteland (which will soon be regenerated and, the suggestion is, become edenic).

Walsh's study of mid-century economic and medical discourse and their relationship with *Great Expectations* shows that the older female body "became available as a potent analogue for economic as well as reproductive 'bankruptcy', the complete foreclosure of the machinery of material production" (711). She sees that Miss Havisham represents the female figure used in popular imagery of the day: "places where economic trouble can be displaced and thereby symbolically disposed of" (714). The greatest ill of the economic body was constriction and blockage: "Because she wrecks the brewery and refuses to sponsor her male relatives, she blocks her financial capital from circulating within the proper channels of investment and trade, thus rendering it economically barren" (717). Walsh goes on to remark that:

> Her perambulations with Pip, as he wheels her about the decayed remains of the wedding feast, not only parody the breakdown of economic "circulation" (the defunct production-and-exchange life of her father's brewery) but also the mental orbits of the older woman trapped in the circular grooves of memory. (717)

There are many examples of industrial gothic or vanities of economic failure in Dickens. In *Oliver Twist*: for example, when Mr. and Mrs. Bumble sell monks the evidence of Oliver's illegitimate birth:

> In the heart of this cluster of huts, and skirting the river, which its upper stories overhung, stood a large building, formerly used as a manufactory of some kind. It had, in its day, probably furnished employment to the inhabitants of the surrounding tenements. But it had long since gone to ruin. The rat, the worm, and the action of the damp, had weakened and rotted the piles on which it stood; and a considerable portion of the building had already sunk down into the water; while the remainder, tottering and bending over the dark stream, seemed to wait a favourable opportunity of following its old companion, and involving itself in the same fate. (335)

The trinket is thrown down into the water:

> the tide foaming and chafing round the few rotten stakes, and fragments of machinery that yet remained, seemed to dart onward,

> with a new impulse, when freed from the obstacles which had unavailingly attempted to stem its headlong course. (335)

We see a similar horror of the tyranny of the junk of manufacturing that we see in Krook's shop and in the streets of the London of *Bleak House* with its continual "stoppage." The factory has become a sick body, tottering to the edge of the river to throw itself in in a suicidal gesture; it is also an old and decrepit body like Miss Havisham's. The notion of darting on with a "new impulse" involves a liberating force. In *David Copperfield* David watches Martha, a prostitute, down by a Thames similarly polluted by the ruins of industry:

> the ground was cumbered with rusty iron monsters of steam-boilers, wheels, cranks, pipes, furnaces, paddles, anchors, diving-bells, windmill-sails, and I know not what strange objects, accumulated by some speculator, and grovelling in the dust, underneath which—having sunk into the soil of their own weight in wet weather—they had the appearance of vainly trying to hide themselves. The clash and glare of sundry fiery Works upon the river side, arose by night to disturb everything except the heavy and unbroken smoke that poured out of their chimneys. (572)

There is an explicit linking of speculation ("some speculator") and industrial waste, that is, a post-industrial waste involving steam-engines which were still in the process of changing both the industrial face of Britain and the aesthetic and economic face of transportation. An aftermath is imagined here in which heaviness, encumbrance, anachronism and monotony is suggested and then linked in the following sentences with slime "ooze and slush" of the "polluted stream." From unspeakable inorganic matter we move to the organic fallen body with "sickly substance . . . like green hair" in the water—which prepares the way for the introduction of Martha who stands "as if she were part of the refuse it had cast out and left to corruption and decay" (572). Martha is linked to hair in the "green hair"—as in the fallen Mary Magdalene—and like Miss Havisham is associated with a site of industrial ruin and also with the fire of the "fiery Works" in the above passage which as in the scene of Miss Havisham's burning is the only dynamic element in all the ruin and decay. Thus the economic body is associated with the female body as Walsh has argued. There is a similar mechanism in the decay described in both *Great Expectations* and *Little Dorrit* of industry along the Thames and in the giant dust heaps in *Our Mutual Friend*.

Thus Miss Havisham might be seen as a focus for these tensions, her body becoming a site for the inscription of many of Dickens's concerns; she is an industrial wasteland in her Gothic decay for she is an aged bride situated in an abandoned manufactory of beer, a piece of the flotsam and jetsam of the failure of speculation, of the shipwreck of great expectations with all the grotesque heterogeneity (an old woman in a virgin bridal dress) of the rubbish dumps of capitalism which we have looked at. That there should be a desire to eradicate her is increasingly logical in a text which constantly presents the reader with the failure of human relationships atomised by capital and commerce. Roston has argued that the fallen woman was the major trope of Victorian society in that she embodied the conflicting notions of, on the one hand, a desire for women to be free from the taint of the market and on the other the impossibility of protecting her from those market forces.[11]

That this eradication should be through fire is also part of an inexorable logic since fire is the emblem of industry as we see it in *Hard Times*, and *The Old Curiosity Shop*: a demonic force but also a liberating one.

Miss Havisham expresses in her person a society moving from an organic model to a mechanic model (Wilt 8). We see in her the rise of the factory to the centre of both economic and social life by 1850 becoming "the economic institution that shaped its [England's] politics, its social problems, the character of its daily life just as decisively as the manor or the guild had done a few centuries earlier." The market becomes the dictator of fortunes rather than the seasons and the "packed and sterile earth of the industrial site" (Heilbroner/Milberg 66) takes the place of farmland as it does at Satis House. The production of goods using capital to provide machines means that the "unaided body" is given "transhuman" (71) dimensions, making the human body (theoretically) into an enduring, resilient machine—or when that system disfunctions into a disastrous monster of a body—a useless and abandoned machine as Miss Havisham becomes.

The Chaos of the World and the Artist's "Fire-Baptism"

Lastly, let us consider the metaphor of blazing light[12] and conflagration which is the hallmark of Carlyle's writing in such phrases as "Behold the World-Phoenix, in fire-consummation and fire-creation" (Roston 14). Roston sees this sort of imagery as being part of Carlyle's prophetic call:

> his prophetic call for a passionate rebirth of the individual soul through the burning away of outmoded fears and allegiances; and inherent in that call is his conception of the poet-preacher as the cultural ignitor of the spark, offering a blazing imaginative vision which should in its turn inflame the hearts and minds of his readers. (15)

Roston studies the way in which Carlyle shared the idea of the vortex with Turner who was criticized for his "frenzies" by the *Athenaeum*: in 1838 "It is grievous to us to think of talent, so mighty and so poetical, running riot into such frenzies" (Roston 16). This referred to Turner's use of brilliant yellows and dazzling brilliance which partook of the solar myth which so captivated artists in the late eighteenth and early nineteenth centuries. We see this in *Regulus* (1828) and *The Burning of the Houses of Parliament* (1835). Turner's *Burial at Sea* (1842) also has brilliant effulgence in contrast to the black hull of ship which is similar to Carlyle's vision of France which "partakes of the same volatile luminosity as Carlyle's ominous image of France, described by him as a fireship packed with brimstone and bitumen, nitre and terebinth, sailing away into the Deep of Time" (Roston 21):

> During this period there is, in both writer and painter, an awareness of potential cataclysm, of latent forces liable to erupt into explosive force, yet at the same time a fascination with the energy and brilliance of the power displayed, however ominous it may be. (Roston 21)

We have seen this awareness in the fire scenes in Dickens already examined in which horror of the destruction of person and property is contrasted with a delight in the movement and energy of that living fire—often personified—and in its capacity to scour the veins of the Victorian urban world. If crisis is in the air then the artist can offer a solution and overcome it since this energy and brilliance is also viewed as an element potentially wielded by the artist to bring meaning and order to the chaos of the world—a new vision of it, a reworking of it based on the *Fiat lux* which Carlyle called "Fire-Baptism."[13]

Pip as the narrator becomes a metaphor for the writer-artist who awakens his imagination from sleep and undergoes a "Fire-Baptism" (Carlyle 167–8): "Divine moment, when over the tempest-tost Soul, as once over the wild-weltering chaos, it is spoken: Let there be Light!" (149). Carlyle also expresses this awakening thus:

> But is there not, human at the heart of all, strangely hidden, sunk, overwhelmed yet not extinct, a light element and fire-element, which if you but awaken it shall irradiate and illuminate the whole, and make life a glorious fixed landscape.[14]

This "inner blaze" (Roston 23) is an artistic energy which brings "aesthetic harmony" (30) to the incoherence of terrestrial events. We witness a movement from the gentle creativity of the moon in Romantic poetry to the blazing sun in Victorian times. Thus the artist is no longer crushed and amazed by the sublime but becomes dominant and self-assertive, his fire—like the fire Miss Havisham is engulfed by—becomes a way of stabilizing a ruinous and an out-of-control social structure. Similarly, Miller sees the spirit of *Deus absconditus* reigning over the writer's world and as obliging the artist to find his own inner means of dealing with the hollowness and bleakness.

Great Expectations contains an energy which is both confident and creative unlike the weariness of the Romantics—yet there is perhaps a strange mixture of the two in Pip's world—both nostalgia and *weltschmerz* as well as a phoenix-like rebirth occasioned by the destruction of Satis House which is symbolically burnt down through Miss Havisham's own demise. There is a weariness in the final reunion with Estella yet the negatively expressed fusion of she and Pip in the novel's last sentence—"I saw the shadow of no parting from her" (358)—is combined with joy at the possibility of change and renewal through fire. This joy is expressed early in the novel in the young Pip's dreams of Miss Havisham's plans for him:

> She reserved it for me to restore the desolate house, admit the sunshine into the dark rooms, set the clocks a going and the cold hearths a blazing, tear down the cobwebs, destroy the vermin—in short, do all the shining deeds of the young Knight of romance, and marry the Princess. (179)

The irony is that the blazing hearth far from being a figure of domestic stability will be a figure of destruction and the Promethean Pip will indeed bring light and fire but not by restoring the house—only by participating in the burning in an ambiguously aggressive manner. However, within the act of saving-or-sacrificing Miss Havisham there is a rising of a phoenix rebirth among the ashes:

> I had a double-caped great-coat on, and over my arm another thick coat. That I got them off, closed with her, threw her down, and got them over her; that I dragged the great cloth from the table for the same purpose, and with it dragged down the heap of rottenness in the midst, and all the ugly things that sheltered there. (299)

The burning symbolises Dickens's attempts in his writing to impose some sort of order on the chaos—the wrestling with the burning female figure is the artist's "Fire-Baptism" in which he sets to rights through the destruction of an old lady the ills of society. Within this struggle there is a redemption through the artist—a figure of promethean vigour and triumph in this case[15]—who like the knight who slays Duessa, a Spencerian personification of deceit and shame in *The Fairie Queene*, fights the ills of his world in the shape of a hideous crone. The immediate consequence is in the microcosm of the fauna of Satis House—an effect in miniature but nevertheless of major semantic importance: the fire drives the endlessly circulating insects out of their wedding cake home and routine and liberates them from their slavish round, setting them off in a different direction. After the fire we are left with the image of "the disturbed beetles and spiders running away over the floor" (300).

Notes

1. Here I have relied on Roston's invaluable work on Turner and Carlyle and their "shared codes and interlocking tropes" in *Victorian Contexts*.

2. We see this quality later in the century with Lucy Westenra's nocturnal barefoot wanderings in *Dracula* which mark her out as a marginal female who will be punished by being made a handmaid of the count. Victorian women whose stultifying domestic prisons help ferment revolt, become symbols of unbridled violence akin to the monomania of a revolutionary crowd. We have such an example just after Mme Defarge's decapitation of the governor of the Bastille: "The sea of black and threatening waters, and of destructive upheaving of wave against wave, whose depths were yet unfathomed and whose forces were yet unknown. The remorseless sea of turbulently swaying shapes, voices of vengeance, and faces hardened in the furnaces of suffering until the touch of pity could make no mark on them" (249).

3. Miss Havisham is a creator of such a murderous woman through Estella whose mother, Molly—her hands the focus of Jaggers' comments as they do womanly domestic work—are hands which have also strangled another human being and are those of a "wild beast tamed." Once again we have a link with Madame Defarge and her knitting since later when Pip realizes that Molly is Estella's mother it is her hands which arrest him first: "the action of her fingers was like the action of knitting" (291).

4. Frost makes the point that Pip's association of Molly with a cauldron and Macbeth shows that "because their strength is negative and is associated with the ability to inflict pain on men, they must be 'bent and broken' before they can win approval, before they can stop being outsiders and can achieve the proper tensionless relationship with Pip" (71). Frost also makes the point that: "Within Satis House adaptation and renewal are not genuine possibilities. The house will later be torn down, not renovated by new owners, and if Miss Havisham is to be purified, the logic is fire, not piety" (77).

5. The uncanny element in Miss Havisham's demise is that from the moment we meet her she is presented in a fashion which suggests she is already dead—"corpse-like" (52) and wearing a shroud" (52)—and buried—"dug out of a vault (50)—and every description of her takes up these motifs again. Strangely then, she is presented to the reader as a corpse and then her death is imagined throughout the novel in different ways and finally we witness the actual destruction of her

body through fire. Orlick's language insists upon burning when he is porter at Satis House: his insolent replies to Pip's questions are "Burn me, if I know!" and just afterwards "Burn me twice over if I can say!!" (180). Pip's body is to be burned in a lime-kiln, his arms and hands still torturing him from the burns received during his struggle with Miss Havisham.

6. The links between the Dutch genre paintings of this period and the nineteenth-century novel have already been established. See Witemeyer.

7. Wheeler in his study of the language of the Revelation in Victorian literature notes that "in *Hard Times* Dickens's use of apocalyptic symbolism is as central to his vision as Blake's or John Martin's" (112). I would suggest that the imagery of *Great Expectations* is also inspired by that of the Revelation.

8. This is the aftermath of the burning of The Warren in *Barnaby Rudge* which underlines the once lively activity of the house: "Silence indeed! The glare of the flames had sunk into a fitful, flashing light; and the gentle stars, invisible till now, looked down upon the blackening heap. . . . Bare walls, roof open to the sky-chambers, where the beloved dead had, many and many a fair day, risen to new life and energy; where so many dear ones had been sad and merry; which were connected with so many thoughts and hopes, regrets and changes—all gone. Nothing left but a dull and dreary blank—a smouldering heap of dust and ashes—the silence and solitude of utter desolation" (508–9).

9. In *Barnaby Rudge* there is both a delight in the movement of the fire and a horror of the destruction of property: "Some searched the drawers, the chests, the boxes, writing desks and closets, for jewels, plate, and money; while others, less mindful of gain and more mad for destruction, cast their whole contents into the courtyard without examination, and called to those below, to heap them on the blaze" (506).

10. The fire might be seen as a machine running on as part of a gratuitous delight in energy. Kucich sees the mechanical in Dickens as a "metaphor for the experience of excess" (201) and as being poised between Arnold, Carlyle and Mill's (and indeed Ruskin's) fear of the inorganic and the machine and his own delight in the gratuity of the energy of mechanical systems. The burning of The Warren, the Vintner's house and Newgate prison in *Barnaby Rudge* all reveal elements of this: "There were men who cast their lighted torches in the air, and suffered them to fall upon their faces, blistering the skin with deep unseemly burns. There were men who rushed up to the fire, and paddled in it with their hands as if in water; and others who were restrained by force from plunging in, to gratify their deadly longing" (508); "the tributary fires that licked the outer bricks and stones, with their long forked tongues, and ran up to meet the glowing mass within . . . the roaring of the angry blaze, so bright and high that it seemed in its rapacity to have swallowed up the very smoke . . . the noiseless breaking of great beams of wood, which fell like feathers on the heap of ashes, and crumbled in the very act to sparks and powder" (507).

11. Erwin Panofsky saw each period having dominant forms or spatial structures: the medieval world had the process of sub-division and classification, Neoplatonism had the sphere while the Enlightenment chose equipoise and symmetry. Roston argues that the central configuration of mid-century literature and art was the Fallen Woman (59). This woman was yearning for forgiveness and compassion. There was a desire at the time to bring back "sacramental spiritualism" (46) in an increasingly materialistic world. The angel of the house as a Victorian symbol was there "to serve as a haven of spiritual refreshment after the pressures of mercantile

activity in the city" (48). This symbolic embodiment of values was under severe strain since the profane business world was incompatible with the morality implied in the domestic angel: "it was to image forth that latter feeling of male guilt that the Fallen Woman emerged in the art and literature of the time" (51). The fallen woman is thus "a grave doubt whether the process of secluding the Christian home from the realities of vigorous competition was feasible after all" (51). The split between Wemmick's public and private world is enfolded into the one person of Miss Havisham since she is a vision of the Victorian home sullied by the filthy lucre of trade. The "soul's sudden conversion to higher ideals, whether religious or secular" (63) at this time is clear in Miss Havisham's pleading for forgiveness of Pip. Roston cites Tennyson's *Mariana*, Millais' representation of this scene, and Trollope's Lily Dale as well as Miss Havisham as some of the many representations in the mid-Victorian era of the forsaken woman, deserted by her lover; the idea of Victorian domesticity frustrated by "the pursuit of wealth, the potential Angel in the House unable to fulfil her desired role" (66).

12. Fire has an additional quality which is part of an aesthetic concern which is a reaction to the turbulence and haphazardness of the human condition at a time when as well as social upheaval of the industrial revolution there was the religious doubt brought about by Lyell's *Principles of Geology* of 1830–33 and the later Darwinian theories and Strauss's *Leben Jesu* of 1835. Most importantly for our study there was an awareness of turbulence which Roston sees in both the vortex element in Turner's paintings and in Carlyle's advocation of charismatic leadership as a way out of universal chaos. His "faith, derived from Fichte, in the powerful will of heroes as the necessary directors and moulders of national affairs" (Roston 12) is to be understood in a background of the "incoherent fortuity of city life" (12) which Dickens expressed in *Barnaby Rudge* and *Oliver Twist.*

13. Roston describes this phenomenon in this way: "the turmoil is countered in his work by a recurrent image of dazzling brilliance, an allusion to the historic moment at Creation when the divine word conjured up light to drive forth the darkness. For him, that act was less a specific event during the formation of the universe than a paradigm offered to mankind, an encouragement to the heroic individual to imitate the divine act by his own visionary and illuminatory power . . . 'Fire-Baptism' was the religiously connotive term he coined for that act, for the soul's self-enfranchisement from its pusillanimous subservience to the authoritarian bonds of tradition" (29).

14. Quoted by Roston (29) from early drafts of Carlyle's incomplete biography of Oliver Cromwell in the Forster Collection of the Victoria and Albert Museum.

15. As Kucich notes: "In nearly back-to-back scenes, Pip confronts his two rivals in battle, against a violent backdrop of fire—Miss Havisham's burning bridal dress and Orlick's limekiln—only to emerge victorious" (111).

Bibliography

Carlyle, Thomas. *Sartor Resartus.* 1833–4. *Complete Works: the University Edition.* New York, 1885.

Dickens, Charles. *A Tale of Two Cities.* 1851. Harmondsworth: Penguin, 1970.

———. *Barnaby Rudge.* 1841. Harmondsworth: Penguin, 1971.

———. *Bleak House.* 1853. Harmondsworth: Penguin, 1971.

———. *David Copperfield.* 1850. New York: Norton, 1990.

———. *Great Expectations*, 1861. Ed. Edgar Rosenberg. New York: Norton, 1999.

———. *Little Dorrit*. 1857. Harmondsworth: Penguin. 1967.

———. *Oliver Twist*. 1837–9. Harmondsworth: Penguin, 1966.

Frost, Lucy. "Taming to Improve: Dickens and the Women in *Great Expectations*." *New Casebooks—Great Expectations*. Ed. Roger D. Sell. London: Macmillan, 1994.

Heilbroner, Robert, Milberg, William. *The Making of Economic Society*. London: Prentice Hall, 1998.

Kucich, John. *Excess and Restraint in the Novels of Charles Dickens*. Athens: U of Georgia P, 1981.

Miller, J. Hillis. *The Disappearance of God: Five Nineteenth-Century Writers*. New York, 1965.

Raphael, Linda. "A Re-vision of Miss Havisham: Her Expectations and Our Responses." *New Casebooks—Great Expectations*. Ed. Roger D. Sell. London: Macmillan, 1994.

Roston, Murray. *Victorian Contexts: Literature and the Visual Arts*. Basingstoke and London: Macmillan, 1996.

Ruskin, John. *Unto This Last and Other Writings*. Published between 1850 and 1884. Ed. Clive Witmer. Harmondsworth: Penguin, 1985.

Walsh, Susan. "Bodies of Capital: *Great Expectations* and the Climacteric Economy." *Great Expectations*, Edgar Rosenberg, ed.

Wheeler, Michael. *Death and the Future Life in Victorian Literature and Theology*. Cambridge: CUP, 1990.

Wilt, Judith. *Secret Lives: The Novels of Walter Scott*, Chicago: U of Chicago P, 1985.

Witemeyer, Hugh. *George Eliot and the Visual Arts*. New Haven: Yale UP, 1979.

CAROLINE LEVINE

Realism as Self-Forgetfulness: Gender, Ethics, and Great Expectations

In 1848, reviewer Edwin Percy Whipple asserted that *Jane Eyre* must have been partly penned by a man. His evidence was that it echoed the style of that decidedly masculine writer—the author of *Wuthering Heights.* Proved emphatically wrong by Charlotte Brontë's revelations of 1850, Whipple had learned his lesson by the time he came to review *Great Expectations* eleven years later. What he claimed to admire most in Dickens's new novel was the fact that the mystery had confounded him:

> In no other of his romances has the author succeeded so perfectly in at once stimulating and baffling the curiosity of his readers. He stirred the dullest minds to guess the secret of his mystery; but, so far as we have learned, the guesses of his most intelligent readers have been almost as wide of the mark as those of the least apprehensive. It has been all the more provoking to the former class, that each surprise was the result of art, and not of trick; for a rapid review of previous chapters has shown that the materials of a strictly logical development of the story were freely given.[1]

Whipple was not the only one to appreciate Dickens's skill in the art of plotting. The *Times* celebrated Dickens "as the greatest master of construction"

From *The Serious Pleasures of Suspense: Victorian Realism and Narrative Doubt*, pp. 84–98, 213–14. © 2003 by the Rector and Visitors of the University of Virginia.

of the era, the most expert at keeping "an exciting story within the bounds of probability." The *Athenaeum* praised him for his adroit sustaining of readerly interest: "Every week almost, as it came out, we were artfully stopped at some juncture which made Suspense count the days until the next number appeared." Even Margaret Oliphant, who dismissed *Great Expectations* as an absurd fantasy, understood that enthusiastic readers found the novel's incidents "strange, dangerous, and exciting."[2] Taken together, these nineteenth-century reviews suggest that suspense may have been the most alluring seduction of *Great Expectations* for the Victorian reader.

This chapter makes the case that Dickens not only thrilled his contemporaries by producing and sustaining a fascinating suspense plot, but he also articulated a clear ethical value for suspenseful plotting. Like *Jane Eyre*, *Great Expectations* brings together the exciting pleasures of suspense with its weighty significance. More surprisingly, perhaps, the novel suggests that in the context of Victorian culture, the gender of suspense was feminine. Dickens claims, as do Ruskin and Brontë, that we cannot unearth the hidden truths of the world without putting aside our most entrenched expectations; in order to know the world we must learn to suspend ourselves. And since Victorian culture insistently cast self-suspension as a quintessentially feminine virtue, women, it seemed, must be the most acute readers of the real. In this light, Biddy emerges as the epistemological ideal of *Great Expectations*.

Great Expectations also allows us to see how the skeptical epistemology of detective fiction moved beyond the literal inclusion of the detective. In order to make the claim that *Great Expectations* belongs in a tradition of detective fiction—quite as much as *Bleak House* or *The Mystery of Edwin Drood*—I start with a brief reading of Poe's "Purloined Letter," which, along with *The Moonstone*, is famous for having launched the genre. Poe shows us how central the suspension of the self is to the accumulation of hidden knowledge. If we read Poe alongside *Great Expectations*, we can see how the earliest detective fictions reveal a shared concern to disseminate a skeptical epistemology.

The Moonstone united the scientist and the detective, and Umberto Eco argues that such a combination is fitting, since they share a skeptical epistemology: they "suspect on principle that some elements, evident but not apparently important, may be evidence of something else that is not evident—and on this basis they elaborate a new hypothesis to be tested."[3] What science and detection have in common, in other words, is a thoroughgoing resistance to the assumption that the truths of world are readily apparent. Dickens broadens the scope of this method to suggest that the scientist's paradigm of suspicion is necessary to solving all mysteries—from formal detection to ordinary reading, including the most commonplace interpretive puzzles of everyday life. Like Brontë, then, Dickens uses the novel to disseminate the critical suspension of judgment and the epistemological project of testing.

The Ethics of Suspense: Poe's "Purloined Letter"

Critics have often claimed that suspenseful plots comfort socially discomfited readers with neat, safe endings. Clive Bloom writes that Edgar Allan Poe's orderly plots are responses to the "decentered and *disordered* society he found himself in." Thus "Poe's art is an antidote to contemporary social displacement on a wide scale." Similarly, Leo Bersani writes that "Realistic fiction serves nineteenth-century society by providing it with strategies for containing (and repressing) its disorder within significantly structured stories about itself."[4] Nineteenth-century novelists supposedly forced the real world to conform, through artful plotting, to historically conditioned conceptual paradigms and ideological oversimplifications.[5]

But this is to miss the lessons of suspenseful narrative. Charlotte Brontë, in her crafty equivocations, taught us to mistrust convention and the workings of our own desire in unearthing the secrets of the world. Before turning to Dickens, we can see the demand for self-suspension as the very first lesson of detective fiction. In "The Purloined Letter," Poe teaches us to recognize the dangers of relying on entrenched assumptions and desires.[6] The crucial error made by the Prefect and his officers, according to Poe's wise Dupin, is that "They consider only their own ideas of ingenuity; and, in searching for anything hidden, advert only to the modes in which they would have hidden it" (12). Like Reynolds and Kant, Ruskin's pre-realist predecessors, the detectives retreat into their own minds in pursuit of the truth. What they refuse to perceive, therefore, is the potential *otherness* of the real. As Jacques Lacan puts it, "the detectives have so immutable a notion of the real that they fail to notice that their search tends to transform it into its object."[7]

Dupin concedes one point to the Prefect and his men: "They are right in this much, that their own ingenuity is a faithful representative of that of the mass; but when the cunning of an individual felon is diverse in character from their own, the felon foils them, of course" (12). Relying on their own preconceptions, which exemplify *general* rules and ideas, the detectives fail to consider what Ruskin would call the "infinite variety" of the real. And this has consequences for method. Unwilling or unable to recognize the world's likely resistance to convention, the detectives never question their habits of detection. "They have no variation of principle in their investigations; at best, when urged by some unusual emergency, by some extraordinary reward, they extend or exaggerate their old modes of practice without touching their principles" (12). To put this another way, they never experiment, obdurately refusing to transform the hypothesis—the principle—even when it does not correspond with the evidence. The result, of course, is that the detectives cannot solve the mystery. Nor can the naïve narrator, who is shocked at Dupin's willingness to overturn convention and exclaims: "You do not mean to set at naught the well-digested idea of centuries?" (13). Here, then, is realism in a nutshell: to know the world one must acknowledge its inaccessibility to traditional rules and conventions—and its basic, unyielding otherness.

It is this emphasis on alterity that leads me to argue that suspense not only offers a potentially subversive politics, as Brontë makes clear, but also disseminates an influential nineteenth-century ethics. Narrative mysteries in the Victorian period teach us to set aside self-interest and personal desire in order to attend to the surprising, unsettling world, a world that may well flout our prejudices and disappoint our expectations. From Poe to Dickens and beyond, the suspense of detective fiction unites ethics and epistemology in a skeptical method intended to teach us a new and more respectful relationship to the world.

Dickensian Suspense

Jaggers, in a perfect example of a plotted "snare," withholds a crucial piece of knowledge from Pip. "The name of the person who is your liberal benefactor remains a profound secret, until the person chooses to reveal it."[8] It is the checking of knowledge that leads directly to the production of Pip's mistaken expectations. And it is the failure to know the truth that gives rise to the desiring motors of the realist plot. We might even say that "great expectations" describes the experience of suspense so perfectly that Pip can only be a figure for the reader of the nineteenth-century novel.

But in fact, Pip and the reader have crucially different experiences of this particular mystery. For the reader, the withholding of the name of Pip's benefactor indicates quite unequivocally that a specific piece of knowledge is missing. By signaling the existence of a secret, Dickens forces us to recognize the fact of our ignorance and so piques a desire for further knowledge. Indeed, even if, as first-time readers, we suspect that it is Miss Havisham who is going to turn out to have been Pip's benefactor, the text offers us an inescapable sign that there is some reason for secrecy. We have to wait and wonder, to speculate and hypothesize, to know that there is something we do not know.

One of Pip's clearest failures in the novel is that he does not experience the moment of his inheritance as suspenseful: unlike the reader, he leaps to the conclusion that his benefactor is Miss Havisham, and he rushes to assume that this is all part of a plot to marry him to Estella. "[Miss Havisham] had adopted Estella, she had as good as adopted me, and *it could not fail to be her intention* to bring us together" (232; my emphasis). Pip, refusing to suspend judgment, sees the world as a reflection of his own hopes and expectations. The result is a drastic misreading. Harry Stone explains that Pip's "topsy-turvy vision" leads him to read the world in reverse.[9] And I would like to suggest that this topsy-turvy structure applies specifically to the text's realism. Pip exclaims: "My dream was out; my wild fancy was surpassed by sober reality; Miss Havisham was going to make my fortune on a grand scale" (137). Inverting the realist experiment, Pip rushes to assume that "sober reality" coincides with his representations. Thus he is in for a rude shock. He will never solve the mysteries of the world if, like Poe's inflexible detectives, he does not put his own methods and assumptions on trial.[10]

The trial—the testing of hypotheses in order to arrive at knowledge. Dickens shows us clearly why we find so many trials, *both* legal and scientific, in the nineteenth-century novel. Trials, whether in the court room or the laboratory, demand the suspension of judgment. Both scientific experiments and courtroom narratives, by their very structure, insist on a delay between initial appearance and more certain knowledge.[11] Both are perfect vehicles for narrative suspense. And perhaps most importantly, both involve plot's ethical imperative: the arresting of arbitrary desires and prejudices in the face of tested knowledge. In *Great Expectations*, Jaggers, the great figure of the law, sounds almost like a broken record in his reiteration of the importance of not leaping to capricious conclusions. Directly before introducing the mystery of Pip's expectations, he offers a disquisition on the legal presumption of innocence to the crowd at the Three Jolly Bargemen. "Do you know, or do you not know, that the law of England supposes every man to be innocent, until he is proved—proved—to be guilty?" (133). The double utterance of the need for proof, here, underscores the fact that the static, unchanging Jaggers will simply repeat the same lesson to Pip, over and over again. "Never mind what you have always longed for, Mr. Pip," Jaggers says, "keep to the record" (138).

Jaggers's instruction to the crowd at the Jolly Bargemen focuses on their leap to assume the guilt of the convict without the rigorous tests of the fair trial. "Are you aware, or are you not aware," asks Jaggers of Mr. Wopsle, "that none of these witnesses have yet been cross-examined?" (133). If to examine is to suspend judgment, then to *cross*-examine is to return to questions already asked and answers already given, to inspect, to question, and often to undermine the evidence. In its exacting methods, legal cross-examination outstrips other models of skeptical interrogation and takes its place as the consummately fair paradigm of knowledge seeking.

But Pip's upbringing has not prepared him for fair trials. The first appearance of the unjust Mrs. Joe reads like a cruel parody of a courtroom examination:

> "Who brought you up by hand?"
> "You did," said I.
> "And why did I do it, I should like to know!" exclaimed my sister.
> I whimpered, "I don't know."
> "I don't!" said my sister. "I'd never do it again. I know that." (9–10)

Assuming Pip's guilt and her own long-suffering goodness, Mrs. Joe's questions are hardly skeptical inquiries: she asks Pip to generate not knowledge but gratitude, not truths but justifications. This is capricious catechism rather than skeptical cross-examination.

In fact, Pip's childhood experience of the trial involves not only the presumption of his guilt and the willful disregarding of the facts, but the evil of questioning itself. "Drat that boy . . . what a questioner he is," Mrs. Joe says irritably, and adds: "Ask no questions, and you'll be told no lies" (14). Mrs. Joe claims to believe that questioning only invites falsehoods from the other. She therefore refuses to countenance inquiry altogether and considers questioning to represent a kind of guilt. "People are put in the Hulks because they murder, and because they rob, and forge, and do all sorts of bad; and they always begin by asking questions," she warns (14).[12] Pip seems to incorporate this lesson immediately, connecting his inquiry to his imminent crime: "I had begun by asking questions, and I was going to rob Mrs. Joe" (14).

On the one hand, Jaggers makes clear that the rigorous questioning of cross-examination is the sign of a fair trial; on the other hand, Mrs. Joe teaches Pip that to ask questions is to be guilty oneself. It is no mystery which of these two is in the right. Mrs. Joe does not even practice what she preaches: when Pip returns from Miss Havisham's, Dickens tells us pointedly that she asks "a number of questions" and shoves Pip's face against the wall for not answering the questions "at sufficient length" (66). She is rewarded with precisely the falsehoods she has claimed to expect when Pip invents a rich fantasy about the house he visits. Carried away with her own self-interest, she speculates greedily, enjoying her wonder about Pip's prospects. Criminalizing Pip's questions and violently insisting on answers to her own, however false, Mrs. Joe casts inquiry itself as a guilty, fruitless act, all the while enjoying it herself. Given this education in the failure of questions, is it any wonder, later, that Pip will not thoroughly interrogate his own "expectations"? He has not been educated in the fruitful patterns of plotted suspense, whether legal, or scientific, or novelistic. Dickens's readers will have the privilege of a different kind of education.

The Gender of Realism

If Jaggers in all his skeptical suspicion of the world is eminently, if impersonally, fair, while Pip's despotic sister criminalizes innocent inquiry, we can begin to draw a Dickensian link between skepticism and justice. Jaggers's presumption of innocence is a model of justice, and thus to be just one must begin by assuming that one does not know the truth, and in order to come to know the truth fairly one must conduct rigorous tests unprejudiced by personal preference and desire. Here is the quintessentially realist union of knowledge, ethics, and experimentation: the skeptical realist demands not so much the real itself, as a rigorously judicious relation to that real.

Yet, Jaggers is hardly the model of sympathetic humanity in *Great Expectations*. And despite his stated philosophy of presumed innocence, in the context of the courtroom Jaggers is not scrupulously fair but rather effectively partisan: it is a good thing when Jaggers is "for" one, no matter how guilty one is. Thus what he attempts to teach Pip is not his own practice but rather the impartial position of the law itself—the fairness of which demands the dual presumption of ignorance and skeptical inquiry. In theory, this ethical relationship to the world is all very well. But the impersonal logic of the law overlooks the force and experience of desire. However articulate a spokesman for abstract justice, the static Jaggers is missing the forward-looking pressures of aspiration and speculation, and so he is a poor model for Pip, whose desires make him all too susceptible to the joys of guesswork. Jaggers neglects the very impulses that motivate not only Pip but also the reader of suspenseful plots: the motors of keen preference and unfulfilled desire. It is easy enough to invoke the presumption of innocence; it is altogether another matter to quell conjecture, extinguish hope, and stifle inclination. The lawyer is not a good figure for the realist reader because, without desire, he does not have to work to set his desires aside; without prejudice, he does not have to labor to transform his prejudices into knowledge.

Unlike Jaggers, the realist text teaches us skepticism *in the face of* desire and prejudice. It is for this reason that realist experimentation is about self-denial, or as Pip calls it, "self-forgetfulness." The term "self-forgetfulness" actually appears in reference to Biddy, that consummate angel in the house, who repeatedly puts her own desires aside in order to attend to the needs of those around her.[13] At first, then, "self-forgetfulness" might seem a politically worrying description, attached as it is to the dangerously self-sacrificing model of Victorian womanhood. The familiar image of the self-denying woman would suggest that only one gender is required to "forget" its desires.[14] But to see Biddy as *only* an angel in the house is to miss her role as the text's most skillful reader, the novel's most expert interpreter of difficult and cryptic signs. In a text packed with misreadings, Biddy's interpretations of the world are sensitive, astute, and just. Quick to spot Pip's bad faith and Joe's pride, she is also adept at the technical skill of reading. Indeed, it is she who actually teaches both Pip and Joe to read in the first place, and it is she who remains Pip's literary equal even without the benefit of his formal education. Pip is perplexed by her superiority to him in this respect: "'How do you manage, Biddy,' said I, 'to learn everything that I learn, and always to keep up with me?'" (125). Biddy is intelligent, and above all, she is an intelligent *reader*.

I would like to suggest that one minor incident in the novel uncovers the ethical-epistemological structure that drives the text as a whole, and it puts Biddy's skill as an interpreter at its center. Mrs. Joe, after her beating, has been communicating by tracing cryptic signs on a slate, including "a character that looked like a curious T." Pip at first interprets it as an initial: "I had in vain tried everything producible that began with a T, from tar to toast and tub." This strategy fails to offer up the truth, and so, in good experimental fashion, he changes tactics, from reading the sign as arbitrary linguistic signifier to reading it as a pictorial referent. Now he is on the right track: "At length it had come into my head that the sign looked like a hammer," a hypothesis to which Pip's sister expresses "a qualified assent" (122–23). We have seen Pip read this way before—on the very first page of the novel he has read his parents' tombstones as if the letters were images. Cannily, then, he shifts reading practices when faced with a mystery and moves a step closer to solving it. This shift does not altogether solve the mystery, however, because Mrs. Joe is not interested in the hammer itself when Pip presents her with it. Pip is stumped. It is Biddy who comes to the rescue. More adept a reader than Pip, she changes reading practices yet again, focusing on the hammer's *associations*. Connecting the hammer with one who wields it in the forge, Biddy presents Mrs. Joe with Orlick. Pip's sister nods vigorously, and so the solution to the mystery is confirmed. The "T" is a metonymic signifier, as well as an ideographic one. The process of discovering this fact has entailed several radical shifts in hypothesis. Indeed, it has meant not only identifying an array of possible solutions to the mystery but also allowing variations in the practice of reading itself.

Consistently, Biddy emerges as the most skillful reader of the signs Mrs. Joe communicates, understanding her confusing signals "as though she had studied her from infancy" (122). It is this responsiveness that earns her a place as Mrs. Joe's caretaker. Thus what makes Biddy a sensitive reader is not only an experimental epistemology but also an ethical acuteness, which allows her to encounter the surprising alterity of the world on its own terms. Her quintessentially feminine labor as Mrs. Joe's nurse and interpreter involves both caring and knowing—both responding to the other and understanding that other. And unlike the abstractly fair Jaggers, Biddy's ethical-epistemological model is supple, *flexible*: she is not bound by written principles—the conventionalized letter of the law—but moves easily among paradigms of interpretation when confronted with the enigmas of the other.[15] Her letter can become metaphor or metonym, picture or arbitrary sign.[16] She can read the mysterious signs produced by Pip's sister because she can put aside her own presumptions to attend to the radical otherness of a mind unlike her own. This, then, is Biddy's "self-forgetfulness," just as it is the substance of experimental realism.[17]

If Biddy seems like a secondary character and her mysteries comparatively inconsequential, the text presents substantial evidence to suggest that her responses to the world should act as a model for both Pip and the reader. Pip, as we know, goes wrong when he does not follow Biddy's experimental example. When faced with the central mystery of his life, he does not test his hypotheses, and thus he imposes his mistaken guesses on the world. And it is Pip's self-absorption that makes him a poor reader: lacking humility, sure of his own judgment, he cannot put aside his own desires to ready himself for surprises. From the perspective of a scientific epistemology, Pip fails to know the hidden truth because he is incapable of what Tyndall calls "self-renunciation." Obviously consumed by self-interested desire, he reads into Jaggers's mystery just what he wants to understand—that Miss Havisham intends both her fortune and Estella for him—and therefore he misses the possibility that the world may not coincide with his expectations.

Biddy's skill at solving mysteries appears in the text directly—and suggestively—after Dickens has introduced a set of official detectives who fail to uncover Mrs. Joe's attacker. Much like Poe's Prefect, Dickens's detectives cannot solve the mystery because they rely entirely on their own ideas, refusing to discard hypotheses when these do not match the evidence. "They took up several obviously wrong people, and they ran their heads very hard against wrong ideas, and persisted in trying to fit the circumstances to the ideas, instead of trying to extract ideas from the circumstances" (121). Like Pip and Ruskin's Old Masters, they begin with the idea and assume that the important truths of the world will reflect the patterns of their minds. A better student of realism, Biddy solves her mysteries by knowing that she does not know, testing guess after guess against the evidence. Refusing rigid conventions and fixed principles, she comes both to know more and to act more compassionately than her novelistic counterparts.

And so, by uniting a sharp perceptiveness with a self-denying femininity, Dickens allows us to rethink the paradigm of the angel in the house. With Biddy as our model, it begins to look as though there might be a connection between Victorian femininity and Victorian science. Both demand a self-denying receptiveness to alterity. Both specifically call for the capacity to suspend desire and preconception in order to come to know the otherness of the world.[18] In this context, it is not surprising that Biddy is an unusually skilled reader in a world of perilously puzzling signs and willful misreadings—responding more skeptically and judiciously than any other character to the mysteries she encounters.[19] With "self-forgetfulness," Dickens is not simply offering us a limiting image of self-sacrificing femininity: Biddy, in responding to the otherness of the world on its own terms, is a model of reading for us readers. The thrusting, self-important hero would do well to learn the heroine's self-denying skepticism, both ethically and epistemologically. And if "self-forgetfulness" is both the foundation of realist knowledge and the ideal quality of Victorian womanhood, then the gender of realism is feminine.

The Lessons of Dickensian Suspense

Pip does finally recognize Biddy's wisdom as he sets off to marry her in the penultimate chapter of the novel, imagining that he will ask her to make him "a better man" (468). Indeed, though much has been made of the two endings of *Great Expectations*, we may say that there are really *three*. Before Pip encounters the lonely Estella in the last chapter, he deliberately and seriously plans to marry Biddy. We are treated to images of the happy home life with Biddy he forecasts for himself, "and of the change for the better that would come over my character when I had a guiding spirit at my side" (473). We are even given a verbatim account of the humble marriage proposal Pip has rehearsed, as if to underscore the earnestness of the plan. Then, the journey home is a suspenseful one: Dickens makes us wait as Pip gives full play to his expectations and finds them slowly disappointed, one by one. First his "hopeful notion of seeing [Biddy] busily engaged in her daily duties" is "defeated" (473); then "almost fearing," he finds the forge closed; and finally he discovers that he has arrived too late. Here, what Pip pointedly calls his "last baffled hope" (474) is not his marriage to Estella, but to Biddy.

Thus Pip fails to bring about the conventional end to the marriage plot—three times, and with two different women. Of the two candidates for marriage, Biddy is even a more credible companion for living happily ever after than Estella, as Dickens makes quite plain in Pip's rosy fantasies of their future together.[20] Furthermore, the suspense the novel builds up with Pip's "last baffled hope" is in direct contrast to the flat unexpectedness of the final meeting with Estella, at least in the first ending. Eleven years after his failed attempt to marry Biddy, Pip tells her that his "poor dream . . . has all gone by" (477), and then he simply happens upon Estella, without anticipation, without particular plans or desires. In the first ending, there is no prospect of a marriage. In this version of the novel, Biddy is indeed Pip's last *hope*—the last of his great expectations, the final object of suspense. Indeed, Dickens called the final meeting with Estella "the extra end . . . after Biddy and Joe are done with."[21] At the advice of his friend Bulwer-Lytton, Dickens then added suspense into his second ending, allowing expectation to sneak back into the text.

Why must Pip endure the suspense and disappointed hope of marrying Biddy and then undergo suspense again with Estella in the second edition of the novel? Why are we still encountering "expectations" in the final paragraphs of the novel?[22] Peter Brooks argues that none of these endings matters terribly much because the plot is effectively over with "the decisive moment" that is the death of Magwitch.[23] But this conclusion overlooks the text's careful teaching of the lessons of skeptical realism. Doubt is not over because the larger mystery of the novel is solved. The fundamental premise of realism is that the otherness of the world is *always* mysterious—always demanding tests, doubts, and guesswork. Thus the text of experimental realism emphatically refuses to let us forget suspense, because it must carry over into our own lives. It does not want to let us rest easy, satisfied with neat answers and conventional closures. We must learn the alterity of the real from these fictional plots and then transfer the practice of skeptical, anti-conventional doubt to the mysteries of our lives.

If the Victorian novel suggests that suspense demands the rigors of self-denial and the pains of self-annihilation, its extraordinary power lies in the fact that it is also *pleasurable*. Dickens focuses our attention on the intriguing seductions of suspense toward the end of the novel. Magwitch has come to stay, and Pip wants desperately to keep his existence a secret. The most important task for him, therefore, is to hide the convict from his domestic servants. Perfectly in keeping with the lessons of "The Purloined Letter," Pip decides that the best way to screen Magwitch is not to try to keep him out of sight, but to display him as something other than what he is:

> The impossibility of keeping him concealed in the chambers was self-evident. It could not be done, and the attempt to do it would inevitably engender suspicion. True, I had no Avenger in my service now, but I was looked after by an inflammatory old female, assisted by an animated rag-bag whom she called her niece, and to keep a room secret from them would be to invite curiosity and exaggeration. They both had weak eyes, which I had long attributed to their chronically looking in at keyholes, and they were always at hand when not wanted; indeed, that was their only reliable quality besides larceny. Not to get up a mystery with these people, I resolved to announce in the morning that my uncle had unexpectedly come from the country. (325)

To conceal is to "engender suspicion," and to keep a room secret is to "invite" curiosity. In other words, a mystery excites alert, skeptical attention. In this case, it is the attention of curious women that is "engendered," and perhaps it is no accident that the small male Avenger has been replaced by two daunting feminine investigators. Pip tries scornfully to divest these thieving domestics of their humanity—referring to them as an "inflammatory old female" and her "ragbag" niece—but one consequence of his scorn is that he narrows our knowledge of the servants to two basic facts: their femininity and their curiosity. Since Pip has markedly failed to indulge such curiosity himself, Dickens hints, once again, that the most canny readers are feminine readers, willing to acknowledge that the world may not match their expectations of it and enjoying the possibility that it might yield more than they know. If the elder servant and the person she "calls" her niece look through keyholes and try to grasp the hidden facts of the environment, Pip and the person he calls his uncle are their masculine others—the flip side of the epistemological coin, readers who fail to be interested in the mysteries around them, subjects of knowledge who do not enjoy the recognition that their desires may or may not match the world.

The female servants are strikingly like us, the readers of suspenseful fiction, and Pip, here, deliberately thwarts their excitement. Thus a knowing Dickens lays bare the structures of suspense: the excitement of interest in the not-self emerges from the knowledge that there is something we do not know. This withholding has a twofold effect: it compels the recognition that the world is other to us, and it acts as a spur to pleasurable, keen inquisitiveness. It is as if Pip, here, has not only learned the truth about his benefactor but also suddenly knows the truth about readerly desire: "to get up a mystery" is the surest way to stimulate the desire to solve that mystery, and, by contrast, to stifle the interest of cunning readers, one must know how to suppress and divert the enigmas of suspense. Pip masterfully disallows the pleasures of doubt—and thereby keeps himself safe from inquisitive reading.

By the time Pip comes to think of marrying either Biddy or Estella, he and the reader have, we hope, learned to doubt properly. We should have learned to enjoy our ignorance, not leaping to assume that our assumptions will be validated by events, not rushing to imagine that we know all of the answers. But just in case we have not learned our lesson, we are offered a coda of suspense, first with Biddy, later with Estella. We must not close the book thinking that there are no more questions, and so we are treated to a series of equally persuasive novelistic outcomes—all of which are plausible, and none quite realized. The conventional marriage plot is circumvented twice, only to reenter the text as an ambiguous, by no means certain, outcome in the second version.[24] If we are still reliant on conventional assumptions even after five hundred pages of suspense, then the multiple ending more or less inescapably leads us to doubt those assumptions. Willy-nilly, we must come to know that we do not know.

Competing endings are a fact of suspenseful plotting: for us readers to feel that there is interesting, unfinished business in the final pages of the novel, it must be plausible for Pip to marry or not to marry, to choose one woman or the other. By the end of *Great Expectations*, it may even be unclear whether it is Biddy or Estella who has all along been the most conventional mate for Pip, so plausible do both options appear. Dickens skillfully throws the conventional ending into question by explicitly including it while showing that it functions as only one alternative among several. Incorporating all manner of endings into the text proper, Dickens thus defamiliarizes suspense itself. We would not enjoy doubts about the narrative's course if it were not possible for it to end in a number of different ways.[25] Thus even conventional closure always takes its place among alternative outcomes, contending with less stable, less neat, less happy conclusions. The anxiety stirred up by suspense proves that we are not so sure that the happy ending is the necessary one. In fact, Dickens suggests that the ending hardly matters at all. Suspense is there to teach us to face the fact that time's unfolding might not offer us what we expect.

Notes

1. [Edwin Percy Whipple], unsigned review, *Atlantic Monthly* (September 1861); in P. Collins, *Dickens*, 428.

2. [E. S. Dallas], unsigned review, *Times* (17 October 1861), in P. Collins, *Dickens*, 432; [H. F. Chorley], unsigned review, *Athenaeum* (13 July 1861), in Dickens, *Great Expectations*, ed. Law and Pinnington, 54; [Margaret Oliphant], "Sensation Novels," *Blackwood's Magazine* (May 1862), in Collins, *Dickens*, 439.

3. Eco, "Overinterpreting Texts," 48–49. For a reading of the relationship between science and detection that focuses on their shared capacity to control and discipline, see Thomas, *Detective Fiction and the Rise of Forensic Science.*

4. Bloom, "Capitalising on Poe's Detective," 17; Bersani, *Future for Astyanax*, 63.

5. The list of critics who have faulted both suspense and realism for imposing too limiting a structure on the frightening disarray of the world is long. Gary Day, for example, sees "Realism, with its emphasis on order, coherence, and limitation" as the "dominant" Victorian mode. He writes: "Although the Victorians were troubled with uncertainty, they preferred to repress their doubts and cling instead to the view that ultimate truths did exist." In "Figuring Out the Signalman," 26.

6. "The Purloined Letter" has attracted a great deal of critical attention in the past few decades. My own brief look at Poe, here, is intentionally condensed and specific. For a rich range of other readings, see Muller and Richardson's *The Purloined Poe*, an excellent critical collection that includes Poe's story, Lacan's famous "Seminar on 'The Purloined Letter,'" Derrida's response to Lacan, and others. All references to the text are taken from this edition.

7. Ibid., 39.

8. Dickens, *Great Expectations*, ed. Margaret Caldwell, 137. All subsequent quotations refer to page numbers from this edition.

9. "He perceives the witch of his life as his godmother; just as that upside-down vision perceives the godfather of his life as his witch." Stone, *Dickens and the Invisible World*, 317.

10. As Graham Daldry puts it, "what [Pip] does not see" is that "the retrospect of the narrative does not necessarily include its anticipation." *Charles Dickens and the Form of the Novel*, 142.

11. Katherine Kearns suggests a similar conclusion, arguing that the alterity of the real gives rise to the novel's concern with legal trials: "The realistic novel's preoccupation with lawyers, court cases, and trials reflects the apprehension of a reality that must be pled into existence." *Nineteenth-Century Literary Realism*, 10.

12. Mrs. Joe is, of course, wrong about this, as we learn later, when Magwitch describes his own childhood, a childhood composed not of questions but of unfair accusations.

13. Biddy's working-class status and initially unkempt appearance might seem to disqualify her from the title of domestic angel, but the trajectory of her plot brings her to become an ideal wife and mother, and this ending is certainly fitting: she has always shown a willingness to sacrifice herself for others, an enthusiasm for education (particularly for literacy), and an industrious, respectable self-reliance. If she does not begin in the middle class, she certainly meets all of the requirements to join it.

14. Intriguingly, Gail Turley Houston argues that Estella too is "self-forgetful": "groomed to be the absent center of the Victorian male's affections." See her *Consuming Fictions*, 159.

15. Jaggers's "fair" system convicts Magwitch, who has indeed broken the law—but who is "innocent" of wrongdoing as far as the reader is concerned. Biddy's more flexible system of knowledge gathering suggests an alternative to the courtroom.

16. Martine Hennard Dutheil argues that Pip "evolves from a naïve reading of signs to a much more skeptical view of language according to which there is more to words than necessarily meets the eye." I would suggest that this argument overlooks the fact that the "naïve" reading is helpful in the effort to make sense of Mrs. Joe's cryptic language, and also that it is reading *flexibility*, a willingness to pull from many competing paradigms of interpretation, that solves the mystery. In other words, the text does not advocate replacing the "naïve" with the sophisticated, but rather it advocates using all tools available for unearthing the secrets of the real. See "*Great Expectations* as Reading Lesson," 166.

17. Kathleen Sell claims that women in the novel repeatedly fail to live up to the model of "selfless" femininity, and Pip blames his own flaws on the failures of Mrs. Joe, Miss Havisham, and Estella. A look at Biddy, it seems to me, must shift Sell's conclusions. "Narrator's Shame," 222.

18. Sharon Aronofsky Weltman argues that Ruskin's science relied on a culturally feminine model rather than a masculine one: "The feminine type is Ruskin's model for scientists who perceive without piercing; who need no phallic swords or dissection tools or engines of war; and who open their hearts to receive the knowledge nature provides." "Myth and Gender in Ruskin's Science," 157.

19. In his impressive look at the theme of reading and interpretation in the novel, Peter Brooks overlooks Biddy altogether, suggesting that Pip learns to read thanks to Mr. Wopsle's aunt and mentioning Mrs. Joe's "aphasic" symbols without discussing who deciphers them. See his *Reading for the Plot*, 131.

20. Robert Garnett suggests that the logic of the text will not permit a marriage to Biddy, since only the emotionally "moderate" men in the novel—Joe, Herbert, and Wemmick—can be paired with moderate women. Pip's passions soften over the course of the narrative, but he never becomes a thoroughgoing moderate and so cannot be properly paired with Biddy. For Garnett, Estella is the more credible companion: "Estella plainly does not belong among the novel's temperate homebodies . . . She is the very antithesis, for example, of Biddy's contented domesticity." "The Good and the Unruly in *Great Expectations*," 34.

21. From a letter to Wilkie Collins (23 June 1861), in Dickens, *Letters* 9: 428.

22. In this respect, *Great Expectations* is a clear exception to Robert Caserio's claim that "However much Dickensian plot cultivates diverse meanings and multiple directions . . . the ending, considered not as finale but as *telos*, organizes all that precedes, explains all suspenseful mysteries and indeterminacies, marshals every detail and contingency, every event and character, into a structure revealed at the last—as purposeful." *Plot, Story, and the Novel*, 169.

23. Brooks, *Reading for the Plot*, 136.

24. When he revised the text, Dickens changed the final phrase, "I saw the shadow of no parting from her," to the more ambiguous ending, "I saw no shadow of another parting from her" (480).

25. Thus suspense troubles Frank Kermode's conclusion that "plotting presupposes and requires that an end will bestow upon the whole duration and meaning." *Sense of an Ending*, 46.

WENDY S. JACOBSON

The Prince of the Marshes: Hamlet *and* Great Expectations

> . . . in *Great Expectations* Pip, haunted by the ghost of a father, goes to see Mr Wopsle in *Hamlet*. (Northrop Frye)[1]

> There needs no ghost, my lord, come from the grave
> To tell us this. (*Hamlet*, 1.5.130–1)

This article attempts to explore a major source for the writing of *Great Expectations*, and possible ways in which the character of Hamlet influences the creation of the partially autobiographical Pip.

To say that *Hamlet* has influenced *Great Expectations* is to state the obvious. Dickens's brilliant burlesque of the tragedy performed by a ridiculous actor and an incompetent theatre company is one of the best-known passages in the language, and one of the funniest. The significance of Shakespeare as Dickens's master is, too, a *donnée* in Dickens studies, and, that *Hamlet* and *Great Expectations* have been examined together so often has made my task a difficult if also an interesting one. As Edgar Rosenberg has said, Dickens 'knew *Hamlet* by heart' (p. 194, fn. 5); he also thinks, and this is rather depressing but must be acknowledged at the start, that 'too much has been made of the *Hamlet* parallel' (p. 407). Nevertheless, and daunting though this warning may be, this paper explores what it is in *Hamlet* that attracts the author of *Great Expectations* into exploiting it as an intertext. Also to be declared at

---

From *The Dickensian* 102, no. 470, part 3 (Winter 2006): 197–211. © 2006 by Wendy S. Jacobson.

once is that the visit by Pip and Herbert to Mr Wopsle's Denmark is referred to here only in passing.

The first allusion to *Hamlet* is not the famous visit to the theatre by Pip and Herbert: there the novel makes its companionship overt, but, right from the start, it is powerfully—if covertly—present. In Mr Wopsle's Denmark, that the one text is invoked by the other is obvious, but in the early chapters 'the intellectual patterns' (Ben-Porat, p. 108) are subverted because we are probably not actually intended to make the connection: the allusions are hidden and the evocations subliminal so that our responses become emotional rather than cerebral. We respond to Pip and to Magwitch as our memory of Shakespeare has taught us to respond to Hamlet and the Ghost. Indeed, it matters not if a reader of *Great Expectations* has no knowledge of *Hamlet*, because Dickens's memory, and not ours, is crucial to the text's formulation, and we recognise the intertext only after detecting its presence through analysis of its indirection.

Because the two texts are not obviously alike, an insistent—perhaps even an impertinent—analysis is required: the visit to the theatre by Pip and Herbert is an evident burlesque of the play and seems arbitrarily imposed. That the two texts are, however, only apparently unrelated emerges after a consideration of what seems a strange moment in the first chapter when Pip is watching Magwitch walk away from him across the marshes:

> . . . . he hugged his shuddering body in both his arms—clasping himself, as if to hold himself together—and limped towards the low church wall. As I saw him go, picking his way among the nettles, and among the brambles that bound the green mounds, he looked in my young eyes as if he were eluding the hands of the dead people, stretching up cautiously out of their graves, to get a twist upon his ankle and pull him in. (1.6–7)

Pip starts to run, 'but presently . . . looked' back before running home without stopping. It is natural that the little boy would think that the man bobbling between the grave stones is grotesque, but, less clear are these words: 'eluding the hands of the dead people, stretching up cautiously out of their graves'. Innuendo mixed with straightforward narrative. There is more: Magwitch gets over the low church wall 'like a man whose legs were numbed and stiff, and then turned round to look for me' (1.7), at which Pip sets off at a run, but, stopping again, is fascinated to see 'him going on again towards the river, still hugging himself in both arms, and picking his way with his sore feet among the great stones' (1.7). Magwitch limps towards the

> . . . gibbet with some chains hanging to it which had once held a pirate. The man was limping on towards this . . . as if he were the pirate come to life, and come down, and going back to hook himself up again. It gave me a terrible turn. . . . (1.7)

The meaning of the pirate, whose emblematic power emanates from legend, fairy story, and children's tales, is clear; what gives one pause, however, is that he is likened to a dead man come to life who must elude 'the hands of the dead people, stretching up cautiously out of their graves . . . to pull him in' (1.7), implying that Magwitch is one of the dead, a ghost who has difficulty in holding 'himself together as he limps towards the low church wall' (1.7), who limps because his legs are chained (like Marley's ghost in *A Christmas Carol*) and who looks around at Pip—as if to say, 'Remember me' (*Hamlet*, 1.5.91).

If he is a Ghost—whose ghost is he? He sets in motion the novel's plot by starting 'up from among the graves' shouting to the little boy who has been crying by the side of his parents' graves (1.4). Not only does his appearance terrify the child, Magwitch also has an extraordinary impact on his life by becoming the creator of his future, of Pip's 'great expectations'. He is, he later claims, his father!

Magwitch is not actually a Ghost, nor does he come from the dead, but the imagery of the man hugging his body together as it he were a ghost and his significance in the opening chapter and for the rest of the story makes an irresistible connection with the following lines:

> Let me not burst in ignorance, but tell
> Why thy canonized bones, hearsèd in death,
> Have burst their cerements, why the sepulchre,
> Wherein we saw thee quietly inurned,
> Hath oped his ponderous and marble jaws
> To cast thee up again. What may this mean
> That thou, dead corpse, again in complete steel.
> Revisits thus the glimpses of the moon.
> Making night hideous, and we fools of nature
> So horridly to shake our disposition
> With thoughts beyond the reaches of our souls?
> Say, why is this? Wherefore? (1.4.25–36)

If a consideration of this encounter between Pip and Magwitch is allowed to affirm *Hamlet*'s presence in the opening chapter of *Great Expectations*, then the novel's intention is fascinatingly extended by a wonderful process of incorporating by allusion other texts into its own. This expands the narrative by a sort of internal allegory when it re-tells an old, beloved, deeply familiar tale within a new and different milieu which is the world of the novel.

That the novel opens with Pip's telling us his father's family name, and that he is reading his father's character from his tombstone, identifies the work's concern with self-knowledge. That the novel is to be initiated by a momentous event is promised in the early sentence: 'My first most vivid and broad impression of the identity of things, seems to me to have been gained on a memorable raw afternoon towards evening' (1.3). The setting is bleak: a graveyard, a cold evening, and the child catapulted into self-awareness because of the traumatic experience of a man leaping out at him 'from among the graves at the side of the church porch' (1.4) thus turning Pip and his world upside down. Like Francisco, in a similarly bleak place, Pip 'is bitter cold' and 'sick at heart' (1.1.8–9), and so, indeed, in the play does a man emerge from the grave to turn Hamlet's world upside down:

> A fearful man, all in coarse grey, with a great iron on the leg. A man with no hat, and with broken shoes, and with an old rag tied round his head. A man who had been soaked in water, and smothered in mud, and lamed by stones, and cut by flints, and stung by nettles, and torn by briars; who limped, and shivered, and glared and growled; and whose teeth chattered in his head as he seized me by the chin. (1.4)

This is a 'fearful man' who 'could a tale unfold' (1.5.15). The colour of the man, all grey, the iron on his leg, and his wet, torn, shivering, limping coldness, betoken his emanating from another world. An escaped convict is not like other men—he does inhabit another planet and 're-visits . . . the glimpses of the moon' (1.4.32) this Christmas Eve because he has escaped the prison ship taking him to the site of his eternal damnation from which the law prohibits his return to England.

The story of Pip, like that of Hamlet, begins with an uncanny encounter with a creature from 'another world'; their visitor makes demands of Pip and Hamlet that are impossibly difficult for them to fulfil. Both Pip and Hamlet have, as it were, great expectations because of their connection to the visitor, but, just as Pip does not carry out to the full Magwitch's expectations, so Hamlet never becomes king of Denmark. Both bear a tragic burden as a result of their connection to the father-figure, which connection profoundly shifts their sense of themselves and their place in the world. Furthermore, both achieve a nobility of character that is perhaps their most valuable shared quality.

The charge of the Ghost—to avenge King Hamlet's murder—is only fulfilled at the end when Hamlet himself is dying—his onerous task can only and at last be achieved at great cost to himself, to his conscience, and his soul. For Pip, the transfer to London and gentility has onerous and ambiguous consequences but his early task—of silence and theft—is carried out also at great cost to himself because his young life is bewilderingly tainted by his connection with the convict who imposes upon him a shame he must hide until and at last Magwitch returns—whereupon Herbert (the friend whose character is drawn from Horatio)[2] shares the burden with him. Pip and Hamlet are alone in their tasks: Magwitch threatens on pain of death: 'You do it, and you never dare to say a word or dare to make a sign concerning your having seen such a person as me' (1.6); so are Horatio and Marcellus made to swear upon the sword of Hamlet with the Ghost '(crying from under the stage)' 'Swear!': 'Never make known what you have seen tonight' (1.5.149, 157).

Shakespeare and Dickens tend to pack their opening scenes with material that points to the rest of the text, so well designed are their works. By the end of the first chapter of *Great Expectations* we know Pip, his story, his fear, and also his sharp perceptiveness and kind heart; we know too that he has been burdened with an obligation he cannot fully understand. Very soon after the opening of *Hamlet* we know that the State of Denmark is disrupted and that a Ghost has appeared to his son to bind him to avenge murder. The atmosphere of the two texts, their characters, and plots emerge from different eras, countries, and classes, but Dickens is remembering *Hamlet* in the very design and language of his novel. Our sympathy with Hamlet and with Pip, and, indeed, with King Hamlet and Magwitch, is firmly in place before we move into the rest of the text. Though the concealment of the allusion is subtly done, in some ways it is not really a puzzle as both novel and play concern themselves with young men whose lives are interrupted by a trauma so major that they will for ever struggle with self-consciousness and conscience; both works explore growth towards self-knowledge; and the process, in both instances, costs them dear.

* * *

There is an interesting sameness which is also a difference, which is the issue of revenge. The visitation from the Ghost of King Hamlet urges upon the young prince the obligation to revenge his father's 'foul and most unnatural murder' (1.5.25), and revenge is also pertinent in *Great Expectations*. Both Pip and Hamlet risk damnation, Pip by stealing and associating himself with the damned of Victorian society, and Hamlet could face the wrath of God—and of the State—were he to kill his uncle. Both characters are constrained to take justice into their own hands and both texts depict the maladministration, even the corruption, of justice in old Denmark and in modern England.

In the novel, Miss Havisham wants revenge against men because she was jilted on her wedding day. She uses Estella to break Pip's heart. Likewise, Magwitch uses Pip to spite 'them colonists' who may own 'stock and land' in Australia but not 'a brought-up London gentleman' (39.317). He thereby avenges a social system that punished him unjustly for crimes committed by Compeyson who receives a lesser sentence because he is posh.

The difference, however, is that the play is designed as a revenge tragedy, whereas in Dickens's bourgeois age there are no more Princes, and duels no longer resolve civil conflicts upon which Victorian courts of law now pronounce. Dickens's text, though it penetrates the drama of revenge, has as a determining motif the assuaging of the effects of revenge by forgiveness. The play's hero attempts throughout and finally succeeds in the vengeance enjoined upon him but he can never fulfil what Fortinbras knows, that 'had he been put on' he would have 'proved most royally' (5.2.350–1). The novel's hero, on the other hand, bestows and achieves love and forgiveness: he is himself, and unlike Hamlet, never motivated by vengeance, which may be in some measure because Victorian law courts are more extensive in their management of justice than they were in Shakespeare's England. Pip's yoke moreover, is different from Hamlet's primarily because the latter's role is public and resolution is in the public arena whereas Pip's is essentially private and he resolves his narrative by turning his grief, loss, and broken pride into an opportunity for Miss Havisham to redeem her own offence. Clearly, what Pip wants is not revenge but justice when he asks her to save, not himself, but Herbert. 'Whether it is acceptable to you or no', he insists on telling her, 'you deeply wrong both Mr Matthew Pocket and his son Herbert', both of whom 'made themselves' his friends 'when they supposed [him] to have superseded them' (44.356). His disinterested love is redemptive and, remembering *Hamlet*'s presence here, is also noble. We learn that Miss Havisham, in a wonderful movement from revenge to forgiveness, has granted Pip's wish; we discover this in a scene that is in keeping with the ending of Shakespeare's play when all the actors are accounted for, and we learn it from a narrator of extraordinary insight—and charm:

> 'Is she dead, Joe?'
>
> 'Why you see, old chap,' said Joe, in a tone of remonstrance, and by way of getting at it by degrees, 'I wouldn't go so far as to say that, for that's a deal to say; but she ain't—'
>
> 'Living, Joe?'

> 'That's nigher where it is,' said Joe, 'she ain't living.'
>
> 'Did she linger long, Joe?'
>
> 'After you was took ill, pretty much about what you might call (if you was put to it) a week,' said Joe; still determined, on my account, to come at everything by degrees.
>
> 'Dear Joe, have you heard what becomes of her property?'
>
> 'Well, old chap,' said Joe, 'It do appear that she had settled the most of it, which I meantersay tied it up, on Miss Estella. But she had wrote out a little coddleshell in her own hand a day or two afore the accident, leaving a cool four thousand to Mr Matthew Pocket. And why, do you suppose, above all things, Pip, she left that cool four thousand unto him? "Because of Pip's account of him the said Matthew." I am told by Biddy, that air the writing', said Joe, repeating the legal turn as if it did him infinite good, '"account of him the said Matthew."' And a cool four thousand, Pip!' (57.459–60).

The minor members of the cast are carefully detailed: Miss Sarah gets £25 for pills, Miss Georgiana 'have twenty pound down', and Mrs 'Camels' £5 for rush lights 'to put her in spirits when she wake up in the night' (57.460).

This is not all—can any writer so astonishingly dispense justice by rendering evil absurd as does Dickens when Joe describes Pumblechook's house being broken into?

> ' . . . and they took his till, and they took his cash-box, and they drinked his wine, and they partook of his wittles, and they slapped his face, and they pulled his nose, and they tied him up to his bedpust, and they giv' him a dozen, and they stuffed his mouth full of flowering annuals to perwent his crying out. But he knowed Orlick, and Orlick's in the county jail.' (57.461)

There are, now, a number of bodies on stage: Compeyson, Magwitch, and Miss Havisham, in a parodied half-remembered fifth act of *Hamlet* taken over by the Pockets and Pumblechook and Orlick in a dispensation of justice that overturns the grief of tragedy to present revenge in burlesque.

The novel's difference, then, from the play is its equal emphasis on forgiveness as on revenge. Forgiveness hardly figures in *Hamlet*: only when Claudius acknowledges that he cannot be pardoned ('May one be pardoned and retain th'offence?' (3.3.56)) does Shakespeare deal with the Christian dogma that denies forgiveness without repentance. The word 'forgiveness' comes once only, in Laertes's dying speech: 'Exchange forgiveness with me, noble Hamlet. / Mine and my father's death come not on thee, / Nor thine on me', whereupon he receives Hamlet's 'Heaven make thee free of it!' (5.2.282–84). Hamlet, in his recognition that 'by the image of my cause I see / The portraiture of his' (5.2.78–9), regrets having 'wronged Laertes' (5.2.179):

> Sir, in this audience,
> Let my disclaiming from a purposed evil
> Free me so far in your most generous thoughts
> That I have shot my arrow o'er the house
> And hurt my brother. (5.2.186–90)

Grace and generosity are comparable in the characterisations of Hamlet and Pip. Revenge has its dreadful course in a Renaissance tragedy, but Dickens moves towards remorse and redemption by rendering forgiveness a recurrent motif, as in Biddy's account of Mrs Gargery's death: 'she laid her head down on Joe's shoulder. . . . And so she presently said "Joe" again, and once "Pardon", and once "Pip". And so she never lifted her head up any more' (35.279). Again, in Estella's confession to Pip that 'suffering has been stronger than all other teaching, and has taught me to understand what your heart used to be', she is recalling the last time they were together when he had said: 'God bless you, God forgive you!' 'And if', she tells him, 'you could say that to me then, you will not hesitate to say that to me now . . . ' (59.478).[3]

Pip, besides, must himself receive forgiveness, from Joe and Biddy, to assuage the haunting remorse of his failure of love and regard: 'pray tell me, both, that you forgive me! Pray let me hear you say the words, that I may carry the sound of them away with me' (58.474) he says before he can leave England to join Herbert in Egypt.

The most compelling plea for forgiveness, however, comes from Miss Havisham. In their last encounter Pip feels the dark place of Miss Havisham's pain to be 'a natural place for me, that day' because in his broken heart Miss Havisham has her revenge: 'I am as unhappy as you can ever have meant me to be' (44.354–5) he has told her. The dreadful damage done by Miss Havisham whose wealthy pride has led her to believe herself entitled to vengeance has rendered Pip 'a part of the wrecked fortunes of [her] house' (49.391). He has nevertheless formulated a different vision because of the knowledge he has of the source of her suffering and his understanding of the 'wounded pride' and 'wild resentment' that has perpetrated 'grievous' damage upon Estella.[4] He is, moreover, aware that 'in shutting out the light of day' Miss Havisham has done something even more grievous to herself:

> ... in shutting out the light of day, she had shut out infinitely more; that, in seclusion, she had secluded herself from a thousand natural and healing influences; that, her mind, brooding solitary, had grown diseased, as all minds do and must and will that reverse the appointed order of their Maker. (49.394)

This passage encapsulates Dickens's belief that, in nurturing 'the vanity of sorrow which had become a master mania' (49.394), Miss Havisham had cut herself off not only from 'The heartache and the thousand natural shocks / That flesh is heir to' but, also and fatally, from the nobler course of having taken 'arms against a sea of troubles, / And by opposing end them' (*Hamlet*, 3.1.63–4, 3.1.60–1).[5]

Hamlet's 'To be, or not to be' soliloquy (3.1.57–89) seems to reflect Pip's sense of Miss Havisham's destructive desire to escape from 'the pangs of disprized love' and 'the law's delay' as well as 'the insolence of office'. His and Hamlet's tragedies are told in terms of the 'whips and scorns of time' and 'The oppressor's wrong'. They both understand 'the spurns / That patient merit of the unworthy takes'. Alas, too, they are both familiar with 'The pangs of disprized love'. The difference is that Pip never considers self-immolation which is Hamlet's great longing in that soliloquy, the longing to escape from the fate that he was born to set right. Rather, Pip accuses Miss Havisham of having escaped the sea of troubles which is life's suffering as well as its potential to heal.

We learn this in Pip's confession of love to Estella when he knows at last that he has been duped by Miss Havisham as well as by his own misplaced desires. The confession is given, oddly, in the presence of Miss Havisham, and Pip is partially aware of her when—in a phrase that takes up the recurrent motif of the heart—she puts 'her hand to her heart' (44.359) and listens to his speech:

> 'It would have been cruel in Miss Havisham, horribly cruel, to practise on the susceptibility of a poor boy, and to torture me through all these years with a vain hope and an idle pursuit, if she had reflected on the gravity of what she did. But I think she did not. I think that in the endurance of her own trial, she forgot mine, Estella.' (44.358)

The gentle generosity of 'I think that in the endurance of her own trial, she forgot mine' comes from what Dickens calls elsewhere an intelligent heart. Recognising this, Miss Havisham puts 'her hand to her heart and' held 'it there ... looking by turns at Estella and at me' (44.358). Later Pip recalls her 'spectral figure' and the 'ghastly stare of pity and remorse' (44.360) upon her face. She puts her hand to her heart and feels, at last, someone else's pain. The same pain, but someone else's, a pain she herself has inflicted and intended to inflict.

I need to return to the first chapters of the novel, when all this begins, and when Pip meets Magwitch on the marshes and is enjoined to bring food and a file under threat of having his heart and liver torn out of him by the convict's companion. This companion is an invention of Magwitch's to terrify Pip, but when Pip sees the second convict he supposes him to be the man willing to tear out a boy's heart and liver. In our first reading, we do not know that this man is Compeyson, and that he will turn out to be the man who broke Miss Havisham's heart. Soon after this encounter, Pip is summoned to Satis House where his first interview with Miss Havisham eerily evokes the trauma on the marshes:

> 'Who is it?' said the lady at the table.
> 'Pip, ma'am.'
> 'Pip?'
> 'Mr Pumblechook's boy, ma'am. Come—to play.'
> 'Come nearer; let me look at you, Come close.' . . . .
> 'Look at me,' said Miss Havisham. 'You are not afraid of a woman who has never seen the sun since you were born?. . . . Do you know what I touch here?' she said, laying her hands, one upon the other, on her left side.
> 'Yes, ma'am.' (It made me think of the young man.)
> 'What do I touch?'
> 'Your heart.'
> 'Broken!' (8.57)

'The young man' of whom Pip thinks when she puts her hands on her heart and whom he saw on the marshes is Compeyson; but we can only understand this brief allusion with hindsight, when we learn Miss Havisham's story. Pip takes on now the terrible lesson he learns from the 'eager look' and the 'strong emphasis' on the word 'Broken!' uttered with 'a weird smile that had a kind of boast in it' (8.57). Much later, when Miss Havisham comprehends the heinousness of her selfish malice and apprehends the bitter fruits of her revenge, she is herself punished by feeling anew the agony of Pip's pain as if it were her own:

> 'Until you spoke to her the other day, and until I saw in you a looking-glass that showed me what I once felt myself, I did not know what I had done. What have I done! What have I done!' (49.394)

This sorrowful moment of acknowledgement interestingly uses Hamlet's image of the mirror in the same way and with the same purpose:

> Come, come, and sit you down. You shall not budge,
> You go not till I set you up a glass
> Where you may see the inmost part of you. (3.4.19–21)

Gertrude's recognition of her calamitous state is expressed with the same repeated motif of the broken heart that we early on associate with Miss Havisham in *Great Expectations*: 'O Hamlet, thou has cleft my heart in twain' (3.4.153):

> O Hamlet, speak no more.
> Thou turn'st mine eyes into my very soul.
> And there I see such black and grained spots
> As will not leave their tinct. (3.4.80–4)

Hamlet wishes to 'wring [her] heart' because he dreads Gertrude's having been hardened to her offence so that, like Miss Havisham, her heart is no longer 'made of penetrable stuff', because 'damnèd custom have . . . brassed it so / That it is proof and bulwark against sense' (3.4.36–9). He is very hard on his mother, and so indeed is Pip upon Miss Havisham. Both Gertrude and Miss Havisham seem afraid of the young men whose lives they have so profoundly disrupted. Miss Havisham fears that Pip may hate her 'too much to bear to speak to' her (49.392) and pitifully asks whether he could 'believe, now, that there is anything human in my heart?' (49.391). Wearily, and earnestly, she guarantees his investment for Herbert, and asks 'is there nothing I can do for you yourself?' (49.393). Then it is she hands him her tablets and speaks the words we hear repeatedly from the Miss Havisham whose pride has all fallen away in her shared suffering:

> 'My name is on the first leaf. If you can ever write under my name, "I forgive her," though ever so long after my broken heart is dust—pray do it!' (49.393)

Pip is amazed at Miss Havisham's passion—'he has never seen her shed a tear before' (49.394). The shift in both these 'false' mother figures is considerable. Miss Havisham seeks expiation of her guilt, and yearns for forgiveness as her only hope of redemption. She fears Pip because she is asking for something of which she herself has never been capable.

> O, speak to me no more.
> These words like daggers enter in my ears.
> No more, sweet Hamlet. (3.4.86–8)

Gertrude's great distress results in the Scene's being interrupted by the Ghost coming his 'tardy son to chide, / That, lapsed in time and passion, lets go by / Th'important acting of [his] dread command' (3.4.99–101). The reminder of the Ghost's need for revenge is like the reminder in the novel that Miss Havisham began the whole sorry business with good intentions but then uses Estella, and also Pip, for her own vengeful ends. The revenge motif is central to both scenes though differently purposed.

The Ghost's concern for Gertrude's dismayed recognition of self is comparable with Miss Havisham's horror in the confession scene in the novel, and, just as Hamlet is urged to pity his mother's distress, so Pip will try to 'step between' Miss Havisham and 'her fighting soul' when he tries to assure her of his forgiveness, even though in the end she cannot hear him:

> But look, amazement on thy mother sits.
> O, step between her and her fighting soul! (3.4.104–5)

We are turned, at this intense moment, towards Pip's assumption of culpability. He contemplates a resemblance between himself and Miss Havisham when he confesses that his own life 'has been a blind and thankless one; and I want forgiveness and direction far too much, to be bitter with you' (49.393). He is aware that his life has reflected a betrayal as profound as hers of the ties by which people are bound. And, recognising this, Miss Havisham uses of him the word 'noble': 'It is noble in you to tell me that you have other causes of unhappiness' (49.392). Pip shares nobility with the Prince of Denmark: the nobility that is in Hamlet is unique in Denmark: in the novel we witness the process by which nobility is achieved by Pip, at last, when grace is affirmed in his acknowledgement of his loyalty to Magwitch: 'when I took my place by Magwitch's side, I felt that that was my place henceforth while he lived':

> For now, my repugnance to him had all melted away, and in the hunted wounded shackled creature who held my hand in his, I only saw a man who had meant to be my benefactor, and who had felt affectionately, gratefully, and generously, towards me with great constancy through a series of years. I only saw in him a much better man than I had been to Joe. (54.441)

When Magwitch suggests that Pip 'should not be knowed to belong to me now' and that he should only visit him in prison, Pip replies:

> 'I will never stir from your side . . . when I am suffered to be near you. Please God, I will be as true to you, as you have been to me!'
>
> I felt his hand tremble as it held mine, and he turned his face away as he lay in the bottom of the boat, and I heard that old sound in his throat—softened now, like the rest of him. (54.442)

This nobility finds, I believe, its source in the greatness of heart that Pip learnt in the forge with Joe, but the mature ability to accept and love Magwitch begins later when Pip explains to Miss Havisham that he has forgiven her. There is every reason for Pip to hate Miss Havisham but he does not do so, because, importantly, he knows her story:

> 'Miss Havisham . . . I believe I may say that I do know your story, and have known it ever since I first left this neighbourhood. It has inspired me with great commiseration, and I hope I understand it and its influences . . .' (49.395)

The motif of knowing and telling one's story is everywhere in this novel, and, in Pip's knowing Miss Havisham's story, he can forgive her; in knowing his father's story, Joe can forgive the beatings; in knowing Magwitch's story, Pip can embrace him.

My argument concludes with Pip's farewell to Satis House. Having 'a presentiment' that he 'should never be there again' (49.396), he walks about before leaving, and in the old brewery shudders 'from head to foot' at a fancy he has of seeing 'Miss Havisham hanging to the beam' (39.397). He returns to the house to be assured that she is safe:

> . . . I saw her seated in the ragged chair upon the hearth close to the fire, with her back towards me. In the moment when I was withdrawing my head to go quietly away, I saw a great flaming light spring up. In the same moment, I saw her running at me, shrieking, with a whirl of fire blazing all about her, and soaring at least as many feet above her head as she was high. (49.397)

In a sense this great flame is a type of purging fire, a baptismal flame, which comes after her agonised begging for forgiveness from both Estella and Pip. There is a symbolic sense of fire signifying deeply repressed and denied emotions—but the catastrophe is also a transcendence: the soaring into destructive flame of all Pip's dreams and ideals and hopes, all his terrible delusions, as the beetles and spiders and rotting cake are consumed; and all the death-in-life upon which Miss Havisham has so stubbornly insisted is also consumed; Pip's corruption is flamed away with the rubbish of years and the pathetic, frayed bridal dress of its owner. She is laid out upon the great table where she had told him 'she would lie one day' (49.398):

> At about six o'clock of the morning . . . I leaned over her and touched her lips with mine, just as they said, not stopping for being touched, 'Take a pencil and write under my name, "I forgive her"'. (49.399)

Pip returns to London, himself wounded and blighted, to fulfil his obligation to Magwitch. Their escape plans are foiled, and they are taken not far from Egypt Bay, where, according to Edgar Rosenberg, 'the prison hulk of the early chapters was moored' (p. 327, fn. 7). The end comes, close to where it had all begun.

Pip begins to heal (although the scars are there to the end) only after Magwitch is dead and after having fallen into delirium, a dark night of the soul, out of which he finally emerges into the protective arms of Joe, Joe who has always been, and now returns as, Pip's guardian angel.[6] Slowly recovering, Pip one day takes courage to ask: 'Is it Joe?', to receive the heart-warming reply from 'the dear old home-voice . . . "which it air, old chap"'. 'O Joe,' Pip says, 'you break my heart!' (57.457).

> Now cracks a noble heart. Good night, sweet prince,
> And flights of angels sing thee to rest. (5.2.312–3)

Pip is not literally at the point of death, but his illness after the fire and the deaths of Miss Havisham, Magwitch, and Compeyson is like a kind of dying. He is, in his weakness, very frail, and we are told that Joe's nursing is 'so beautifully proportioned to my need, that I was like a child in his hands'. As if Pip has gone back to his childhood, he recognises the 'old home-voice', and, as he recovers, 'we looked forward to the day when I should go out for a ride, as we had once looked forward to the day of my apprenticeship' (57.461). Pip is as a child again, born again.

His noble heart, like Hamlet's, cracks. Hamlet dies and his tragedy concludes; but Pip's heart must mend, and his dark night of the soul must return him to life. Their stories have to be told. Pip's own account can be deconstructed in its self-consciousness from the start when the first words that are spoken in his telling of his story are 'Hold your noise!' cried out in 'a terrible voice' (1.4).

In Hamlet's play, he cannot die in peace were Horatio to drink the poisoned wine because of the injunction he must make to the one man he can trust to tell his story aright:

> O God, Horatio, what a wounded name,
> Things standing thus unknown, I leave behind me!
> If thou didst ever hold me in thy heart,
> Absent thee from felicity awhile,
> And in this harsh world draw thy breath in pain,
> To tell my story. (5.2.297–302)

Notes

1. p. 75.

2. And perhaps, is Tommy Traddles and also Mortimer Lightwood?

3. These words are movingly echoed in the original ending when Estella's 'touch gave me the assurance, that suffering had been stronger than Miss Havisham's teaching, and had given her a heart to understand what my heart used to be' (Appendix, p. 482).

4. 'Miss Havisham . . . you may dismiss me from your mind and conscience. But Estella is a different case, and if you can ever undo any scrap of what you have done amiss in keeping a part of her right nature away from her, it will be better to do that, than to bemoan the past through a hundred years' (49.395).

5. To be, or not to be—that is the question:
Whether 'tis nobler in the mind to suffer
The slings and arrows of outrageous fortune,
Or to take arms against a sea of troubles,
And by opposing end them? To die, to sleep—
No more; and by a sleep to say we end
The heartache and the thousand natural shocks
That flesh is heir to—'tis a consummation
Devoutly to be wished: to die, to sleep.
To sleep, perchance to dream. Ay, there's the rub;
For in that sleep of death what dreams may come,
When we have shuffled off this mortal coil,
Must give us pause. There's the respect
That makes calamity of so long life.
For who would bear the whips and scorns of time,
The oppressor's wrong, the proud man's contumely,
The pangs of disprized love, the law's delay,
The insolance of office, and the spurns
That patient merit of the unworthy takes,
When he himself might his quietus make
With a bare bodkin? (3.1.57–77)

6. The Working Notes describe Joe as a 'Ministering Angel': 'Pip arrested', the Notes say, 'when too ill to be moved—lies in the chambers in Fever. Ministering Angel Joe' (Cardwell edition, Appendix B, p. 485).

Bibliography

Ben-Porat, Ziva. 'The Politics of Literary Allusion', *PTC: A Journal for Descriptive Poetics and Theory of Literature* (1976), pp. 105–128.

Dickens, Charles. *Great Expectations* (1861), edited by Margaret Cardwell (Oxford: Oxford University Press, 1994).

Frye, Northrop. 'Dickens and the Comedy of Humors' in *Experience in the Novel*, edited by Roy Harvey Pearce (New York and London: Columbia University Press, 1068), pp. 49–82.

Rosenberg, Edgar, editor. *Great Expectations*, by Charles Dickens (New York: Norton, 1999).

Shakespeare, William. *Hamlet*, edited by G. R. Hibbard (Oxford: Oxford University Press, 1997; 1998).

STEWART JUSTMAN

Great Expectations: *"Absolute Equality"*

Democracy of Ignorance

The Greek romance, of which *Callirhoe* is one, has been called "a latter-day epic for Everyman" the expression of an "equalitarian" age and outlook—and this in the derogatory sense that it adapted itself to "all kinds of values high and low" (as might be said of the mass media today) and addressed itself to readers reduced to an equal degree of insignificance.[1] But for whatever reason—perhaps romance's receptivity to values high and low—more sophisticated fiction has long felt a paradoxical attraction to romance as both its own origin and its favorite object of parody. Beginning with Heliodorus, author of the *Ethiopian Story*, and his ironic play on Chariton, a tradition of parody has shadowed romance like a double.[2] The pinnacle of the tradition is *Don Quixote* with its ridicule of romance, yet the energy of parody also runs through Fielding and Austen, Flaubert and Joyce, as if it were really inseparable from the novel itself. Each of the moderns discussed at length here composed anti-romances. In the case of Tolstoy we leave aside the anti-romance of *Anna Karenina* (its heroine like Callirhoe in the impossible position of being "married" to two men at once) to concentrate on two other works, one of which really is a latter-day epic, the other about a man of no apparent significance whatever. Both *Great Expectations* and *The Brothers Karamazov* are novels in which someone erroneously imagines himself a hero of romance and which draw power from fictions exposed

From *Literature and Human Equality*, pp. 48–69, 150–53. © 2006 by Northwestern University Press.

as fictions. It is to the first of these anti-romances that this chapter addresses itself. Romantic visions bring forth in Pip, the hero of *Great Expectations*, the fraudulence, luxury, and loss of independence that Rousseau traces to inequality. Instead of anatomizing some institution like the law courts or the bureaucracy as in *Bleak House* and *Little Dorrit*, Dickens in *Great Expectations* investigates this original evil. Not only the content, however, but important compositional features of *Great Expectations*—in particular, its denial of privileged knowledge to anyone, including the reader—reflect the ideal of human equality.

If in the original romance, the *Odyssey*, knowledge is distributed unequally like a privilege (with the hero enjoying the patronage of a goddess who "know[s] all things" [13.417]), the anti-romance of *Great Expectations* institutes a kind of democracy of ignorance. Late in the novel, as the sun slants in on a group of condemned prisoners as well as the man who sentenced them, Pip remarks that both the judged and the judge "were passing on, with absolute equality, to the greater Judgment that knoweth all things and cannot err" (56.465). No one in *Great Expectations* knows all. Everyone seems in the dark on some critical point. Miss Havisham doesn't know where her ward Estella came from; Jaggers, otherwise so knowing, doesn't know the identity of Estella's father. (He "knew nothing" of Miss Havisham's design to use Pip as a plaything, either [44.363].) Estella herself knows nothing of either parent. Magwitch doesn't know of his daughter's existence.[3] Of Magwitch, Miss Havisham. seems to know only the identity of his lawyer (44.363) and the sole condition attached to Pip's legacy, that he keep his name (19.160); of Miss Havisham, Magwitch knows nothing. Neither knows they have a common betrayer. Magwitch, on his return to England, "had no perception of the possibility of [Pip's] finding any fault with [his] good fortune" (41.343), and dies without realizing that his property, his life's work, is forfeited to the crown. Herbert knows the story of Miss Havisham only in part and doesn't know that Pip, and later Miss Havisham, have underwritten him. Asked to relate the story of Jaggers's housekeeper, Wemmick answers, "I don't know her story—that is, I don't know all of it" (48.398). Joe doesn't know Pip's history with Magwitch or, later, his feeling for Biddy. As befits the hero of such a tale of blindness, Pip himself is a sort of concentrated essence of ignorance, unaware of the identity of his patron, unable to fathom Miss Havisham's campaign against a world that made her suffer ("she was perfectly incomprehensible to me," he says after his first visit to Satis House [9.65]), and prey to his own delusions.

Lest Pip's ignorance induce in us the complacency of superior knowledge, however, we ourselves discover things only as he does. The privileges of "Helios, who sees all things" are not ours. In recounting his visit to Circe's island, Odysseus describes the transformation of his men into swine even though he never witnessed the event and received no report of it. As Homer's deputy, he simply assumes a temporary privilege of omniscience. Only after the fact, when it is too late, can Pip put together the tale of his youth, and in so doing he takes pains to reveal only so much as he actually knew at each stage of it.[4] In this respect *Great Expectations* differs from Dickens's other "autobiographical" novel, *David Copperfield*, where "although every scene is brilliantly rendered through David's eyes, as it seemed to him at the moment, there is . . . often a kind of lucid double exposure shading it with the hidden future."[5] Dostoevsky once observed that if an artist imagines an event from the past, he will imagine it "in its completed aspect, that is, with the addition of all its subsequent developments that had not yet occurred at the historical moment in which the artist was trying to depict a person or event."[6] *Great Expectations* resists this fallacy of the historical imagination at every point. Those of us who grew up with the tale and take its construction for granted (and now read back into the unfolding plot what we already know of its outcome, under the influence of the effect Dostoevsky describes) may have lost sight of the subtlety and boldness of Dickens's experiment. The experiment consists in subjecting the reader, Pip, and everyone else in *Great Expectations* to one and the same condition of ignorance, and doing so in recognition of their—our—common humanity. It was Dickens's belief that we are all "connected by fate without knowing it."[7]

In his influential *Theory of Justice*, John Rawls presents a contract theory wherein persons in a condition of equality establish the very principles of justice. But in order for this to take place, each of these founders can have no knowledge of the benefits to be derived from any particular principle.

> For example, if a man knew he was wealthy, he might find it rational to advance the principle that various taxes for welfare measures might be counted unjust; if he knew that he was poor, he would most likely propose the contrary principle. To represent the desired restrictions, one imagines a situation in which everyone is deprived of this sort of information.[8]

Ignorance is the correlate of equality. But how could a person be rich or poor and not know it? This question doesn't really concern John Rawls, as he proposes such conditions as a conceptual device, nothing more. It would take a Dickens to work out situations where someone is rich or poor without knowing it. In *Great Expectations* Pip thinks he is rich until he discovers otherwise, and, as noted, his patron Magwitch dies without knowing that his wealth is not his. In *Great Expectations* the veil of ignorance, as Rawls calls it, is no exercise in abstraction but a given of experience—a condition binding, moreover, on the reader and narrator as though they were themselves parties to a literary contract.

Perhaps the first narrative in our literature where the reader is kept in uncertainty for the purpose of building up interest and suspense is the last of the surviving Greek romances, Heliodorus's *Ethiopian Story*, an artfully constructed tale of the ordeals of love and the revelation of identity. Mindful of the *Odyssey*, Heliodorus begins in the middle of things, but this time we must wait to understand the beginning. Only later do we discover how it is that two lovers, Theagenes and Chariclea, happen to be found by brigands at the mouth of the Nile. But despite its drama and delayed revelations, such a romance as the *Ethiopian Story* is not really a template for *Great Expectations*. I don't mean solely that the *Ethiopian Story* tells a tale of love and *Great Expectations* of love unreturned, or that the former is set well in the past and the latter on the verge of the present, or even that a divine plan governs events in the ancient novel while the plot of the modern is driven by mortals. Chariclea discovers her identity when we do, in book 4 of a tale in ten books, and what she discovers is that she is the daughter of the king and queen of Ethiopia. In Pip there is no royalty, and his way of making the reader his equal in knowledge and fellow in discovery seems connected with the critique of an unequal society posed by his tale. The *Ethiopian Story* has been called a tale of "incomplete cognition."[9] In *Great Expectations* people fail to know not because destiny is written in riddles but because they themselves are fallible and their corrupted world lacks transparency; or as we might say, in an unequal world defective understanding is the last equality. Under the power of this sentiment, Dickens reinvents the novel in *Great Expectations* as the narrative form of imperfect knowledge.[10]

How the world lost transparency Rousseau attempts to explain in the *Discourse on Inequality*. Once "the inequality of fortunes [and] the use and abuse of riches" became an established fact, "it was necessary in one's own interest to seem to be other than one was in reality. Being and appearance became two entirely different things, and from this distinction arose insolent ostentation, deceitful cunning, and all the vices that follow in their train."[11] In other words, it is due to the corruption of moral sentiments as a result of the evolution of property that the world now presents treacherously misleading appearances of the kind that prove so fateful in Pip's story. Of Rousseau's exposé of civilization, John Stuart Mill wrote within two years of *Great Expectations*:

> There lay in [it], and has floated down the stream of opinion along with it, a considerable amount of exactly those truths which the

> popular opinion wanted; and these are the deposit which was left behind when the flood subsided. The superior worth of simplicity of life, the enervating and demoralising effect of the trammels and hypocrisies of artificial society, are ideas which have never been entirely absent from cultivated minds since Rousseau wrote.[12]

And these ideas are written into *Great Expectations*. The fawning, parasitism, insolence, and insincerity rife in *Great Expectations* are the unmistakable signs of a corrupted and unequal society, just as the different treatment received at the hands of the law by Magwitch and his partner—actually superior—in crime exposes the system of vicious distinctions in the tale's world. At their first meeting Pip and Estella play Beggar My Neighbor. Beggaring your neighbor is the very theme and logic of civilized life, according to Rousseau.[13] When Rousseau goes on to remark that under the regime of corruption even masters are slaves, he chronicles before the fact Pip's relation to his own liveried servant ("the Avenger") in London.

Along with the loss of transparency goes the disappearance of what Jean Starobinski in his study of Rousseau terms immediacy: the state in which nothing comes between self and others.[14] In *Great Expectations* the loss of immediacy reveals itself in the use of agents, intermediaries, pawns, doubles (the two Wemmicks), displacements (as Pip stands in for the male sex in the eyes of Miss Havisham), as well as masks of all kinds. With so much virtually bureaucratic complication besetting their relations, no wonder people in *Great Expectations* labor behind a veil of ignorance. This satiric profusion of false relationships is a symptom of a disordered world. With Joe Gargery, a man who speaks and acts for himself and neither exploits others nor employs masks, we get immediacy, and it is significant that Joe's occupation of blacksmithing is virtually a form of undivided labor in *Great Expectations*. Rousseau associates the inception of inequality with the division of labor.

Once civilization is envisioned as a kind of joint-stock company of hypocrisy, conspiracy theory becomes a possibility, and Rousseau in fact came to believe in the existence of a conspiracy against himself. As Dickens's vision darkened, he "developed a view of the world as almost totally in the grip of a gigantic conspiracy which takes myriad forms but of which the sole effect is to thwart and stifle human freedom."[15] But the critic here quoted applies this observation to *Bleak House* and *Little Dorrit*, among other works, not to *Great Expectations*. It does not apply to *Great Expectations* because, as noted, that novel does not anatomize the institutions of oppression so much as search out the evil—inequality—responsible for oppression in the first place. What is more, while Pip is caught in two schemes that fit perfectly quite as if their authors had plotted it all out like conspirators, the fact is that Magwitch and Miss Havisham inhabit different spheres, never meet, never concert their plans, are too obsessed in any case to coordinate their actions with anyone, and know nothing or next to nothing about one another. Such is the ignorance that runs through this tale of persons linked without knowing it.

Standard Categories and Fixed Distinctions

Considered by many the summit of Dickens's art, *Great Expectations* is the troubled story of Pip—his early and lasting association with a convict, his hopeless love of the marmoreal Estella, his weakness of character in the face of those who prey on his romantic illusions and use him for their own ends. It is a tale of wonders, roughly evocative of the Greek original of the modern novel (which also features orphaned children exposed to the force of events). In the open narrative space of the Greek romance such motifs as the fateful coincidence, the reversal of fortune, and the dramatic recognition figure large, released from the logic and compression of tragedy. In *Great Expectations* it is as though these motifs resumed their tragic significance. Both *Great Expectations* and the ancient romance can be described as an extended tale, told for its own sake, relating "the adventures or experiences of one or more individuals in their private capacities and from the viewpoint of their private interests and emotions."[16]

In one respect, indeed, *Great Expectations* is truer to this definition than the original, for it really is told in the first person. If a Greek romance were told in the words of either the hero or the heroine, the parity between the two, both spiritual and erotic, might well be disrupted. As it is, such concordance exists between these figures that they fall in love at the same moment. As chance would have it (and the factor of chance figures ironically, in one way or another, in all of the nineteenth-century works considered here), Callirhoe and Chaereas "walked headlong into each other at the corner of a narrow intersection—a meeting contrived by the god to make sure that they saw each other. They fell in love at first sight: . . . beauty had been matched with nobility" (*Callirhoe* 31). So it is in the *Ethiopian Story* as well: love comes in at the eye. "At the moment of meeting the young pair [Theagenes and Chariclea] looked and loved, as though the soul of each at the first encounter recognized its fellow. . . . [They gazed] with eyes intently fixed on each other, as if they had had some previous knowledge or sight which they were recalling to memory."[17] While Pip feels a profound affinity with Estella, with whom his memories are bound up, she does not with him.[18] That imbalance alone indicates the tale's ironic attitude toward the ancient conventions of romance that still influence its shape. Pip's hopeless infatuation with this inanimate being might be taken as a darker variant of the sort of imprisonment within a private mental system that makes others in the Dickens world comical.

Theagenes and Chariclea, Chaereas and Callirhoe are carried off to distant places; Estella is herself distant, remote, alien.

Besides being told in the first person, *Great Expectations* is distinguished from the ancient romance by a number of factors, one of which claims special notice. In the most dramatic scene of *Callirhoe*, where Chaereas (presumed dead) comes forward in a courtroom, the spectators feel exactly what the actors in the scene do. They rejoice with the defendant, now proven innocent; grieve with the plaintiff; and "about Callirhoe they were baffled" (267), as she herself is. Readers of *Callirhoe* are assumed to have the same set of responses. Dickens is not content that the readers of *Great Expectations* should feel what Pip felt, but additionally, and in contrast to Chariton, makes sure that we know only what Pip knew at each moment. So conscious is Pip of his duty not to smuggle later knowledge into his narration that he apologizes for introducing into his first description of Miss Havisham details that he registered perhaps a minute later.

> It was not in the first few moments that I saw all these things, though I saw more of them in the first moments than might be supposed.... It was when I stood before her, avoiding her eyes, that I took note of the surrounding objects in detail. (8.57)

In allowing us to know only what he himself knew at the time, not what he came to know afterward, Pip gives the tale the character of a drama of discovery and makes us a partner in that discovery. Or as we might say, by denying the reader all knowledge except that acquired by the hero in the stages of his experience, Dickens grounds *our* knowledge in experience. Locke in the preface to the *Essay Concerning Human Understanding* likens himself not to Newton but to "an under-labourer ... clearing the ground a little, and removing some of the rubbish that lies in the way to knowledge." In its modesty and reduced ambition, this statement has something in common with the note of *Great Expectations*, itself a tale of the clearing of illusions. (The Lockean principle that "each individual has a radically private language"[19] yields in Dickens's pages a society of solipsists—people enclosed in their own mental world, whether like Joe, who can read only his own name and really does speak a dialect all his own, or Miss Havisham, a woman of passion forever dwelling on her own injury.) If Locke seeks to ascertain the scope and limits of human knowledge, Dickens brings home to us the imperfect nature of our knowledge not only by denying complete knowledge to anyone in the tale, including its prime movers, but by having our narrator report things as they appeared to him at the time—a fictional version of Locke's historical method. Locke's concern is to settle the foundations of human knowledge, Dickens's to authenticate, as it were, both Pip's knowledge and our own by the living-through of illusion.

The principal source of the young Pip's illusions is his assumption that his life is following the script of romance word for word—that he has been vouchsafed a conventional remarkable destiny. "She reserved it for me ... to do all the shining deeds of the young Knight of romance, and marry the Princess" (29.234). With the formulas of romance stamped indelibly on his imagination, he misinterprets appearances in a kind of quixotic manner and dupes himself as completely as the grotesques of the Dickens world driven by fictions of their own invention. At the root of his error is the belief that he has for some reason been singled out for the high privileges of romance, and still more fundamentally a belief that conventions of romance laid down long ago govern his life in the present moment. By the time of the tale's telling he has outgrown these delusions of his youth (being capable of change, unlike those Dickensian creations who seem like stuck clocks) and shares his author's sense of the insufficiency of standard formulas and categories. If Wordsworth, transposing the revolutionary critique of artificial distinctions to literature, disputed the categorical distinction between poetry and prose, *Great Expectations* throws into question the social differences that anchor the traditional distinction between comedy and tragedy. The work has both tragic and comic passages. Not even the primary distinction between narrative and drama remains quite secure in *Great Expectations.*

A novel told in the first person, in the voice of "a man speaking to men," possesses something of the charged immediacy, the powerful illusion of presence, of the drama.[20] Moreover, even while telling of change over time (a "pip" after all being a seed), *Great Expectations* employs what we might call dramatic time—the foreshortening that makes for the swift catastrophes of tragedy and the sudden, non-naturalistic reversals of drama generally. Pip's near-death in the attempt to smuggle Magwitch out of England ushers in a change of character almost as dramatic, in the strict sense of the word, as Hamlet's conversion to a man of action aboard a ship bearing him to England and his own death—a change of the greatest consequence, too, for the Pip who emerges from this disaster is in fact the narrator of *Great Expectations.* At certain points of crisis like this one in *Great Expectations*, time loses the gradualism that otherwise governs a long tale of a boy becoming a man. Events themselves become dramatic. That Pip lives to tell of his trials, and tell of them in the voice of a composed self, means only that *Great Expectations* does not conform to the model of tragedy which dictates that the hero die. A fictional autobiography, a tragedy with comic inflections, an anti-romance that cannot abandon romance itself, *Great Expectations* will not be encompassed by any conventional category, instead fusing different categories into a unity corresponding to that of a person qualified by his unusual nature to speak as a man to men.

According to M. M. Bakhtin, neither can the hero of a novel be fitted into a single category. Such a hero "cannot become once and for all a clerk, a landowner, a merchant, a fiancé, a jealous lover, a father, and so forth," lest he lose both the capacity *for* becoming and the "surplus of humanness" that distinguishes him from a lesser figure.[21] In keeping with his own "surplus of humanness," Pip (who never does become a blacksmith) possesses a mixed nature and an abundance of conflicting potentials. Capable of warmth and frigidity, loyalty and ingratitude, generosity and meanness, impulse and delay, he is characterized by his friend Herbert Pocket as "a good fellow, with impetuosity and hesitation, boldness and diffidence, action and dreaming, curiously mixed in him" (30.251). And just as it is the singularity of his nature, and the unique contradictions of a character "at once effeminate and inflexible"[22] that give the story of Rousseau—the great defender of human equality—its claim to universality, so the curious mixture of Pip's qualities serves to make him an exemplary figure. If Pip is a kind of Everyman, this is not because he is a bare shell of a human being but on the contrary because of his "surplus" of conflicting possibilities. And if he himself were not so overfilled with potential, so indeterminate, his tale would be less charged with uncertainty as well.

Ironically, what qualifies Pip to speak in the first person as the narrator of *Great Expectations* is exactly the lack of that identity certified by tokens like the hero's pin, scar, and bow in the *Odyssey*, or confirmed by trial in the Greek romance—the identity unaltered by events. A mark of Pip's unsettled identity is the multitude of his names and titles, from Handel to Sir to Dear boy to the incongruous Mr. Pip. When Joe calls Pip both Sir and Pip in the same utterance as though addressing both a friend and a superior (27.225), he touches on a division in Pip's being even as he dramatizes his own fantastic oddity. Finally Pip suffers not from an excess of names but from false consciousness—that state of self-delusion known to literature well before it became the malady of those in denial of the political truth. The identity behind the first-person narration of *Great Expectations* is not given from the beginning and does not await the hero at the end as the reward of his labors, but constitutes the record of those labors themselves, the living-through of his delusions. But this is also to say that his is the identity of one at variance with himself.

As Bakhtin writes of the Greek novels, "the hammer of events shatters nothing and forges nothing—it merely tries the durability of an already finished product."[23] Hammer and forge figuring as potent images within its pages, *Great Expectations* tells a different story. Not only is Pip scarred by his ordeals both physically and morally (for events in all their violence register on him deeply), but these ordeals do not test an identity already in place but confound the formation of identity itself. It is Estella who seems to possess the unchanging nature of a constructed thing. She virtually refers to herself as a finished product. ("I am what you have made me," she says to Miss Havisham [38.308–9].) Pip for his part is exposed to pressures from so many sides, and is so liable to delusion, that he barely comes to identity at all, and even that is shattered by the return of Magwitch. Magwitch's scheme is internally contradictory to boot. Bestowing his fortune on Pip because the young Pip "acted nobly" (39.321) but fostering all that is least noble in him by feeding his pretensions, Magwitch deepens the "confused division of mind" (18.147) that was Pip's even before his change of fortune and elicits the conflict of motives that makes Pip the roundest character in *Great Expectations*. One describable as "a good fellow, with impetuosity and hesitation, boldness and diffidence, action and dreaming, curiously mixed in him" is far from a finished identity.

Fittingly for one of so mixed a nature, Pip also seems innocent and guilty in the same measure. He is innocent in the sense of being unaware of others' designs on him at the very time that he loses his innocence to luxury and dissipation. Though he really is the plaything of other wills, caught up in plots he doesn't understand or even know of, in neither his own nor the reader's eyes is Pip blameless. In accordance with its ironic handling of the conventions of romance (conventions that still live in its pages, however), *Great Expectations* thus troubles the question of innocence in ways that romance itself cannot contemplate. Most ironically, Pip is responsible for playing out his role in Magwitch's design in spite of being ignorant of its existence. As further evidence of his "surplus of humanness," innocence and guilt are curiously mixed in Pip.

When his improbable sister is struck down with the shackle once worn by the convict Magwitch, Pip blames himself since he was the one who supplied Magwitch the means to file it off. As the novel progresses and Pip is drawn ever more deeply into the role of unwitting player in others' designs, the guilt here linked so strangely with innocence itself comes into its own. Supposing Miss Havisham his sponsor when in fact his money comes from Magwitch ("I worked hard that you should be above work" [39.324]), he starts to become the spoiled child of privilege that he imagines his appointed character. Guilt preys on him all the same. "I lived in a state of chronic uneasiness respecting my behaviour to Joe. My conscience was not comfortable by any means about Biddy" (34.275). "My lavish habits led [Herbert's] easy nature into expenses that he could not afford, corrupted the simplicity of his life, and disturbed his peace with anxieties and regrets" (34.276). When Magwitch returns and declares himself, he is met with the frigid snobbery he unintentionally helped nurture. Yet Pip's crime of ingratitude, first to Joe and Biddy, then to Magwitch, begins in the naive belief that he is following a script that has been laid down for him. Where innocence in the Greek romance is the seal of identity, now the very innocence of Pip's romantic delusions makes for his betrayal of both others and self. That he really believes himself chosen to rise in life (that is, rise above others), because circumstances conspire against his weak points and play tricks on his mind, makes him invest himself all the more in the role of the chosen one. It is as if Dickens turned innocence against itself, much as Tolstoy turns the blamelessly conventional (and also falsely scripted) life of the hero against him in "The Death of Ivan Ilych" a tragedy in prose. It is tragedy after all that searches the paradox of guilt in innocence, that portrays a hero both sinned against and sinning, blind to his own actions (as with Oedipus) but responsible all the same. All of this is true in some sense of Pip in *Great Expectations*, guilty of much but subjected to fire, flood, and at last delirium, beyond all deserving. And the last of these crises reads like a deprivation of knowledge. "I knew [illness] was coming on me now, and I knew very little else" (57.468). "Whether I had two or three times come to myself on the staircase with great terror, not knowing how I had got out of bed"—this in itself Pip does not know (57.469). Confronted by two men arresting him for debt, he says, "I don't know you." "I don't know what they did, except that they forebore to remove me" (57.469). As though his very knowledge had to collapse like his fantasy of distinction, the purgation of Pip's pride calls for the destruction of his knowledge as well.

Not only, then, does Dickens make an unknown the hero of *Great Expectations*, but he subjects that unknown to overpowering, virtually tragic forces. Naturally, though, this is tragedy with a difference. First of all, simply as a tale that keeps us in uncertainty, *Great Expectations* cannot be a tragedy where fate descends on a hero inevitably—inevitably, if only because known to the audience in advance. In this respect the original tragic figures are the warriors at Troy, caught up in a fate that became legendary. Tragic are the tales of Achilles, who gets his wish that the Greek forces should feel his absence of Hector, whose death is his city's ruin. In the case of Agamemnon's fatal homecoming we have a tale so completely foreknown that in the first book of the *Odyssey* it is already taken to be common knowledge. In the clarity of retrospect we watch each figure—Achilles, Hector, Agamemnon—somehow achieving his own destruction. The original heroes of tragic drama likewise belonged to the past, their tales in some sense already given. Tragic heroes are also subjected to fatal forces. By making Hamlet so reluctant to execute his father's decree (as though he sought to preserve his freedom in the face of the role imposed on him by tragedy itself), Shakespeare introduces a new suspense into the tragic form. *Great Expectations* is in that tradition, except that Pip receives no decree at all.

Then too, Pip is not the only one in *Great Expectations* to be exposed to overpowering forces. The same principle of equality responsible for Dickens's choice of a commoner to present his autobiography (as Rousseau, a former valet, had done) also dictates that Pip cannot have the honors of tragic distinction to himself. For if Pip seems singled out for suffering, what of Magwitch, his tormentor and patron? Like a tragic figure who undergoes simply too much suffering, Magwitch in the course of his lifelong ordeal undergoes hunger, imprisonment, exile, self-imposed hard labor, recapture, and sentence of death, the greater part of his life being dedicated to the tragic, because self-defeating, passion of revenge. The uncomplaining way in which Magwitch meets his death sentence, and death itself, not only illustrates tragic acceptance but sets a precedent for the ironic but unembittered tone of Pip's very narrative; and just as Magwitch "never . . . tried to bend the past out of its eternal shape" (56.463), so Pip refuses to falsify the past by revealing what became known only later.

As *Joseph Andrews* nears its contrived resolution (whereby the identities of the lovers are established following the ancient conventions of romance), hero and heroine "felt perhaps little less anxiety . . . than Oedipus himself whilst his fate was revealing."[24] In *Great Expectations* Pip really is seized with anxiety as the sponsor of his fortunes reveals himself, and the reader seized with suspense. Here discovery is stripped of the comic character it assumes in *Joseph Andrews* and invested with the power of a tragic effect.[25] (Both Pip and Magwitch, like Oedipus, run into the very thing they are in flight from.) In this scene, of which it has been said that "Dickens seems to draw together lines from the whole of his created universe to make [it] the highest manifestation of his artistic capacity,"[26] the former convict Magwitch, returned from Australia, claims Pip as his foster son, first asking him what property, and whose property, the young man has inherited. "I don't know" is the answer given to both questions (39.323). At that point Magwitch confronts him with indisputable evidence that he, Magwitch, and no one else has been the young man's underwriter. As if Dickens had completely ironized the romance tradition originating in the *Odyssey* of the use of tokens to confirm identity, the returned convict presents his proofs to a "son" overcome with horror and disgust.

> "Concerning a guardian," he went on. "There ought to have been some guardian or such-like, whiles you was a minor. Some lawyer maybe. As to the first letter of that lawyer's name, now. Would it be J?"
>
> All the truth of my position came flashing on me; and its disappointments, dangers, disgraces, consequences of all kinds,

> rushed in in such a multitude that I was borne down by them and had to struggle for every breath I drew. (39.323–24)

Maybe it is a flaw in *Great Expectations* that it places Pip in the tragic position of one who experiences a shattering recognition (and "recognition is best when it occurs simultaneously with a reversal," according to Aristotle), when the greater capacity for both action and suffering belongs in fact to Magwitch. But it can be argued that Dickens divides the honors of the tragic position between Pip and Magwitch—that he is too modern, too un-Ptolemaic as a matter of literary practice, to make the tale revolve around a single hero who engrosses all of its tragic potential.

The description of Pip as a kind of impulsive John-a-dreams—one with "impetuosity and hesitation, boldness and diffidence, action and dreaming, curiously mixed in him"—establishes him as a descendant, however remote, of the richest and most enigmatic self in literature, the exemplar of hesitation but also a bold antagonist, Hamlet. At one point Pip attends a farcical performance of *Hamlet* in which, when the Prince asks whether it is nobler in the mind to suffer, "some roared yes, and some no, and some inclining to both opinions said 'toss up for it'" (31.257). For the reader and for Dickens there is a lot more of *Hamlet* in the surrounding pages of *Great Expectations*, with its tale of a young man enlisted into his foster father's campaign of revenge against the destroyers of his life. (So too, when Pip remarks on Herbert Pocket's untroubled way of bearing "all blows and buffets" [22.186], that companion and confidant momentarily becomes Horatio, the troubled mind belonging to Pip-Hamlet.) Hamlet is at cross-purposes with himself, Pip subjected to the conflicting purposes of others and made miserable by a "confused division of mind" (18.147).[27]

If Pip with his erratic shifts between "action" and "dreaming" necessarily brings to mind Hamlet, the convict who makes his entrance among the graves, as though one of the walking dead, and whose Christian name Abel speaks of fratricide, conveys echoes of the Ghost. In the commands of the Ghost, the will of the dead threatens to dominate the will of the living, and had Magwitch been less driven, he might have taken the conventional way of rewarding Pip: by leaving him a fortune in a will, also an instrument by which the dead have their way with the living. That Magwitch seeks in life what is a prerogative of death suggests that he himself exists in a state of death-in-life. And so it proves. Doomed by a society with one law for the rich and one for the poor, Magwitch leads the existence of a living ghost in *Great Expectations*, appearing from nowhere, disappearing for a large stretch of the tale though haunting Pip all the same, then reappearing to Pip and Herbert, whom he swears to secrecy like the Ghost in *Hamlet*, while all but invisible to the world at large. With his return from penal exile for the purpose of seeing Pip, Magwitch is liable to arrest and execution at any moment. Tragedy gravitates to the boundaries of human existence—in *Hamlet*, the edge of a cliff, the verge of suicide, the bank of a fast-running stream, the brink of a grave, the limits of endurance. More than anyone else, it is the commoner Abel Magwitch, living as if in the presence of death, who dramatizes those boundaries in *Great Expectations*.

Unknowns

Driving the plot of *Great Expectations* is not divine providence or the abstract power of Fortune but the designs, the plots, of human agents, especially Miss Havisham's scheme to enslave Pip's heart to Estella and Magwitch's project of making a gentleman of him, also for purposes of revenge. Miss Havisham tortures him, Magwitch pampers him. (That these two—one born to wealth and one to poverty—are similarly driven and have the same betrayer, that their lives converge on Pip, that one goes from wealth to self-imprisonment and the other from imprisonment to wealth—this is Dickens's Discourse on Inequality.) Because Pip does not understand these designs and because they work together as if their authors conspired, each exploiting a weakness of his constitution (romantic infatuation on the one hand, snobbishness on the other)—their combined effect is to sap his autonomy and confuse him to the core. The dramatic effect of the recognition scene is the greater for his entanglement in this fantastic web.

It is thus the coincidence of two plots—Miss Havisham's revenge against the male sex and Magwitch's revenge against the society that cast him out—that places the young Pip at the mercy of forces he can neither master nor even comprehend, a mariner shaken by two Poseidons. And what makes the coincidence a genuine one (44.363) is that despite their both having been betrayed by one Compeyson, neither Miss Havisham nor Magwitch really knows anything of the other. In a work whose author attended carefully to the question of who knows what, this mutual ignorance is clearly essential to the narrative design. Knowledge itself in *Great Expectations* seems to be qualified with ignorance. When, over their first dinner together, Herbert tells Pip the story of Miss Havisham, he ends with a string of disclaimers.

> "[What was in the letter Miss Havisham received] I can't tell you, because I don't know.... Indeed I know only so much, through piecing it out myself.... Mind! I don't know that.... I don't know.... I know no more." (22.183–84)

When the returned Magwitch delivers his story to Pip and Herbert, in the process mentioning that his nemesis Compeyson "had been in a bad thing with a rich lady some years before" (42.351), he seems not even to know the woman's name. It is Herbert, after the recital, who informs Pip, "Compeyson is the man who professed to be Miss Havisham's lover" (42.356). So too, although Miss Havisham adopts Magwitch's daughter, she has no knowledge that she is Magwitch's daughter. She simply informs the lawyer Jaggers

> "that I wanted a little girl to rear and love, and save from my fate.... He told me that he would look about him for such an orphan child. One night he brought her here asleep, and I called her Estella." (49.406)

Later, Pip informs Jaggers, "I know more of the history of Miss Havisham's adopted child than Miss Havisham herself does" (51.416). In sum, neither of the revengers who use Pip for their own conflicting ends knows even the name of the other, much less the depths of the other's motivation. So fully committed is Dickens to the portrayal of unknowns that he makes these two movers of *Great Expectations* unknown to one another. Had Dickens (or Pip) made known from the beginning just how events fit together in *Great Expectations*, the reader would have been placed in the position of understanding what no one in the world of the tale does—not even Jaggers, who numbers both Miss Havisham and Magwitch among his clients, and who habitually acts as if he "knew all kinds of things" to the disadvantage of everyone else (18.140; 20.165). In the novel as we have it, such false superiority is precluded.

Pip's ignorance is our own, then; and all of the ignorance in *Great Expectations* seems to converge in Pip—a Hamlet now oppressed by a lack of knowledge. Underlying all the affinities between *Hamlet* and *Great Expectations*—the irresolution of the heroes (each burdened with guilt), the haunting of each by a "father" who somehow returns from the land of no return (in the case of the exiled Magwitch, Australia)—is the reduction of Hamlet and Pip to instruments of another's vengeful will, with the critical difference that Pip doesn't even know he is being used, and used by two implacable wills and not just one. (However, we might regard the two revenge plots of *Great Expectations* as a reflection of the kind of doubling that is everywhere in *Hamlet* itself.) Hamlet of course is subjected to the demand—delivered with the greatest possible rhetorical force—that he avenge the murder of his father. With some two months elapsing between his receipt of this solemn charge and the beginning of act 2, Hamlet's hesitation suggests an attempt to preserve his own freedom in the face of an irresistible force. The drama of the play deepens as Hamlet, even after verifying the Ghost's word, delays the execution of his revenge.

Unlike Hamlet, Pip does not delay the execution of a vengeful command but fulfills only too well, if unwittingly, the role assigned him in Magwitch's vendetta against the society that ruined his life. An unknowing instrument of revenge, Pip also serves as an object of Miss Havisham's vendetta against the male sex (Dickens's concern in both cases evidently being the complete subjection of a life to the purposes of another). Suspense comes with the working out of these cross-plots, the resolution of identities, and Pip's shattering discovery of the truth about his rise to wealth and imaginary distinction. Hamlet's shattering discovery is made in his conference with the Ghost in act 1; later, after considerable intrigue, the Ghost is discovered to be the spirit of Hamlet's father that he appeared to begin with. The suspense of *Hamlet* is not the suspense of awaited discovery. While both Hamlet and Pip are trapped in a riddle, the first suffers from an excess, the second from a deficiency of knowledge. But in a sense, not-knowing is a fit response to a world where the traditional certainties of social position seem to have given way. If Pip had become a blacksmith (as Joe did, following in the footsteps of his father), if Magwitch had never reinvented himself as a sheep farmer in Australia, if Miss Havisham had accepted the role of a spinster that misfortune seemed to consign her to—if the social positions of an unequal world remained stable—Pip's experience would probably never have supported a tale of suspense and surprise in the first place. In this respect it is the shock to traditional distinctions that is responsible for *Great Expectations*.

In the course of Pip's discoveries we ourselves learn just how little we knew about Magwitch, and how viciously he has been dealt with by the authorities whose public face is one of rectitude. Pip himself is unknown to history, and it may be fitting that while tested to the limits of endurance and beyond, he experiences the humble and anticlimactic fate of survival rather than a tragic death. (Somewhat analogously, in *War and Peace* the city of Moscow burns and comes back to life rather than suffering a tragic death like the Homeric city of Troy.) As an unknown, Pip does not have the sort of visibility that makes the godlike heroes of Horner a spectacle for the gods themselves—though at the same time objects of divine enmity—and makes the tragic hero a lightning rod for forces greater than human life can bear. The greatness of tragic figures places them as it were too near the gods for their own good, gods who then remind them that they are merely human. Hamlet's father had

> Hyperion's curls, the front of Jove himself,
> An eye like Mars, to threaten and command,
> A station like the herald Mercury
> New lighted on a heaven-kissing hill (3.4.56–59),

only to die miserably in a state of sin. In the ironic world of tragedy, it is death that sets the final seal of greatness on a human life. There is something of the antihero in Odysseus, not just because he appears before us in rags as one beneath notice but because (according to the prophecy of Tiresias) he will die "in / some altogether unwarlike way . . . in the ebbing time of a sleek old age" (11.135–37).

Only survivors can tell their story. After he and Penelope resume "their old ritual" (23.296), Odysseus tells her the story of his adventures. The hero whose greatness is sealed with death must have his story told by another, as Horatio lives on at Hamlet's request to tell his (Hamlet's) story to the world. To bring out the distinction between Tolstoy and Dostoevsky's views of death, Bakhtin asks himself how the latter would have composed Tolstoy's tale "Three Deaths." He can only conclude that "Dostoevsky would never have depicted three *deaths*" in the first place, for in Dostoevsky's world "death cannot function as something that finalizes and elucidates life," as in tragedy.

> Death in the Tolstoyan interpretation of it is totally absent from Dostoevsky's world. Dostoevsky would not have depicted the deaths of his heroes, but the *crises* and *turning points* in their lives; that is, he would have depicted their lives *on the threshold*.[28]

Death itself cannot be depicted because events in the Dostoevskian world are presented as though in the words of the characters themselves—the author having renounced the pretense of standing above them and writing about them—and no one can narrate his or her own death.[29] Autobiography cannot end in death; and Pip, as a fictional autobiographer, cannot have a classically tragic fate. (In this he is upstaged by Magwitch, who dies in a state of acceptance, beyond all excuses, defenses, and arguments.) Like a character in Dostoevsky, who in fact has a definite affinity with Dickens,[30] Pip is shown in crises and at turning points; and in accordance with the prosaics of the novel, the humble task of telling his story falls not to Horatio but to Pip himself.

Tragic and Comic

Among the great ironies of the *Iliad* is that between the two warring armies there is no distinction in ethos or valor, which is to say that they are each worthy of the other—equally heroic. Heroism itself, it seems, implies a certain standard of equality At one point in book 12 of the *Iliad*, the well-matched armies are likened to equal weights of wool in the hands of a woman laboring for her children (12.430–36). To say that the *Odyssey* lacks the tragic character of the *Iliad* is to note, among other things, that it contains no equal or rival against whom Odysseus can be tested. (For that matter, neither does it feature the contest of god against god, as in the *Iliad*.) But if heroes are to be measured against one another on the field of war, does this not imply that heroism itself is in some way self-negating?

In the twelfth book of the *Iliad*, the middle of the poem, Hector leads a counterattack against the Greek forces. He does not know—although we do, privy to the intentions of Zeus and the vision of the future—that the Trojans' success will be temporary and in fact self-defeating, as it will rouse Achilles from his tent; that Troy itself will perish as a result; and that the race of heroes that includes both Achilles and Hector will pass from the earth by the will of Zeus.[31] All of these ironies generate a complex music akin to that of a tragedy where one greater than ourselves knows less than ourselves, if only because his very story is already known. Greatness revealed in its human weakness makes for poignancy and paradox. The tragic irony associated with the Homeric view of heroes blind to their own future and the purposes of Zeus is transformed in *Great Expectations*. In accordance with the dictate of equality, we share Pip's blindness. At no point in *Great Expectations* is the future revealed to us but not to him or any other character; indeed, it is not revealed to anyone. (Even the official ending of *Great Expectations*—"I saw no shadow of another parting from her" [59.493]—does not amount to a revelation of the future. It is the statement of a person, that is, one subject to error.)[32] Discussing the cardinal literary distinction between force and fraud, Northrop Frye associates the first with the violence of tragedy and the second with the ruses of comedy. "As *forza* is open violence, tragedy seldom conceals anything essential from audience or reader," while in comedy (Frye seems to be thinking of New Comedy in particular) identities may be concealed from the audience.[33] In *Great Expectations* the identity of Pip's sponsor is concealed from the reader because it was concealed from Pip, and its disclosure—the tale's peripateia—approximates a tragic effect. At the same time, the strain of comedy in *Great Expectations* seems to tell us that the hereditary distinction between the tragic and the comic—the one concerned with lofty and the other with common persons and matters—no longer applies. The warriors on the plains of Troy and the woman weighing her wool exist in separate worlds; but in *Great Expectations* the tragic and comic live practically side by side.[34] Dickens in fact conceived the novel as a tragicomedy.[35]

And the mixing of tragic and comic tones in *Great Expectations* in defiance of traditional literary decorum implies a rejection of the social orderings on which literary classification was grounded. Depicting a fall from a political height, tragedy centers on the great, while comedy concerns itself with the inferior, according to Aristotle. A century before Dickens wrote *Great Expectations*, it was already apparent to some that the fixed distinction between tragic and comic subjects rests on nothing more solid and creditable than a double prejudice, a hereditary error of the brain that works in favor of the great and against the poor.[36] To Dickens, the system that stands on such fallacies is itself false, and particularly in the story of Magwitch, whose life was ruined by one who knew exactly how to play on the prejudice against the poor, he explodes the social presumptions underwriting tragedy and comedy as literary categories.

Systems and Prisons

In *Gulliver's Travels* the hero's habit of assimilating himself to his masters, even to the point of adopting the gait and neigh of a horse, makes for a satiric illustration of the way a mind without innate moral sense falls captive to whatever system it finds itself in. "Any system can become a prison," writes Denis Donoghue.

> *Gulliver's Travels* is only superficially about big men and little men: it is really about entrapment; and the most disturbing episode in the book deals with the Struldbruggs, those people in Luggnagg who are immortal in the appalling sense that they get older but can't die. They can't leave the system.[37]

Upon hearing that the Struldbruggs are immortal, Gulliver naively assumes that being exempt from death they "have their Minds free and disingaged."[38] In point of fact, they become the hopeless prisoners of their own deformed passions, envying those lucky enough to die. The grotesques of Dickens are like mortal Struldbruggs, speaking a sort of private language where the Struldbruggs lose the use of words. Even Pip has something of the Struldbrugg in him: where they are mocked by their own desires, he is condemned to live in a perpetual state of desire he himself understands to be futile. Like the tale of the Struldbruggs, the Dickens world is ruled by the irony of captivity. Not long before *Great Expectations*, Dickens devoted *Little Dorrit* to the paradox of the willing prisoner, illustrating the theme unforgettably in William Dorrit, who wears mind-forged manacles when free and can only expand his spirit, it seems, when immured in the safety of the Marshalsea; in the willed paralysis of the Miss Havisham–like Mrs. Clennam; in the entrapment of Miss Wade within her own resentment of imagined injuries; even in a kind of abdication of sexual being by Arthur Clennam, another hero divided in mind and haunted by failure.[39] These, however, are but special cases of characters locked within their own constructs. The Dickens world abounds with beings who can't leave the system—not necessarily the system they find themselves in, but one they author, the warped expression of their own powers. In the manner of Prince Vasili in *War and Peace*, who "like a wound-up clock, by force of habit said things he did not even wish to be believed" (4), the grotesques of the Dickens world have become human mechanisms. Much of the comedy of *Great Expectations* is vested in these inhabitants of a private system, these creatures of habit whose "humors" in the satiric sense—their oddities—have taken possession of them. In this respect, and in keeping with the author's practice of mixing moods, the very comedy of *Great Expectations* is serious: a comment on minds entrapped in some illusion of their own creation, like Mrs. Joe in the fantasy of her oppression, and entrapped the more completely for that reason. (By contrast, Mrs. Pocket's delusions of nobility were instilled by her father, "who had invented for himself a conviction that his deceased father would have been made a Baronet" but for opposition in high places [23.190]. In a parody of hereditary privilege, Mrs. Pocket inherits a fiction.) In portraying those who immure themselves in their own mental Marshalsea, Dickens is as concerned with the renunciation of freedom as Dostoevsky in his legend of the Grand Inquisitor. As to Pip, had he remained a prisoner of his own ignorance and pretension, he might never have been able to tell a tale in good clear language in the first place. His tone itself speaks to us of experience gained and illusions surrendered. Others in *Great Expectations* remain so locked in their own mental world that they speak a kind of language of one that would never do for telling a tale. Presumably these distortions of language support and are supported by the grotesque social relations that are evident to the reader from the first pages of *Great Expectations.*

If the grotesque shuts himself in the system of his own "humor," a Miss Havisham—shut in her room as well as in the mania of a consuming passion—brings out the more tragic side of the forfeiture of freedom. The tragic figure, writes Northrop Frye, uses freedom "to lose freedom. . . . This happens to . . . Hamlet when he accepts the logic of revenge."[40] Imprisoned of her own free will and, even worse, surrendering in rapture to the logic of revenge, Miss Havisham dramatizes the perversion of freedom. While plotting revenge employs Odysseus's powers so fully as to constitute a mode of self-expression, vengeance makes a grotesque of Miss Havisham; and while in the Homeric world revenge serves as a way of making one's name (as in the case of Orestes) or making oneself known (as Odysseus reveals himself to the suitors when he sets about slaughtering them), Miss Havisham's revenge is indirect and secretive.[41] It is an aggravated form of the "deceitful cunning" and the "dark propensity to injure" associated by Rousseau with the evils of inequality.[42] Miss Havisham's sole rival in obsession in *Great Expectations* is Magwitch, who also sacrifices his freedom to the will to revenge. "Single-handed I got clear of the prison-ship; I made a dash, and I done it. I could ha' got clear of these death-cold flats likewise—look at my leg: you won't find much iron on it—if I hadn't made the discovery that *he* [Compeyson] was here. Let *him* go free?" (5.36). And these two powerful, perverse wills, each too wrapped up in itself to recognize the other, converge on the young Pip. In an important sense, he too loses freedom. He does so by enslaving himself to Estella—the link between Miss Havisham and Magwitch if only they knew it—in spite of her inanimate nature and in fact her own warning. Like a grotesque, Pip too is trapped in the absurdity of obsession. It was presumably because this fate was too dark that Dickens rewrote the ending of *Great Expectations* to raise the prospect of his reunion with Estella. ("I saw no shadow of another parting from her.") For Dickens, the image of a human being locked in a mental system can be comic or tragic or perhaps both.

If a system is said to be rational when all of its parts are disposed "in accordance with a unifying central criterion," a Dickens character commanded by some single fiction of his own invention becomes a sort of Swiftian figure lost in a private system.[43] In its very composition, *Great Expectations* disputes the rationality that subjects all to a single criterion. Being a romance and a satire *on* romance, and heightened with color both tragic and ludicrous, the work seems to repudiate uniformity itself as if that too were the result of confinement in a single perspective. Dickens is a Shakespearean novelist, and it bears remembering that in the playwright's time tragedy, history, and comedy were not hard-and-fast categories. In Shakespeare's problem plays these genres bleed into one another notoriously, yielding in *Measure for Measure* an enigmatic comedy acted out in the shadow of the executioner's block, and in *Troilus and Cressida* an indeterminate composition that was originally classified now as history, now comedy, now tragedy. But *Hamlet* too is a problem play, the hero himself being the problem, and *Great Expectations* takes place under the shadow of this figure who resists our efforts to understand him because he never seems identical to himself. Even *Hamlet* has a dash of dark comedy. To Dickens a strictly "tragic" version of *Great Expectations*—a *Great Expectations* with no admixture of the comic—would have seemed rigid and one-sided. To the closed logic of system, he opposes a work of abundant life that overflows literary divisions and categories. To the grotesque who reads everything in one way, he opposes a work bound to no single literary perspective in spite of being told by one person.

"Man is born free; and everywhere he is in chains": a principle with both comic and tragic applications in *Great Expectations*. On the one hand are minds manacled to absurdities of their own creation, like Mrs. Joe's image of herself as a woman oppressed. On the other hand is the brute oppression of Magwitch, victim of society's double standard. Magwitch, it seems, was not many years in this world before he was locked up. "When I was a ragged little creetur as much to be pitied as ever I see . . . I got the name of being hardened. 'This is a terrible hardened one,' they says to prison wisitors, picking out me" (42.349). From the fastening of this epithet on Magwitch to his leg-iron in the marsh to the very linkage of his story to Pip's, the fact of the chain figures powerfully in *Great Expectations.* And arguably, the character in *Great Expectations* who breaks out of his own mental system most dramatically is the very man we meet shackled, the one whose tale is bound to Pip's for good and with whom Pip divides the laurels of tragic experience: Magwitch. Toward the end of *Great Expectations*, even before capture and conviction force resignation upon him, Magwitch accepts his lot with a peace of mind nothing like the resentment that possesses him for most of the tale—a state of both rest and readiness akin to the tragic wisdom that lies beyond rationalizations and the fury of argument. "I'm quite content," Magwitch says after his arrest (54.454). To the judge who condemns him as a "scourge of society"—the very description he once resented so bitterly—he replies, more in sorrow than in anger, "My Lord, I have received my sentence of Death from the Almighty, but I bow to yours" (56.465). Guilty of murder but also sinned against, Magwitch takes on a resemblance to those tragic figures including Hamlet's father, a victim of murder with sins on his head, who confound the categories of guilt and innocence governing the romance world. His story adds a dimension of depth to *Great Expectations.* Like Pip and like the work itself, he too is a curious mixture, at once victim and victimizer, remembering both kindnesses and injuries, passing from obsession to peace.

Literary Leveling

The novel, it has been said, "is always expanding to meet the new and widening interests and outlook of its time, tending to absorb and to supplant in popular favor all other forms, especially poetry and drama and whatever in artistic literature is intense or concentrated, and to become for the open society of the cosmopolitan world what the old epic was for the closed society of tribal and patriarchal days—everything."[44] We cannot fail to be struck by the epic length of some of Dickens's novels, as well as their ambition to mirror a world in its entirety. In *Great Expectations* the drive to encompass all makes for prose with the heightened quality of poetry and the immediacy of drama, for a certain crossing of tragic and comic moods, and for both the fulfillment and frustration of the original romantic conventions of the novel itself. The literary name given to the power that flows through all of the divisions of literature almost as if they weren't there is satire. Confined to no single tradition, indifferent to drama and narrative, prose and verse, and capable of adapting itself to both tragic and comic expression, satire has strong anti-generic potential.[45] Satire turns the act against the actor, revealing us as the captives of our own folly, pretense, and delusion, like Pip in *Great Expectations* and others to come on our list of "heroes."

In *The Dialogic Imagination* Bakhtin unearths a tradition of comical satire that poses "a critique on the one-sided seriousness of the lofty direct word" and reminds us that reality "is always richer, more fundamental and most importantly *too contradictory and heteroglot* to be fit into a high and straightforward genre," an opinion Dickens would have seconded.[46] Belonging to this tradition is "the comic Hercules," identified by Bakhtin as "one of the most profound folk images for a cheerful and simple heroism, and . . . an enormous influence on all of world literature."[47] The comic Hercules of *Great Expectations*, as already noted, is Joe Gargery, "a sort of Hercules in strength, and also in weakness" (2.6). A vivid example of cheerful simplicity, Joe is also the human image of the spirit of equality in *Great Expectations*, not only in his lack of snobbery but in the more positive sense that he acts like the equal of the child Pip (7.49) and speaks for "equal justice betwixt man and man" (7.46). But even as he carries the "direct word" of equality into *Great Expectations*, Joe Gargery embodies a "contradictory and heteroglot" mix of qualities—not just strength and weakness, or manhood and childhood, but wisdom and folly. Pip refers to the abundance and wealth of his nature (57.474).

Also suggesting abundance, "satire" comes from the Latin word for "full," as though at root it referred to something overflowing, not to be contained within any single vessel or category. Dickens is drawn to satire as a disbeliever in the literary laws marking off one domain from another: satire cuts across literary differences roughly as the principle of equality cuts across differences in social position. The next novelist before us was not so much an antinomian as an iconoclast, possibly the most complete in literature, and among the idols he shatters is the form of the novel itself. It has been said of *War and Peace* that it "satirizes all historical writing, and all novels."[48] Tolstoy does not satirize for the joy of destruction, or not solely for that reason, but because only satire can expose the insufficiency of systems and tear away the pretenses of the great and the falsehood of artificial distinctions. And with these ends Dickens might have agreed.

Late in his life, Tolstoy wrote to a correspondent (in English), "I think that Charles Dickens is the greatest writer of the nineteenth century, and that his works, impressed with the true Christian spirit, have done and will continue to do a great deal of good to mankind."[49] Such was his esteem of Dickens that it survived his rejection of art. His early works *Childhood* and *Boyhood* were written under the immediate influence of Rousseau and the Dickens of *David Copperfield*. Perhaps by the time Tolstoy wrote *War and Peace* he was beyond literary influences. Nevertheless, there is still an affinity with Dickens. Inasmuch as the adult Pip, like David Copperfield, carries within him the child he was, we see things in *Great Expectations* to some extent through the eyes of a child not yet accustomed to the imbecility of human conventions and the practices of a grotesque world. Of Tolstoy too some say that he reveals things in their strangeness, as if the reader were seeing through the eyes of one unfamiliar with human practices—a strategy that serves Tolstoy's satiric purposes.

Notes

1. Perry, *Ancient Romances*, 48–49.
2. John J. Winkler, "The Mendacity of Kalasiris and the Narrative Strategy of Heliodoros' *Aithiopika*," *Yale Classical Studies* 27 (1982): 93–158.
3. Additionally, at the novel's crisis "the mother and father [of Estella], unknown to one another, were dwelling within so many miles, furlongs, yards if you like, of one another" (*Great Expectations* 51.420).
4. Significantly in this connection, "Provis" suggesting "provide" and thus "foresee," is the false name taken by the returned Magwitch.
5. Edgar Johnson, afterword to *David Copperfield*, by Charles Dickens (New York: Signet, 1962), 873.
6. Cited in Joseph Frank, *Dostoevsky: The Mantle of the Prophet, 1871–1881* (Princeton: Princeton University Press, 2002), 111. On the difference between real time and retrospect, see Sherwin Nuland, *The New Republic*, September 13 and 20, 2004, 38: "Looking back with unbridled condemnation on the beginnings of racial hygiene does not enlighten today's thoughtful man or woman in regard to how he or she might have responded at the time."
7. As reported by Dickens's friend and biographer John Forster; cited in Donald Fanger, *Dostoevsky and Romantic Realism* (Cambridge, Mass.: Harvard University Press, 1965), 92.
8. John Rawls, *A Theory of Justice* (Cambridge, Mass.: Harvard University Press, 1971), 18–19.
9. Winkler, "Mendacity of Kalasiris," 95.
10. By keeping the narrative "solution" from the reading audience for months on end, serialization is well adapted to the conveyance of imperfect knowledge.
11. Jean-Jacques Rousseau, *A Discourse on Inequality*, trans. Maurice Cranston (Harmondsworth, Eng.: Penguin, 1984), 119.
12. John Stuart Mill, *On Liberty* (New York: Norton, 1975), 45–46.
13. "It is thus that we each find our profit at the expense of our fellows; and one man's loss is nearly always the good fortune of another" (Rousseau, *Discourse on Inequality*, note I, p. 148).
14. Jean Starobinski, *Jean-Jacques Rousseau: Transparency and Obstruction*, trans. Arthur Goldhammer (Chicago: University of Chicago Press, 1988).
15. Garis, *Dickens Theatre*, 97.
16. Perry, *Ancient Romances*, 45.
17. Heliodorus, *Ethiopian Story*, trans. Sir Walter Lamb (Rutland, Vt.: Everyman, 1997), 70.
18. "You are part of my existence, part of myself," Pip says (*Great Expectations* 44.368).
19. Hans Aarsleff, *From Locke to Saussure: Essays on the Study of Language and Intellectual History* (Minneapolis: University of Minnesota Press, 1982), 27.

20. William Wordsworth, preface to the *Lyrical Ballads*, in *The Great Critics*, ed. James Harry Smith and Edd Winfield Parks (New York: Norton, 1951), 506.

21. Bakhtin, *Dialogic Imagination*, 37. This observation appears in an essay investigating the difference between the still-evolving genre of the novel and the finished world of epic, only novels being capable of moving toward an unknown outcome. Presumably Bakhtin would agree with the judgment that the *Odyssey* lacks suspense, as in fact he notes the complete irrelevance to the *Iliad* of questions like "How does the war end? Who wins? What will happen to Achilles?" In *Great Expectations* the already closed tale of Pip's youth is delivered exactly like a tale moving toward an unknown destination. If the question of how the Trojan War ends is of no interest because everyone already knows how it ends, Pip is a complete unknown whose tale is also fraught with the unknown.

22. Jean-Jacques Rousseau, *The Confessions*, trans. J. M. Cohen (Harmondsworth, Eng.: Penguin, 1953), 232.

23. Bakhtin, *Dialogic Imagination*, 107.

24. Henry Fielding, *Joseph Andrews* (Harmondsworth, Eng.: Penguin, 1985), 315.

25. Discovered not to be brother and sister as they feared, Joseph and Fanny are free to marry; Pip and Estella, adopted son and natural daughter of a criminal both sinned against and sinning, are estranged by a force as strong as that binding the other two. Where Fielding diversifies the romance plot with a satiric medley of materials, Dickens seems to apply a satiric corrective to romance as such.

26. Bernard Schilling, *The Rain of Years: "Great Expectations" and the World of Dickens* (Rochester: University of Rochester Press, 2001), 94.

27. "I loved [Estella] against reason, against promise, against peace, against hope, against happiness" (*Great Expectations* 29.234), in fine, against himself.

28. Bakhtin, *Problems of Dostoevsky's Poetics*, 73.

29. Exceptions are the Ghost in *Hamlet* and Agamemnon in the *Odyssey*.

30. Anny Sadrin, *Parentage and Inheritance in the Novels of Charles Dickens* (Cambridge, Eng.: Cambridge University Press, 1994), reads *Great Expectations* as a novel haunted by parricide. What might the author say of *The Brothers Karamazov*?

31. Clay, "Whip and Will of Zeus," 40–60.

32. See Phillip V. Allingham, "Shadows of 'Things That Have Been and Will Be' in *Great Expectations*," *ELN* 41 (2004): 55.

33. Northrop Frye, *The Secular Scripture: A Study of the Structure of Romance* (Cambridge, Mass.: Harvard University Press, 1976), 66, 71.

34. On Dickens's ironization of the Homeric simile, see Bakhtin, *Dialogic Imagination*, 305–6.

35. On *Great Expectations* as tragicomedy, see Meckier, *Dickens's "Great Expectations,"* chap. 1.

36. Adam Smith, *Lectures on Rhetoric and Belles Lettres* (Indianapolis: Liberty Classics, 1985), 124: "Kings and Nobles are what make the best characters in a Tragedy. The misfortunes of the great as they happen less frequently affect us more. There is in humane Nature a Servility which inclines us to adore our Superiors and an inhumanity which disposes us to contempt and trample under foot our inferiors. We are too much accustomed to the misfortunes of people below or equal to be greatly affected by them." Elsewhere Smith observes that "in ease of body and peace of mind, all the different ranks of life are nearly upon a level, and the beggar, who suns himself by the side of the highway, possesses that security which kings

are fighting for" (*Theory of Moral Sentiments* [Indianapolis: Liberty Classics, 1982], 185). Smith's sometimes-dinner companion Dr. Johnson observed characteristically in an *Idler* paper on sleep that "there is reason to suspect that the distinctions of mankind have more shew than value, when it is found that all agree to be weary alike of pleasures and of cares, that the powerful and the weak, the celebrated and the obscure, join in one common wish, and implore from Nature's hand the nectar of oblivion" (*The Idler* no. 32, November 25, 1758).

37. Denis Donoghue, *The Practice of Reading* (New Haven: Yale University Press, 1998), 182. On some of the bonds between Swift, and Dickens, see Stewart Justman, *The Springs of Liberty: The Satiric Tradition and Freedom of Speech* (Evanston, Ill.: Northwestern University Press, 1999).

38. Jonathan Swift, *Writings* (New York: Norton, 1973), 178.

39. The tragic element appears in *Little Dorrit* in the form of strong echoes of *King Lear*, the title character being an unmistakable Cordelia.

40. Frye, *Anatomy of Criticism*, 212.

41. Odysseus begins the slaughter of the suitors at the banquet table. Miss Havisham imagines the suitors for her wealth feasting on *her*, laid out on the banquet table (88). This is surely a bizarre way of disappointing their great expectations.

42. Rousseau, *Discourse on Inequality*, 119. In the state of nature, Rousseau believed, people do not experience the desire for revenge. See note O, p. 168.

43. Edward Shils, *Tradition* (Chicago: University of Chicago Press, 1981), 291.

44. Perry, *Ancient Romances*, 29.

45. Arguably, it is the satiric energy of *Ulysses* that makes it, in Northrop Frye's words, a "complete prose epic." A work that is all at once "novel, romance, confession, and anatomy" (*Anatomy of Criticism* 314) does not really belong to any given genre.

46. Bakhtin, *Dialogic Imagination*, 55.

47. Ibid.

48. Morson, *Hidden in Plain View*, 83.

49. Letter written by Tolstoy in 1904 to one James Ley.

ANDREW SANDERS

Great Expectations

In early October 1860, Dickens gave Forster this account of the novel he was writing: "The book will be written in the first person throughout, and during these first three weekly numbers you will find the hero to be a boy-child, like David [Copperfield]. Then he will be an apprentice. You will not have to complain of the want of humour as in *The Tale of Two Cities*" (*Letters* 9: 325). The essence of *Great Expectations* was therefore already distilled in Dickens's mind. It was to be an autobiography like *David Copperfield*, but published in weekly parts rather than in monthly numbers. Unlike the central character of *David Copperfield*, the new boy-hero was to be born into the social class where becoming apprenticed to a trade was normative. David, the "young gentleman" to his workmates at Murdstone and Grinby's, had been obliged to experience being *déclassé* and had found the process agonizing. Pip, by contrast, would follow the artisan norms of his class. The new novel would also be essentially *humorous* unlike its predecessor in *All the Year Round*. Forster must have privately expressed his disquiet at the "want of humour" in *A Tale of Two Cities*, and he was to reassert this criticism when he later wrote that "there was probably never a book by a great humourist . . . with so little humour and so few rememberable characters" (Forster bk. 9, ch. 2). *Great Expectations* was therefore to revert to an established Dickens

From *A Companion to Charles Dickens*, edited by David Paroissien, pp. 422–32. © 2008 by Blackwell Publishing, editorial material and organization © 2008 by David Paroissien.

type: the humorous, first person narrative, but with a distinctively working-class central character.

In the same letter of October 1860, Dickens expanded on his conception of the nub of the plot and the essential narrative mode of *Great Expectations*:

> I have made the opening . . . in its general effect exceedingly droll. I have put a child and a good-natured foolish man, in relations that seem to me very funny. Of course I have got in the pivot on which the story will turn too—and which indeed, as you will remember, was the grotesque tragi-comic conception that first encouraged me. To be sure I had fallen into no unconscious repetitions, I read *David Copperfield* again the other day, and was affected by it to a degree you would hardly believe. (*Letters* 9: 325)

Weeks earlier, Dickens had outlined this "very fine, new and grotesque idea" to Forster and had evidently shown him the manuscript in order to give substance to the themes that the novelist enthusiastically described as "opening up" before him. His serial, he declared, would revolve around what he called his "grotesque" idea "in a most singular and comic manner" (*Letters* 9: 310). Writing later to Mary Boyle on December 28, 1860, Dickens repeated his emphasis on the comic and the droll elements. The first chapters, he reported, were "universally liked" probably because the novel "opens funnily and with an interest too" (*Letters* 9: 354). It seems to me, in view of a tendency to ignore this emphasis on the comic, worth pursuing two issues. First, just how "droll" is the "grotesque" side of *Great Expectations*? Secondly, what significance lies in the effort Dickens made to distinguish his new novel from the earlier, and ostensibly sunnier, *David Copperfield*?

Forster seems to have remained persuaded that *Great Expectations* was essentially comic both in its conception and its achievement. Comparing it with *A Tale of Two Cities*, he insisted in his anonymous review of the novel in the *Examiner* in July 1861 that "its contrivance allows scope for a fuller display of the author's comic power" (Forster 1861: 452). A decade later, after offering a complimentary account of the characterization of Joe and Magwitch, Forster went on to comment on other aspects of the dramatis personae of *Great Expectations*. He was particularly delighted by Daggers and by Wemmick ("both excellent, and the last one of the oddities that live in everybody's liking for the goodheartedness of its comic surprises"); he found the Pumblechooks and Wopsles "as perfect as bits of *Nickleby* fresh from the mint"; and he considered the scene in which Pip and Herbert make up their accounts as "original and delightful as Micawber himself" (Forster bk. 9, ch. 3).

Like other nineteenth-century critics, Forster preferred the earlier, breezy, optimistic Dickens novels over the later, darker, ambiguous ones. When he reaches out for flattering parallels he finds them in *Nickleby* and *Copperfield.* The early reviews of *Great Expectations* are generally complimentary, though one dissenter, writing in the *Westminster Review* in 1862, insisted that nothing "but the talisman of Mr. Dickens's name, would induce the general public to buy and read 'Great Expectations.'" He then went on to declare that "there is not a character or a passage" in the whole novel "which can afford enjoyment to anybody twenty years hence" (Anon 1862: 286–7).

What other reviewers noted, however, was not the familiar Dickensian rehash that the partisan *Westminster* had complained about, but a happy return to an earlier, essentially comic manner. The *Saturday Review* commented that "after passing under the cloud of *Little Dorrit* and *Bleak House* . . . *Great Expectations* restores Mr. Dickens and his readers to the old level. It is . . . quite worthy to stand beside *Martin Chuzzlewit* and *David Copperfield*" (quoted in Collins 1971: 427). E. S. Dallas rejoiced that "Mr. Dickens has good-naturedly granted to his hosts of readers the desire of their hearts . . . [he] has in the present work given us more of his earlier fancies than we have had for years . . . there is that flowing humour in it which disarms criticism." Dallas concluded his review in *The Times* by stressing the restored triumph of Dickens's "rare faculty of humour" (quoted in Collins 1971: 430–1, 434). A similar expression of relief at being delivered from gloom permeates the review in the *Dublin University Magazine* of December 1861 ("Expecting little, we gained on the whole a rather agreeable surprise . . . The favourite of our youth still stands before us . . . the old humour still peeping playfully from lip and eye"). Moreover, the reviewer insisted that *Great Expectations* presented readers with "an entertainment got up by the oldest, yet still the first of our living humorists" (quoted in Collins 1971: 435–6).

Critics today tend not to share these views. Instead, they ignore Dickens's professed intentions and read the novel as an expression of pessimism occasioned by the novelist's personal estrangement from and disillusion with society. Social bankruptcy, non-communication, guilt, and confession number among the topics frequently explored in the current literature about the novel.

Certainly there is ambiguity in the comedy of *Great Expectations.* The opening chapters, for example, are recounted with a degree of "double-take." Pip's account of the threat presented by Magwitch's supposed companion ("That young man has a secret way pecooliar to himself, of getting at a boy, and at his heart, and his liver") can be read in two ways. From the perspective of a child's world it remains truly terrifying, but adult perceptions tend to diminish the menace much as adults suppress fear of the imagined dangers and perils of the night. The funny, if slightly melancholy, Christmas dinner scene in chapter 4 can be seen as serving to condition those memorably jolly earlier Dickensian Christmasses at Dingley Dell and at the Cratchits. Nevertheless, the *dénouement* of Christmas at the forge has a brilliantly contrived ambiguity as Pip runs for the door only to be stopped by the party of soldiers ("one of whom held out a pair of handcuffs to me saying, 'Here you are, look sharp, come on!'"). As readers were to learn at the opening of the next number, it is not Pip who is to be arrested, but Magwitch for whom Pip has committed the "crime" of stealing the brandy and the pork pie.

Other primarily "comic" scenes share something of this ambiguous edge. Most notable is Wopsle's chilling revelation to Pip that Compeyson has been observed seated behind him in the waterside theater to which Pip had repaired one evening for light entertainment (ch. 47). Nevertheless, what Forster and Victorian critics admired as evidence of Dickens's return to a predominantly "humorous" mode should surely be acknowledged to be as vital in determining the nature of the novel as the melancholy which has informed so many latter-day readings. One might cite here, as Forster did, the characterization of Herbert Pocket and of Wemmick, and especially the comic delicacy with which Dickens explores Wemmick's "commuter" mentality, delineates his relationship with the Aged P, and delights in his semi-clandestine marriage (an example, perhaps, of what Forster meant by "the goodheartedness of the comic surprises").

A further key to the way *Great Expectations* was originally read as predominantly *comic* may lie in the ending Dickens gave to the published version. Not till Forster printed the original last paragraphs of the novel in 1874 did Victorian readers have access to Dickens's first, bleaker, and far less ambiguous conclusion. The fact that Dickens so readily acceded to Bulwer-Lytton's suggestion that he change the ending indicates that Dickens himself was never really happy with what he had first written. He was rarely so responsive to friendly criticism and never before had he reacted either so positively or so radically. His original three hundred odd words were scrapped in favor of a more extended meditation of some thousand words which, as Dickens explained to Bulwer-Lytton, arose from his need to avoid "doing too much." As he went on to say: "My tendency—when I began to unwind the thread that I thought I had wound for ever—was to labour it, and get out of proportion. So I have done it in as few words as possible; and I hope you will like the alteration that is entirely due to you" (*Letters* 9: 428–9).

He had earlier told Wilkie Collins that he felt that his change was "for the better," and a week later he wrote to Forster insisting that he had "put in as pretty a piece of writing as I could, and I have no doubt the story will be more acceptable through the alteration" (*Letters* 9: 432–3). Dickens was not simply throwing a sop to his middlebrow readership by rendering the new ending more "acceptable." By having so scrupulously "unwound" the thread of his first ending, he was effectively obliged to reweave a number of threads that had run through the story from its inception. His new emphasis was not on alienation, or loneliness, or estrangement but on Pip's shaky achievement of a kind of wholeness and integrity. Estella may remain as distantly unachievable as she always was, but Pip himself seeks to aspire to a new set of "expectations" which are founded not on economic exploitation but on emotional achievement.

The new ending does not serve to resolve the Pip/Estella story (though it does not emphatically deny that there *might* be some happy resolution of it); what it properly does for readers is to suggest that Pip has moved on, and retains the potential for further growth. The revision stands as a development of, and from, what had gone before. The rising morning mists are now rising evening mists, and "the broad expanse of tranquil light" contains, as far as Pip sees it, no "shadow." He may be wrong, of course, but surely Dickens implies that Pip's experiences have matured him, and that this achievement of maturity is essentially integral to a predominantly *comic* narrative rather than a *tragic* one. Jack may, or may not, have Jill, but that is not the only issue at stake in this bitter-sweet revision. The change may not strike many readers as artistically satisfying as the original, but it must be conceded that it is quintessentially Dickensian.

It seems to me that the revised ending serves to move readers on from the earlier resolution of the two other key relationships in Pip's life: the "exceedingly droll" and "very funny" relationship with Joe and the "grotesque tragi-comic" one with Magwitch. As Dickens noted in his letter to Collins of June 23, 1861, he had only changed concluding matter dealing with events "after Biddy and Joe are done with" (*Letters* 9: 428). Whether or not Pip might have proposed to Biddy much earlier in the novel, and whether or not Biddy would have accepted him, is not the issue at stake. What matters is Joe's improved status—a mutually responsive marital relationship and birth of his own child—both of which had been denied him in his marriage to the first Mrs. Joe. Also made clear before this final chapter is the extent to which Pip and Joe are reconciled. As so often in the latter stages of *Great Expectations*, the process is built not simply on expressions of love and acceptance, but also of repentance (on Pip's part) and ready forgiveness (on Joe's), themes that remain firmly grounded in the novel:

> "But I must say more. Dear Joe, I hope you will have children to love, and that some little fellow will sit in this chimney corner of a winter night . . . Don't tell him, Joe, that I was thankless; don't tell

> him, Biddy, that I was ungenerous and unjust, only tell him that I honoured you both, because you were both so good and true . . .
>
> "I ain't a going," said Joe, from behind his sleeve, "to tell nothink o' that nature, Pip. Nor Biddy ain't. Nor yet no one ain't."
>
> "And now though I know you have already done it in your own kind hearts, pray tell me, both, that you forgive me! . . .
>
> "Oh dear old Pip, old chap," said Joe. "God knows as I forgive you, if I have anything to forgive!" "Amen! And God knows I do!" echoed Biddy. (ch. 58)

The Christian language here is hardly arbitrary. It echoes the parallel confessions and reconciliations presented in the account of Magwitch's last hours in Newgate prison and Pip's final prayer asking for forgiveness for his benefactor (ch. 56). Neither scene comes off as "humorous" or "droll." Nor is there any suggestion of the "tragi-comic." But we should surely recognize that Pip's reconciliation first with Magwitch and then with Joe suggests that he is also reconciled with his past. Such a steady movement toward that end cannot properly be described as "tragic." It may not offer the neat resolutions of *Nicholas Nickleby* or *Martin Chuzzlewit*, to which some Victorian critics sought to compare it. But the last chapters of *Great Expectations* can be seen as profoundly "comic" in the sense that they allow for a new potential in Pip and for something of a happy and unexpected resolution to his "expectations." If some critics find Pip as "disillusioned" at the end of his narrative, it seems to me that Dickens's revised ending allows us to see a man not only chastened by experience but also one reconciled both to the strengths and to the weaknesses of his character.

G. K. Chesterton scores a direct hit when he describes *Great Expectations* as a book in which "for the first time the hero disappears." Chesterton sees the narrative as a whole as possessing "a quality of serene irony and even sadness" and he accredits this to the particular nature of Dickens's development as a novelist. Early in his career, Dickens had presented readers of *Nicholas Nickleby* with an updated version of the hero of Romance whom Chesterton typifies as a "demi-god in a top hat." This figure, according to Chesterton, continues to evolve through Kit Nubbles, Walter Gay, David Copperfield, and Sydney Carton, as each becomes less heroic and more complex. "The study of Sydney Carton," writes Chesterton, "is meant to indicate that with all his vices, Sydney Carton was a hero."

> The study of Pip is meant to indicate that with all his virtues Pip was a snob. The motive of the literary explanation is different. Pip and [Thackeray's] Pendennis are meant to show how circumstances

> can corrupt men. Sam Weller and Hercules are meant to show how heroes can subdue circumstances. (Chesterton 1911: 198–9)

As ever, Chesterton resorts too readily to the aphoristic manner, but his central point remains valid: Dickens was attempting something new in *Great Expectations* and much of that novelty depended on the character and manner of its narrator. Pip's is the dominant consciousness in the novel, but as a describer, delineator, and analyst, both of himself and of his circumstances, he is essentially flawed and "un-heroic." This lack of "heroism" may have contributed to what critics have seen as the novel's "gloom" and to what has been interpreted as estrangement and guilt, but it can also be read as integral to Dickens's humorous "tragi-comic conception."

This leads us back to Dickens's determination to make Pip and his narrative distinct from that of David Copperfield. Pip was to be of a lower social class than David, and, ostensibly, he was almost certainly to be far less of a surrogate Dickens. The novelist's confession to Forster that he was "affected by it to a degree you would hardly believe" by re-reading his earlier work suggests not only the extent to which his own private emotions had molded the "personal experience" of David Copperfield but also the fact that he now sought to distance himself from Pip's experiences, both personally and artistically. This was not how George Bernard Shaw saw it. In comparing Pip with David in 1937, Shaw gave the distinction between the two a distinctly socio-political edge. He insists that in the ten years that separate the two novels, Dickens had developed both as an artist and as a critic of himself and the world about him. Dickens's "reappearance" in the character of a blacksmith's boy, Shaw famously asserted, "may be regarded as an apology to Mealy Potatoes," one of David's work associates at Murdstone and Grinby's. For Shaw, the shades of Warren's Blacking fall darkly over the whole novel, as Dickens re-explores an embarrassing secret with a renewed and more perceptive sense of guilt (Shaw 1958: 45–6).

To clinch his point, Shaw may have selected the peculiarly named Mealy Potatoes as the object of Dickens's "apology" rather than the more likely figure of Mick Walker. Mick's original, Bob Fagin, was the senior boy worker at Warren's, who had proved to be particularly attentive to Dickens. By contrast, Mealy's original, Poll (Paul) Green, seems to have had a vague air of romance about him because his father worked as a fireman "at one of the large theatres." No such romance is associated with Mick/Bob. As Dickens's autobiographical fragment reveals, it was Bob Fagin who had attempted to assuage the pain in the boy Dickens's side with blacking-bottles filled with hot water and who had attempted to see the boy safe home. It was of Bob Fagin too that Dickens disarmingly remarks "I took the liberty of using his name, long afterwards, in *Oliver Twist.*" This admission has served to disconcert many latter-day readers (how could Bob's kindness have been rewarded with such despicable associations?). The answer seems to lie in Dickens's boyhood fear that somehow associating himself with the likes of Bob and Poll might taint him socially and trap him for ever in a working-class world in which he felt acutely ill at ease. Readers must remember how Dickens (and David) express their distress at the loss of status represented by the real Warren's and the fictional Murdstone and Grinby's. "No word can express the secret agony of my soul," Dickens wrote, describing how he sunk into the companionship of common men and boys and how he felt his hopes of growing up "to be a distinguished man" crushed in his bosom (*David Copperfield* ch. 11).

But it *was* written, twice over, both as a record of fact and as fiction, and we must surely appreciate the force of Dickens's phrasing and choice of words. This world of boyhood drudgery represents a fall from middle-class grace. Instead, a proletarian hell predominates where gestures of kindness and fellow-feeling are distorted into Mephistophelian entrapments. Shaw's assumption that what Pip's narrative represents is some kind of apology to Mealy Potatoes may indeed find justification in the reference by Joe on his visit to London that he and Mr. Wopsle have made a point of seeking out "the Blacking War'us" (though the one they visited is Warren's rival, Day and Martin's). The reference compounds Pip's embarrassment before Herbert at this point in the story, but it may also indicate something of Dickens's own uneasiness at a stirring of uncomfortable associations with the past.

Since Shaw's time, issues of social class have come to dominate the discussion of *Great Expectations*. Critics have all too often chosen to concentrate on ideas of class guilt or Marxist ideas of alienation and class betrayal, thereby distorting readings of the novel. As Dickens indicated in the outline he sent to Forster, Pip was to become an apprentice. This obviously distinguishes him both from David Copperfield and from Dickens himself. If David appears to have been born into the gentlemanly class, Dickens's own lower-middle-class origins suggest a rather more tenuous grasp on gentility. While John Dickens consistently aspired upwards, the family's fall in 1822 seems to have marked Charles all the more severely given the social and educational ambitions he took for granted. Pip wants to be a gentleman, just as Emily had wanted to be a lady, but neither was born with the assumptions instilled in the boy Dickens. Precarious as those assumptions were to prove, we must accept that Dickens seems to have been brought up to see himself as a cut above Mick Walker and Mealy Potatoes.

It does not seem to me that Dickens shaped *Great Expectations* as an apology for his earlier social aspirations, as Shaw insisted. Rather, he wanted to explore a new fictional idea. Pip is not of his own class, just as he is not of

David's, but he will be given a series of false economic and social expectations that he will have to work out. Pip's promotion to the status of a gentleman by means of Magwitch's money makes an artificial and socially inadequate man of him (at least in Dickens's eyes). Everything depends on work, and Magwitch effectively, if temporarily, removes Pip from the world of work. What is required of Pip as his narrative develops is sound *professional* promotion rather than mere *status* promotion. Pip's work as a clerk, and later a partner, in Clarriker and Co., gives him a role in society; Magwitch's manipulation of him merely takes him out of the forge and, in making him a "gentleman," gives him nothing to do.

The word "gentleman" has its ambiguities even for Magwitch. It is thus that he defines his arch-enemy, Compeyson, when the pair are arrested together on the marshes. "He's a gentleman, if you please, this villain. Now, the hulks has got its gentleman again, through me." When, later in the novel, he explains to Pip what he has done for him, Magwitch claims that he has sought not only to lift his protégé above the world of work but also to possess the thing that he could never himself be: "Yes, Pip, dear boy, I've made a gentleman on you! It's me wot has done it! I swore that time, sure as ever I earned a guinea, that guinea should go to you . . . I lived rough, that you should live smooth; I worked hard, that you should be above work" (ch. 39).

It is not that Magwitch is taking revenge on all the gentlemanly Compeysons through Pip, as Miss Havisham is taking revenge on all the manly jilters though Estella. But somehow he *does* want to claim a vicarious place among the gentlemen in order to prove that their gentility is not innate but manufactured. "The blood horses of them colonists might fling up the dust over me as I was walking," he explains to Pip, and "what do you say? I says to myself, 'I'm making a better gentleman nor ever *you'll* be!'" (ch. 39). In a sense, the "gentleman" Pip is a product of the kind of "trade" that real Victorian gentlemen pretended to despise. Perhaps worse, he is a product of "speculation" by a transportee, tainted by the associations of crime, the hulks, indenture, and colonial venture.

Until Magwitch's revelations at the end of the novel's second stage, Pip has, of course, been unquestioningly happy with what he sees as his good fortune and his social advancement. Since his boyhood meeting with Estella, he had aspired to rise above the class into which he was born and his un-named benefactor has enabled him to realize richly his ambitions. He has also willingly, and to him "naturally," altered his perspectives:

> "Since your change of fortune and prospects, you have changed your companions," said Estella.
>
> "Naturally," said I.

> "And necessarily," she added, in a haughty tone, "what was fit company for you once, would be quite unfit company for you now." (ch. 29)

Coldly and astutely, Estella puts her finger on Pip's new-found snobbery, and, on this particular occasion, Pip readily abandons any thought of visiting Joe at the forge. What readers have to place against these manifestations of Pip's snobbish assumptions, however, is the fact that though, by any moral and human standard, he ought to remain the intimate of a blacksmith, he can now never resort to working as a blacksmith's apprentice. His own inclinations, as much as his "expectations," have prepared him for something different. What he must learn is that he cannot afford to feel superior. In a telling exchange with Biddy, as he sets out to begin his new and snobbish life in London, Pip professes himself determined "to do something for Joe" in view of his own higher prospects. In the garden at the forge, Pip asks Biddy to help Joe on "a little." Asked to explain "how," Pip is forced to say that Joe's "learning and manners" lacked something and that if he were to remove Joe into "a higher sphere" when he comes fully into his property, Joe would need to be improved. "And don't you think he knows that?" Biddy asks, plucking a blackcurrant leaf and then rubbing it to pieces in her hands. "Have you never considered that he may be proud?"

> "Proud?" I repeated, with disdainful emphasis.
>
> "Oh there are many kinds of pride," said Biddy, looking full at me and shaking her head; "pride is not all of one kind—"
>
> "Well, what are you stopping for?" said I.
>
> "Not all of one kind," resumed Biddy. "He may be too proud to let anyone take him out of a place that he is competent to fill, and fills well and with respect. To tell you the truth, I think he is: though it sounds bold in me to say so, for you must know him far better than I do." (ch. 19)

This is perhaps the most crucial exchange in the whole novel. Biddy throws the responsibility for understanding back on Pip, but, at the time, Pip fails to grasp this responsibility. We know that he *will* come to understand the import of the conversation because of Dickens's introduction of the blackcurrant leaf, the smell of which will bring back the memory, freshly and involuntarily. What Pip has to learn is that Joe not only accepts his role in life: he is *proud* of it and of the respect it earns him. Joe has an integrity that, at this stage in his expectations, Pip singularly lacks. It is not a matter of Joe "knowing his place" but of Joe being happy with what he is.

It is obvious to Pip and Biddy in this scene that although Joe represents a moral standard, he does not offer either a model of professional or class aspiration. Pip has to learn the distinctions that Biddy wisely intuits, but we need to acknowledge that at no stage in the novel does Joe seek social promotion or possess expectations. Those expectations are given to Pip, and the novel is about what he does with them. Dickens knew this when he hit on the name for his story and when he announced that his hero was to be a boy-child, "then he will be an apprentice." Pip is not to *stay* an apprentice.

But, having acquired the status and manners of a gentleman, nor is he to stay the kind of "gentleman" that Magwitch wanted to make him. Pip has to learn about a different kind of status, one defined by work, rather than by a distaste for work. *Great Expectations* is not, in the end, a novel about disillusionment, or alienation, or non-communication, or estrangement, but one concerned with finding one's place in the world of work and, as so often in Dickens's novels, being defined by work. Pip is obliged to discover the middle way between the working artisan and the workless gentleman. The novel's focus on class is ultimately, and unromantically, about the process of *embourgeoisement*. This is why, to a critic like Chesterton, Pip can never emerge as "heroic," and why, to Marxists, the story seems to dwell darkly on social estrangement.

During their last encounter, Pip admits to Estella that he works "pretty hard for a sufficient living" and therefore he does "well." These words perhaps reflect Samuel Smiles's comments about the character of "The True Gentleman" in the last chapter of his popular ethical manual *Self Help* (1859): "Riches and rank have no necessary connection with genuinely gentlemanly qualities. The poor man may be a true gentleman—in spirit and in daily life. He may be honest, truthful, upright, polite, temperate, courageous, self-respecting, and self-helping—that is, be a true gentleman" (Paroissien 2000: 420). For Smiles, all work was "noble" whether it be manual labor, administration, composition, or cerebration. This was, of course, an echo of Carlyle's insistent demand that work should be seen as giving meaning both to the individual and to society.

Much as Carlyle had outlined in his 1840 lectures on *Heroes, Hero-worship and the Heroic in History*, David Copperfield was given a mission to find his own "heroism" in becoming a man of letters. David's first sentence asks whether or not he will be the "hero" of his own life, and his narrative shows him developing both independence and social standing through writing. David was also to be an example of the Dickensian self-made man, one who overcomes disadvantage in order to prove himself worthy of happiness. Pip's realization of his destiny is to be equally a matter of struggle and self-help, but his destiny lacks the glamour of literary success. To work oneself up from a clerk to a partner in Clarriker and Co. may seem to lack flamboyance and romance, but that is precisely what becomes the "unheroic" Pip. In his own eyes, he has done "well" by dint of "hard work."

Readers may baulk at the subdued nature of the novel's ending, and may see Pip's occupation as a sign of his disillusion, but that is not how Victorian readers seem to have taken it. There is certainly nothing for tears in either ending that Dickens provided, though so few latter-day critics feel stimulated to do justice to the "flowing humour" and the "entertainment" that contemporary readers rejoiced in. In some ways, *Great Expectations* is a typical Dickensian comedy of manners in which the worthy central character loses illusions in order to find his true *métier*. Pip sees mists rising at the end of his narrative and he interprets them as portending no shadow of a parting from Estella. What they may also portend is a future in which men like Pip build a world that dispenses both with class assumptions and with assumptions about class.

References and Further Reading

Anon (1862). Review of *Cloister and the Hearth. Westminster Review*, 77, 286–7.

Cheadle, Brian (2001). The late novels: *Great Expectations* and *Our Mutual Friend*. In John O. Jordan (Ed.), *The Cambridge Companion to Charles Dickens* (pp. 78–91). Cambridge: Cambridge University Press.

Chesterton, G. K. (1911). *Appreciations and Criticisms of the Works of Charles Dickens*. London: J. M. Dent.

Collins, Philip (Ed.) (1971). *Dickens: The Critical Heritage*. London: Routledge and Kegan Paul.

[Forster, John] (1861). Review of *Great Expectations. The Examiner*, July 20, 452–3.

Miller, J. Hillis (1958). *Charles Dickens: The World of his Novels*. Cambridge, MA: Harvard University Press.

Moynahan, Julian (1960). The hero's guilt: the case of *Great Expectations. Essays in Criticism*, 10, 60–79.

Paroissien, David (2000). *The Companion to Great Expectations*. Robertsbridge: Helm Information.

Ricks, Christopher (1962). *Great Expectations*. In John Gross and Gabriel Pearson (Eds.), *Dickens and the Twentieth Century* (pp. 199–211). London: Routledge and Kegan Paul.

Shaw, George Bernard (1958). Foreword to *Great Expectations*. In Dan H. Laurence and Martin Quinn (Eds.), *Shaw on Dickens* (pp. 45–59). New York: Frederick Ungar (original work published 1937; text revised 1947).

Chronology

1812	Charles John Huffam Dickens, the second of eight children, born February 7 to John and Elizabeth Dickens.
1814	John Dickens, a clerk in the Navy Pay Office, is transferred from Portsea to London. During these early years, from 1814 to 1821, Charles Dickens is taught his letters by his mother, and he immerses himself in the fiction classics of his father's library.
1817	John Dickens moves family to Chatham, where Charles Dickens attends Dame School with his sister Fanny.
1821	Begins at the Rev. William Giles School. Remains at this school for a time even after his family is transferred again to London in 1822.
1822	Composes his first tragedy, *Misnar, the Sultan of India*, modeled on *The Tales of the Genii.*
1824	Father is arrested for debt and sent to Marshalsea Prison, accompanied by his wife and younger children, who take up residency at the jail. Charles soon finds lodging in a poor neighborhood and begins work at Warren's Blacking Factory. Father is released three months later.
1824–26	Attends Wellington House Academy, London, until he is again forced to leave because of his father's financial embarrassments.
1827	Works as a law clerk.

1830 Meets Maria Beadnell, daughter of George Beadnell, a prosperous banker. He eventually falls in love with her, but by 1832, her parents begin to discourage the relationship. Upon her return from a trip to Paris in 1833, Maria loses interest in him.

1831 Becomes a reporter for the *Mirror of Parliament*.

1832 Becomes a staff writer for the *True Sun*.

1833 First published piece, "A Dinner at Poplar Walk," appears in December issue of the *Monthly Magazine* under the pen name "Boz."

1834 Becomes staff writer on the *Morning Chronicle*. His "street sketches" begin to appear in the *Evening Chronicle*. Meets his future wife, Catherine Hogarth. Father is arrested again for debt.

1836 *Sketches by Boz*, illustrated by George Cruikshank, published. Marries Catherine Hogarth in April. First play, *The Strange Gentleman*, runs for two months at the St. James's Theatre. Second play, *The Village Coquettes*, is produced at the same theater. In late 1836, becomes editor of a new magazine, *Bentley's Miscellany*. Meets John Forster, who becomes a lifelong friend and his biographer.

1836–37 *Pickwick Papers* published in monthly installments from April through the following November.

1837 *Pickwick Papers* appears in book form. *Oliver Twist* begins to appear in *Bentley's Miscellany*. Success of *Oliver Twist* enables Dickens to rent a terrace house in Bloomsbury. *Is She His Wife?* produced at the St. James's. First child, a son, born, and the family moves to Doughty Street. Catherine's sister Mary, deeply loved by Dickens, dies suddenly.

1838 *Nicholas Nickleby* appears in installments and is completed in October 1839. First daughter born.

1839 Moves with his family to Devonshire Terrace. Second daughter is born. *Nickleby* appears in book form.

1840 Edits *Master Humphrey's Clock*, a weekly periodical, in which *The Old Curiosity Shop* appears.

1841 *Barnaby Rudge* appears in *Master Humphrey's Clock*. Another son born.

1842	He and his wife tour America from January to June. Publishes *American Notes*.
1843	*Martin Chuzzlewit* appears in monthly installments (January 1843 through July 1844). *A Christmas Carol* published.
1844	Tours Italy and Switzerland. Another Christmas book, *The Chimes*, completed. Third son is born.
1845	Produces *Every Man in His Humour* in England. *The Cricket on the Hearth* is written by Christmas. Fourth son is born.
1846	Creates and edits the *Daily News* but resigns as editor after 17 days. *Dombey and Son* appears in 20 monthly installments (October 1846 through April 1848). *The Battle of Life: A Love Story* appears for Christmas.
1847	Begins to manage a theatrical company and arranges a benefit tour of *Every Man in His Humour*. Fifth son is born.
1848	Daughter Fanny dies. Theatrical company performs for Queen Victoria. Last Christmas book, *The Haunted Man*, published.
1849	Begins *David Copperfield* (published May 1849 through November 1850). Sixth son is born.
1850	*Household Words*, a weekly periodical, established with Dickens as editor. Third daughter is born and dies within a year.
1851	Father dies.
1852	*Bleak House* appears in monthly installments (March 1852 through September 1853). First bound volume of *A Child's History of England* appears. Last child, his seventh son, is born.
1853	Gives first public readings, from the Christmas books. Travels to France and Italy.
1854	*Hard Times* published in *Household Words* (April 1 through August 12) and appears in book form.
1855	*Little Dorrit* appears in monthly installments (December 1855 through June 1857). Travels with family to Paris, where he meets other leading literary and theatrical persons.
1856	Purchases Gad's Hill Place.
1857	Is involved primarily with theatrical productions.

1858 Begins first public readings for profit. Announces separation from his wife, about which he writes a personal statement in *Household Words* to dispel rumors of his having an affair with Ellen Ternan.

1859 Concludes *Household Words* and establishes a new weekly, *All the Year Round. A Tale of Two Cities* appears there from April 20 to November 26 and is published in book form in December.

1860 Begins series of papers, *The Uncommercial Traveller* for *All the Year Round. Great Expectations* under way in weekly installments (December 1860 through August 1861).

1861 *The Uncommercial Traveller*, a collection of pieces from *All the Year Round*, published. First installment of *Great Expectations* published in *Harper's Weekly* in November.

1862 Gives many public readings and travels to Paris.

1863 Continues his readings in Paris and London. Daughter Elizabeth dies, and his own health is seriously declining, showing symptoms of thrombosis.

1864 *Our Mutual Friend* appears in monthly installments for publisher Chapman and Hall (May 1864 through November 1865).

1865 Suffers a stroke that leaves him lame. Involved in a train accident with Ellen, which causes him to change the ending of *Our Mutual Friend. Our Mutual Friend* appears in book form. Second collection of *The Uncommercial Traveller* is published.

1866 Gives 30 public readings in the English provinces.

1867 Continues the provincial readings, then travels to the United States in November, where he reads in Boston and New York. Invited to a meal at the White House with President Andrew Jackson. This tour permanently breaks Dickens's health.

1868 In April, returns to England, where he continues to tour and entertains American friends at Gad's Hill.

1869 First public reading of the murder of Nancy (from *Oliver Twist*) performed, but his doctors recommend he discontinue the tour.

1870 Gives 12 readings in London. Six parts of *Edwin Drood* appear from April to September. Dies at age 58. Buried in the Poets' Corner, Westminster Abbey.

Contributors

HAROLD BLOOM is Sterling Professor of the Humanities at Yale University. Educated at Cornell and Yale universities, he is the author of more than 30 books, including *Shelley's Mythmaking* (1959), *The Visionary Company* (1961), *Blake's Apocalypse* (1963), *Yeats* (1970), *The Anxiety of Influence* (1973), *A Map of Misreading* (1975), *Kabbalah and Criticism* (1975), *Agon: Toward a Theory of Revisionism* (1982), *The American Religion* (1992), *The Western Canon* (1994), *Omens of Millennium: The Gnosis of Angels, Dreams, and Resurrection* (1996), *Shakespeare: The Invention of the Human* (1998), *How to Read and Why* (2000), *Genius: A Mosaic of One Hundred Exemplary Creative Minds* (2002), *Hamlet: Poem Unlimited* (2003), *Where Shall Wisdom Be Found?* (2004), and *Jesus and Yahweh: The Names Divine* (2005). In addition, he is the author of hundreds of articles, reviews, and editorial introductions. In 1999, Professor Bloom received the American Academy of Arts and Letters' Gold Medal for Criticism. He has also received the International Prize of Catalonia, the Alfonso Reyes Prize of Mexico, and the Hans Christian Andersen Bicentennial Prize of Denmark.

STANLEY FRIEDMAN taught at Queens College, City University of New York. He is the author of *Dickens's Fictions: Tapestries of Conscience* and a co-editor of several volumes of the *Dickens Studies Annual.*

GAIL TURLEY HOUSTON is professor and chairperson of the department of English language and literature at the University of New Mexico. She has written three books: *Consuming Fictions: Gender, Class, and Hunger in Dickens's Fiction*; *Royalties: the Queen and Victorian Writers*; and *From Dickens to Dracula: Gothic, Economics, and Victorian Fiction.*

JOHN CUNNINGHAM is the author of *Elizabeth and Early Stuart Drama*, *Chaucer's "Miller's Tale"* in the Penguin Critical Studies series and other titles.

MARGARET FLANDERS DARBY is associate professor of writing and rhetoric and chairperson of the department at Colgate University. She authored *From Dickens to Dracula: Gothic, Economics, and Victorian Fiction* and *Consuming Fictions: Gender, Class and Hunger in Dickens's Novels.*

ROBERT R. GARNETT is a professor at Gettysburg College. He has published a book on Evelyn Waugh and is working on a longer study of passion and spirituality in Dickens's novels.

SARA THORNTON is a professor of English at the University of Paris 7 Denis-Diderot and is the author of *Advertising, Subjectivity and the Nineteenth-Century Novel: Dickens, Balzac and the Language of the Walls.*

CAROLINE LEVINE is a professor teaching in the English and political science departments at the University of Wisconsin–Madison. She is co-editor of *From Author to Text: Re-reading George Eliot's "Romola."*

WENDY S. JACOBSON is a retired associate professor at Rhodes University in South Africa. She is the author of *Dickens and the Children of Empire* and *The Companion to* The Mystery of Edwin Drood.

STEWART JUSTMAN is a professor in the liberal studies program at the University of Montana. Among his works are *Shakespeare: The Drama of Generations* and *The Springs of Liberty: The Satiric Tradition and Freedom of Speech.*

ANDREW SANDERS is a professor at Durham University. Among his publications are *Charles Dickens: Resurrectionist* and *Dickens and the Spirit of the Age.*

Bibliography

Baumgarten, Murray. "Calligraphy and Code: Writing in *Great Expectations*." *Stanford Humanities Review* 8, no. 1 (2000): 226–238.

Bloom, Harold, ed. *Charles Dickens*. Updated ed. New York: Chelsea House Publishers, 2006.

Brinton, Ian. *Dickens's* Great Expectations: *A Reader's Guide*. London; New York: Continuum, 2007.

Brooks-Davies, Douglas. *Fielding, Dickens, Gosse, Iris Murdoch, and Oedipal Hamlet*. New York: St. Martin's Press, 1989.

Brown, Carolyn. "'Great Expectations': Masculinity and Modernity." *Essays and Studies* 40 (1987): 60–74.

Campbell, Elizabeth. "*Great Expectations*: Dickens and the Language of Fortune." *Dickens Studies Annual* 24 (1995): 153–65.

Cheadle, Brian. "Sentiment and Resentment in *Great Expectations*." *Dickens Studies Annual* 20 (1991): 149–174.

Cohen, William A. "Manual Conduct in *Great Expectations*." *ELH* 60, no. 1 (1993): 217–259.

Cottom, Daniel. *Text and Culture: The Politics of Interpretation*. Minneapolis: University of Minnesota Press, 1989.

Craig, David M. "The Interplay of City and Self in *Oliver Twist*, *David Copperfield*, and *Great Expectations*." *Dickens Studies Annual* 16 (1987): 17–38.

Craig, Randall. "Fictional License: The Case of (and in) *Great Expectations*." *Dickens Studies Annual* 35 (2005): 109–32.

Crowley, James P. "Pip's Spiritual Exercise: The Meditative Mode in Dickens' *Great Expectations*." *Renascence* 46, no. 2 (1994): 133–143.

Dutheil, Martine Hennard. "*Great Expectations* as Reading Lesson." *Dickens Quarterly* 13, no. 3 (September 1996): 164–174.

Edgecombe, Rodney Stenning. "Violence, Death and Euphemism in *Great Expectations*." *Victorians Institute Journal* 22 (1994): 85–98.

Friedman, Stanley. *Dickens's Fiction: Tapestries of Conscience*. New York: AMS, 2003.

Hannon, Patrice. "The Aesthetics of Humour in *Great Expectations*." *Dickensian* 92, no. 2 (1996): 91–105.

Hara, Eiichi. "Stories Present and Absent in *Great Expectations*." *ELH* 53, no. 3 (Fall 1986): 593–614.

Hardy, Barbara. *Dickens and Creativity*. London; New York: Continuum, 2008.

Holbrook, David. *Charles Dickens and the Image of Woman*. New York: New York University Press, 1993.

Houston, Gail Turley. *Consuming Fictions: Gender, Class, and Hunger in Dickens's Novels*. Carbondale: Southern Illinois University Press, 1994.

Johnston, Judith. "Women and Violence in Dickens' *Great Expectations*." *Sydney Studies in English* 18 (1992/93): 93–110.

Kappel, Lawrence, ed. *Readings on* Great Expectations. San Diego: Greenhaven Press, 1999.

Krzemienski, Ed. "For Fun or Function? Recreation and Class in *Great Expectations*." *Aethlon* 16, no. 2 (1999): 85–96.

MacKay, Carol Hanbery, ed. *Dramatic Dickens*. New York: St. Martin's, 1989.

Macleod, Norman. "Which Hand? Reading *Great Expectations* as a Guessing Game." *Dickens Studies Annual* 31 (2002): 127–57.

Maglavera, Soultana. *Time Patterns in Later Dickens: A Study of the Thematic Implications of the Temporal Organization of* Bleak House, Hard Times, Little Dorrit, A Tale of Two Cities, Great Expectations *and* Our Mutual Friend. Amsterdam; Atlanta: Rodopi, 1994.

McFarlane, Brian. *Charles Dickens'* Great Expectations: *The Relationship between Text and Film*, edited by Imelda Whelehan. London: Methuen Drama, 2008.

Meckier, Jerome. "Charles Dickens's *Great Expectations*: A Defense of the Second Ending." *Studies in the Novel* 25, no. 1 (1993): 28–58.

———. *Dickens's* Great Expectations: *Misnar's Pavilion versus Cinderella*. Lexington: University Press of Kentucky, 2002.

———. "*Great Expectations*: Symmetry in (Com)Motion." *Dickens Quarterly* 15, no. 1 (1998): 28–49.

Morgan, Monique R. "Conviction in Writing: Crime, Confession, and the Written Word in *Great Expectations*." *Dickens Studies Annual* 33 (2003): 87–108.

Morris, Christopher D. "The Bad Faith of Pip's Bad Faith: Deconstructing *Great Expectations*." *ELH* 54, no. 4 (Winter 1987): 941–55.

Newey, Vincent. *The Scriptures of Charles Dickens: Novels of Ideology, Novels of the Self.* Aldershot, England: Ashgate, 2004.

Newlin, George. *Understanding* Great Expectations: *A Student Casebook to Issues, Sources, and Historical Documents.* Westport, Conn.: Greenwood Press, 2000.

Park, Hyungji. "Criminality and Empire in *Great Expectations.*" *Journal of English Language and Literature* 49, no. 4 (Winter 2003): 707–29.

Phelan, James. "Reading for the Character and Reading for the Progression: John Wemmick and *Great Expectations.*" *Journal of Narrative Technique* 19, no. 1 (1989): 70–84.

Rosenberg, Edgar. "'Murder' 'Shot!' 'Drowned!': A Note on Dickens's Descriptive Headlines." *Q/W/E/R/T/Y* 9 (October 1999): 87–95.

Sanders, Andrew. "Dickens and the Idea of the Comic Novel." *Yearbook of English Studies* 36, no. 2 (2006): 51–64.

Schilling, Bernard N. *The Rain of Years:* Great Expectations *and the World of Dickens.* Rochester, N.Y.: University of Rochester Press, 2001.

Sell, Kathleen. "The Narrator's Shame: Masculine Identity in *Great Expectations.*" *Dickens Studies Annual* 26 (1998): 203–26.

Sell, Roger D. "Blessings, Benefactions, Bear's Services: *Great Expectations* and Communicational Narratology." *European Journal of English Studies* 8, no. 1 (2004): 49–80.

Shattock, Joanne, ed. *Dickens and Other Victorians: Essays in Honor of Philip Collins.* New York: St. Martin's (1988).

Spurgin, Timothy A. "'It's Me Wot Has Done It!': Letters, Reviews, and *Great Expectations.*" *Dickens Studies Annual* 27 (1998): 187–208.

Stein, Robert A. "Repetitions during Pip's Closure." *Dickens Studies Annual* 21 (1992): 143–56.

Stolte, Tyson. "Mightier Than the Sword: Aggression of the Written Word in *Great Expectations.*" *Dickens Studies Annual* 35 (2005): 179–208.

Thurin, Susan Schoenbauer. "The Seven Deadly Sins in *Great Expectations.*" *Dickens Studies Annual* 15 (1986): 201–220.

Tritter, Daniel F. "Mr. Jaggers at the Bar." *Dickens Quarterly* 14, no. 2 (June 1997): 92–107.

Acknowledgments

Stanley Friedman, "Estella's Parentage and Pip's Persistence: The Outcome of *Great Expectations*." From *Studies in the Novel* 19, no. 4 (Winter 1987): 410–21. © 1987 by *Studies in the Novel.*

Gail Turley Houston, "'Pip' and 'Property': The (Re)Production of the Self in *Great Expectations*." From *Studies in the Novel* 24, no. 1 (Spring 1992): 13–25. © 1992 by *Studies in the Novel.*

John Cunningham, "Christian Allusion, Comedic Structure, and the Metaphor of Baptism in *Great Expectations*." From *South Atlantic Review* 59, no. 2 (May 1994): 35–51. © 1994 by *South Atlantic Review.*

Margaret Flanders Darby, "Listening to Estella." From *Dickens Quarterly* 16, no. 4 (1999): 215–29. © 1999 by the Dickens Society.

Robert R. Garnett, "The Good and the Unruly in *Great Expectations*—and Estella." From *Dickens Quarterly* 16, no. 1 (March 1999): 24–41. © 1999 by the Dickens Society.

Sara Thornton, "The Burning of Miss Havisham: Dickens, Fire and the 'Fire-Baptism.'" From *Q/W/E/R/T/Y* 9 (October 1999): 105–14. © 1999 by Publications de L'Université de Pau.

Clare Pettitt, "Monstrous Displacements: Anxieties of Exchange in *Great Expectations*." From *Dickens Studies Annual* 30 (2001): 243–62. © 2001 by AMS Press.

Caroline Levine, "Realism as Self-Forgetfulness: Gender, Ethics, and *Great Expectations*." From *The Serious Pleasures of Suspense: Victorian Realism and Narrative Doubt*, pp. 84–98, 213–14. © 2003 by the Rector and Visitors of the University of Virginia.

Wendy S. Jacobson, "The Prince of the Marshes: *Hamlet* and *Great Expectations*." From *The Dickensian* 102, no. 470, part 3 (Winter 2006): 197–211. © 2006 by Wendy S. Jacobson.

Stewart Justman, "Great Expectations: '*Absolute Equality*.'" From *Literature and Human Equality*. © 2006 by Northwestern University Press.

"Great Expectations" by Andrew Sanders. From *A Companion to Charles Dickens*, edited by David Paroissien. © 2008 by Blackwell Publishing, editorial material and organization. © 2008 by David Paroissien.

Every effort has been made to contact the owners of copyrighted material and secure copyright permission. Articles appearing in this volume generally appear much as they did in their original publication with few or no editorial changes. In some cases, foreign language text has been removed from the original essay. Those interested in locating the original source will find the information cited above.

Index

3 1333 03920 3987